ASMUS BOYSEN
AND HIS
DAM PROBLEMS

ASMUS BOYSEN AND HIS DAM PROBLEMS

Lawrence Woods

LAWRENCE WOODS

authorHOUSE®

AuthorHouse™
1663 Liberty Drive
Bloomington, IN 47403
www.authorhouse.com
Phone: 1-800-839-8640

Published by AuthorHouse   01/23/2013

ISBN: 978-1-4817-0672-8 (sc)
ISBN: 978-1-4817-0674-2 (hc)
ISBN: 978-1-4817-0673-5 (e)

Library of Congress Control Number: 2013900713

INTRODUCTION

The State of Wyoming and the U. S. government have placed the name of Boysen on a dam and several physical features in Wyoming, with only the briefest mention of an earlier Boysen dam located nearby. There is a great deal more to the story.

Asmus Boysen was not yet eighteen when he stepped off the ship in New York in the spring of 1886, and he was surely glad to leave behind his troubled Danish homeland, to make his fortune in the free environment of the United States. And in a remarkably short time, he did just that, marrying a beautiful and wealthy woman, building a considerable estate, and making many friends, some of them very influential in the political life of the country.

But fickle Fate lured him to an Indian reservation in the middle of Wyoming, where he used his newly-acquired political influence to lease a huge tract of land to look for coal. When the search for coal proved unrewarding, Boysen parlayed his tenuous claim to the lease into a square mile of mineral land athwart a rugged canyon, where he hoped to find precious metals. Alas, that hope proved to be doomed, as well, and he then committed his fortune (and the money of others as well) to a dam and power plant, hoping to recover it all and more from the sale of power to the anticipated mining industry and the crowd of settlers he expected on the reservation land that had just been opened to public settlement.

The story is further complicated by the appearance in Boysen's world of Nebraska lawyer John T. Clarke, who successfully claimed and tenaciously clung to a share in Boysen's property. Asmus Boysen and Clarke might have become friends at first—we cannot be sure of that—but they became locked in a struggle that brought them before a number of courts—a struggle that exhausted both their fortunes. In the end, neither was a winner, as a railroad, the State of Wyoming and the river conspired to rob both men of the hoped-for pot of gold.

The dam Boysen built is gone, but the Boysen State Park includes some of Boysen's land, and the mountain sheep that roamed the area before Boysen intruded on their pasture can once again be seen grazing there. In an ironic vindication of Boysen's original dream, the government built a much larger Boysen dam, just upriver from Boysen's location—mute testimony that it made sense to erect a dam and power plant there, if the builder was rich enough and powerful enough to deal with the objections raised by the railroad and the river.

This is more than a story of looking for precious metals, or building a dam and selling electric power, or trying to bring Danish farmers to settle in Wyoming, although Boysen did all those things. This is also the story of the struggle among five opponents: two individuals, a powerful railroad, the State of Wyoming and the river, each with inconsistent objectives. And the objectives of two of the three most powerful opponents were not at all clear for a long time.

Indeed:

- The railroad did not really know whether it would build alongside Boysen's dam during the entire critical period when he was constructing it, and
- the State of Wyoming wanted *both* a dam and a railroad, and finally adopted a plan that did not meet the needs of either.

Finally, the objectives of the third powerful opponent, which was the river, were unknown and unknowable during the entire time Boysen was trying to restrain it.

Except for the river, all of the other opponents used and abused the judicial system to advance their several objectives, and often the opportunity to delay was shamelessly exploited to prevent what should have been inevitable results. The story of this remarkable legal tangle involves more than sixty cases, requiring the attention of more than thirty lawyers and judges in courts ranging from a county justice of the peace to the Supreme Court of the United States (with many others in between), over a period of more than forty years. While I make no claim that this story of overdone litigation is unique, it certainly ranks among the most egregious examples, and the blame for it must be shared among all of the four major parties (leaving out the river, which was not concerned with lawyers and judges).

BEFORE THE
BOYSEN DAM

1

THE GOOD YEARS

Asmus Boysen's grandfather was Peter Boysen, a navigation instructor born about 1797 in the old duchy of Slesvig (Schleswig in the German spelling), which was ruled by the Danish king. Peter and his wife, Ingeborg Matthiesen had a son, Hans Jes Boysen, who married Maren Mathilde Vildfang in 1863, in the port town of Aabenraa, which was the home of Denmark's third largest trade fleet, serving trade all over the world.[1]

The town of Aabenraa dated back to 1450, and in 1860 was the home to more than 5,000 people. Unfortunately, the year of Hans Boysen's marriage was the last year that Aabenraa was under Danish rule. Prussia, under the leadership of Otto von Bismarck, had designs on the duchies of Slesvig and Holstein, because of their German population, and also because of their strategic location between the North Sea and the Baltic.[2]

Unfortunately, when the Danish government tried to merge Slesvig with Denmark in 1863, Bismarck seized upon this excuse to claim both Slesvig and Holstein for the Prussian crown. The subsequent war was a disaster for Denmark, for the weak Danish government was ill prepared to face the combined military might of Prussia and Austria,

---

[1]   Hans Jes Boysen was born April 24, 1839, and married Maren Mathilde Vildfang on May 22, 1863 in Aabenraa, Aabenraa County. She was born in Aabenraa on July 19, 1845.

[2]   The duchy of Slesvig had a large Danish population, and Holstein was heavily German.

and in the treaty ending the war, both Schleswig and Holstein fell under Prussian rule.[3]

The expected invasion by Prussian and Austrian forces may well have been the impetus for Hans Boysen to move with his bride from Slesvig further up the Jutland peninsula to the town of Skanderup in Denmark's Ribe county. In any case, when their daughter Anna Christine was born in February, 1864, Prussian troops were already in Holstein, on their way north into Denmark proper.

Skanderup, located north and west of their former home at Aabenraa, was a town of a few more than 1,000 souls. The parish was an agricultural area, growing wheat, rye and barley, and Hans Boysen found work at Drabæk Mølle, a nearby grist mill. It was in Skanderup that Maren gave birth to their second child and first son, Asmus, in the summer of 1868.[4]

Although Hans Boysen moved his family to Denmark, the Boysens relatives who remained in Aabenraa fell under Prussian rule, and with the approach of the Franco-Prussian War of 1870, Danish men in Schleswig faced military duty in the Prussian army, and many refused to fight the French. Hans Boysen's younger brother Adolph (only two years older than his nephew Asmus) was 23 in 1870, and we do not know where he went when he left Schleswig, but in 1872, he took passage for New York, the first member of the Boysen family to emigrate.[5]

By 1876, Adolph Boysen was in Milwaukee, where he used his family's knowledge of the grain business to become a grain commission

---

[3] Anna Christine Boysen was born February 18, 1864, in Skanderup.

[4] Asmus Boysen was born July 11, 1868 and christened July 26, 1868, in Skanderup. The second son, Jacobi Frederik Boysen, who was born in Skanderup on January 15, 1870, and the fourth son, Nis Peter Boysen, who was born July, 1877, both later followed Asmus to the United States.

[5] Adolph Boysen arrived in New York from Glasgow on June 24, 1872. His entry on the passenger list gave his nationality and origin as Swedish, so that he may have spent some time in Sweden before booking passage to New York.

merchant, and in 1880 his prominence in the Danish community earned him appointment as Danish Vice Consul for Michigan and Wisconsin, with office in Milwaukee. By 1882 he was a land agent for the Northwestern railroad in Minnesota and Iowa, and his brother-in-law, George Koch, joined in this business. Adolph worked from offices in Milwaukee and Chicago, and he had a home in Evanston, Illinois (where the family spent winters), and another in Lake Benton, Minnesota, where his wife apparently spent the summers.

Adolph Boysen's work as a railroad land agent included efforts to encourage Danish colonization on railroad lands in Iowa and southern Minnesota. In the fall of 1885, Adolph Boysen went back to Denmark to promote Danish colonies in the United States, and there he found the Danish economy was suffering from the fall of grain prices after the opening of the Suez Canal and the Pacific railway in the U. S.[6]

When his uncle appeared in Denmark with stories of success in selling land to settlers, those stories must have ignited great enthusiasm in the heart of the 17-year-old Asmus. Certainly the prospects for a young man in the United States sounded much more promising than those in Denmark, and when Adolph left again for the United States in March 1886, Asmus was not far behind.[7]

Asmus Boysen came to the United States in 1886, aboard the three-masted steam ship *Pieter Caland*. The ship had both first and second class cabins, but Asmus was in steerage, because he could not afford the first class passage Adolph had enjoyed on his voyage. When Asmus stepped off the ship in New York with one piece of luggage he was two months shy of his 18th birthday; the manifest gave his occupation as "cook." We know nothing of his whereabouts in the next

---

[6] Adolph Boysen worked on Danish colonization in Emmet County, Iowa, and in southern Minnesota he made arrangements with the Danish Evangelical Lutheran Church to locate a Danish colony in Lincoln County. *Lake Benton News,* June 30, 1885, Enok Mortensen, *The Danish Lutheran Church in America: The History and Heritage of the American Evangelical Lutheran Church* (Philadelphia, 1967), 77 and John Danstrup, *A History of Denmark* (Copenhagen, 1947), 122.

[7] Adolph Boysen arrived in New York on the *Elbe* on March 20, 1886.

three years, but at the end of 1889, we find Asmus in Illinois, where he made a very favorable marriage to Anna Leet, the daughter of William Leet, a wealthy businessman who at one time controlled a considerable grain trade along the Burlington railroad in Illinois and owned banks and real estate in Iowa. At the time of Anna's marriage the Leet family was living in Aurora, Ill., although Leet went to work in Chicago every day.[8]

When they married, Asmus Boysen was 21 and Anna was 18. Their son Allan was born in Illinois in 1890, before the family moved to Manning, in Carroll County, Iowa, where their daughter Helena was born the following year. While living in Manning, Asmus was already involved in selling real estate, and we know he embraced his uncle's peripatetic business lifestyle. The Manning *Monitor* later noted that he was absent "most of the time on extensive land deals." It was a lifestyle that made for a lonely existence for the Boysen wives.[9]

In the spring of 1892, Asmus purchased a house in Audubon, Iowa, so that Anna would be closer to her brother's family there when he was away on business. While living in Audubon, Asmus sold Burlington railroad lands in Nebraska, both for his own account and as agent for the railroad. He had a real estate office in Omaha in the years 1893-95, and this was the time when Boysen likely met his future lawyer, John N. Baldwin, who later was attorney for the Union Pacific.[10]

In the spring of 1894, Anna was delivered of a second daughter. Asmus continued traveling extensively, including a "land exploring expedition through the South," and in the fall of 1894 he was conducting "home-seeking" parties of prospective settlers to look at railroad land in southern Minnesota. He also shared an office in Chicago with his

---

[8]   Asmus Boysen arrived in New York from Rotterdam on the *Pieter Caland* on May 15, 1886. Anna Leet was born March 21, 1871, and she married Asmus Boysen in Chicago on December 20, 1889.

[9]   Allan Boysen was born July 16, 1890 and Helena Boysen was born November, 20, 1891. Also, *Manning Monitor,* April 16, 1892.

[10] At this time, Baldwin was practicing law in Council Bluffs, and Asmus Boysen's younger brother, Jacobi Boysen, was also practicing medicine in Council Bluffs.

uncle, Adolph Boysen. Asmus moved his family again, this time to Gray, Iowa, in Audubon County, where he bought a farm, and in 1897, he moved his family to a house he bought in Chicago, although they returned often to Audubon County.[11]

Asmus was a handsome man and easily made friends with his "cheerful, open-hearted" demeanor, "always shaking hands, and he soon achieved some prominence. Boysen's ambitions soon extended beyond the task of building his fortune. In 1897 he made his first foray into politics, seeking the nomination on the Republican ticket for state representative to the Iowa legislature from Audubon County. He achieved a plurality on the fifth and sixth ballots, and although he failed on the seventh ballot the smile on his face afterward signaled that he would try again.[12]

When Boysen entered the Iowa political circles, that state was in its "golden age" as a formidable force on the national political scene. In the Iowa Republican party Senator William B. Allison reigned supreme, and the Allison machine was also closely linked to the railroads. Grenville M. Dodge of Council Bluffs was a part of the Union Pacific group, and he backed Allison's first appointment to the Senate. Of equal importance in Iowa politics was the Burlington railroad group, represented by general counsel Joseph W. Blythe, who was conveniently the son-in-law of Iowa Senator John Henry Gear, as well as the brother of James Blythe, the chairman of the Iowa Republican Central Committee.

In the Congress, Iowa Senator Allison was a member of the "Big Four" who dominated the U. S. Senate, and at the end of 1899, Allison's aide, Col. David Bremner Henderson, was named Speaker of the House of Representatives. The Iowa delegation in the House included Congressman John Fletcher Lacey, who was a member of the Public

---

[11] *Audubon County Journal* (Exira, Iowa), July 22, 1897. By 1900, Anna had been delivered of nine children, but only four survived to adulthood. Anna Marie Boysen was born March 5, 1894, and Rosa Darlene was born in February 1900. Also, *Manning Monitor,* October 6, November 24, 1894.

[12] *Audubon County Journal* (Exira, Iowa), November 4, 1897, November 27, 1902 and August 27, 1903.

Lands Committee, and chairman of that committee for twelve years, while another Iowa congressman who later assisted Boysen's efforts was Smith McPherson.[13]

In the Executive Branch, James Wilson of Iowa was Secretary of Agriculture, and when Theodore Roosevelt replaced McKinley's secretary of the treasury, Iowa Governor Leslie M. Shaw was appointed to that post. Below cabinet level, the Director of the Mint and the Solicitor of the Treasury were both Iowans, and there were several Iowans in the diplomatic service. This powerful Iowa presence in Washington was of great help to Boysen in his later dealings with the U. S. government.[14]

It is remarkable that even before he held elective office in Iowa, Asmus Boysen had already entered the inner circle of the Iowa Republicans, which also gave him access to the powerful Iowa presence in Washington. For his next project, he would need help from official Washington, and he knew where to get that help.

---

[13] The "Big Four" in the Senate during the McKinley and Roosevelt administrations were Allison, Nelson W. Aldrich of Rhode Island, John C. Spooner of Wisconsin and Orville H. Platt of Connecticut.

[14] George E. Roberts was Director of the Mint and Maurice D. O'Connell was Solicitor of the Treasury; both men were from Fort Dodge, Iowa. Leland Sage, *William Boyd Allison: A Study in Practical Politics* (Iowa City, 1956), 277, 284. Shaw was appointed as Secretary of the Treasury on January 9, 1902.

2

THE WIND RIVER
RESERVATION LEASE

It was during a business trip to eastern Arkansas at the beginning of 1899 that Boysen became interested in minerals prospecting. The trip began as a survey of real estate opportunities, but he and Frank Leet then learned of the discovery of lead near Mena, Arkansas, and of a rumored gold discovery. Prospects were encouraging enough to cause a mining district to be formed and an ore crusher built to serve the anticipated mines. After sending an Iowa man down to Arkansas to look over the situation, Boysen and Leet incorporated the Audubon Mining and Development company of Mena, but riches eluded the company, and we hear no more about it.[15]

However, while Boysen was still in Arkansas, he launched his next minerals venture. Using borrowed stationery of the Iowa state legislature, he wrote to the U. S. Interior Department, asking permission to go on the Shoshoni Indian reservation in Wyoming (*i.e.,* the Wind River reservation) to negotiate a lease to mine coal and other minerals. We do not know the intervening details, but on March 1, the Audubon newspaper reported that Boysen was home from a "long" business trip, which may well have included a short trip to Wyoming.[16]

---

[15] The partners sent Martin N. Esbeck, a fellow Dane, who was the owner of a hardware store in Audubon, and also was the Audubon County Recorder.

[16] Boysen's first letter was dated February 16, 1899, and he would have had to borrow the stationery because he was not even nominated for the

Although Boysen was looking for hard minerals in Arkansas, his Wyoming venture ostensibly was a search for coal, and the "other minerals" phrase in his letter was very possibly suggested by someone who also had other objectives. The lease he was seeking was huge, and was located in a sparsely settled area, with few substantial markets for coal, so it seems likely that Boysen was being encouraged by a railroad that would welcome a coal deposit adjacent to its line. We know that Boysen had contacts with Burlington officials from the years when he was dealing in that railroad's land. At this time Burlington management was seriously considering a connection to Salt Lake City that would be shorter than the Union Pacific's main line across southern Wyoming, and such a survey of a line from Guernsey, Wyo. to Salt Lake City was completed in December, 1900. If that line were built, it would pass the Wind River reservation on its way, and an abundant coal supply in that area would be welcome, and would certainly justify support for Boysen's coal lease efforts. These facts, plus the Wyoming rumors that claimed the Burlington was backing Boysen, make that railroad as the probable source of the money Boysen hoped to make from the coal on his lease.[17]

The Wind River Reservation, located in central Wyoming, is the only Indian reservation in the state, established for the Shoshoni tribe by the treaty of 1868, and also the home of the northern Arapaho tribe in 1878. The first public indication that something was afoot on the reservation came in April, 1899, when the Lander *Clipper* reported on a flurry of speculations, noting rumors that a syndicate was "trying to get hold of the surplus land of the Wind River reservation," by long term lease. Several rumors connected this activity to the railroads, and

---

legislative seat until July of 1899.

[17] Richard C. Overton, *Burlington Route: A History of the Burlington Lines* (New York, 1965), 233. While Boysen also had contacts with the Union Pacific, that railroad went into bankruptcy in 1893, and was not in financial condition to build extensive new lines.

one article mentioned that an "agent" of the Burlington railroad was on the reservation.[18]

We know that Boysen was at Fort Washakie on April 1, 1899, but this time the Audubon newspaper was silent on his travels. It is clear from subsequent developments that while Boysen requested the meeting with the government, in all likelihood he did not select the land to be leased, nor did he contact the other eleven "partners" whose names appeared in the syndicate agreement he was to sign. The man responsible for those important "details" was undoubtedly Col. John T. Wertz, an eloquent, charming, well-dressed and well-groomed former traveling clothing salesman from Omaha, whose full-time job on the reservation was supposed to be that of allotting agent for the U. S. government. Wertz was very familiar with the reservation land and undoubtedly he both selected the land to be leased and organized the syndicate to develop it.[19]

Wertz was well connected with Nebraska's Senator John M. Thurston, who may have secured Wertz's appointment on the reservation, and also may have been involved in smoothing the way for the 1899 meeting on the reservation. Since Thurston was the general attorney of the Union Pacific before he was elected to the Senate in 1896, that connection would explain the press rumors involving the Union Pacific in the lease, as there is no indication that railroad was interested in the matter.[20]

---

[18] The Lander *Clipper* reported that the Burlington "agent" was asking for a 30-year lease, but that the Indians, who had met in council, only wanted to lease for 10 years. *The Clipper* (Lander), April 21, 1899.

[19] We do not know when Wertz met Boysen, but at the end of 1898, Wertz took leave from his work on the reservation to go to Omaha, where his wife and their new baby were living, and this may well have been the time when Wertz met Boysen and proposed the idea for a mining lease to him. While Wertz was called "Colonel" (and sometimes "Captain" or "Major"), we have found no record of any military service.

[20] A rumor quoted by the *Clipper* from the Cheyenne *Tribune* said that the Union Pacific was alert to the Burlington moves in the Wind River country, and had its own surveyors out to "head off" the Burlington in

John Wertz was appointed as special allotting agent and special disbursing agent on the Wind River Reservation in July, 1897, but he did not issue many allotments, and some of those he did issue were of questionable validity. However, he later said that he convinced the government to authorize a $12,000 survey to identify prospective mineral deposits on the reservation, and he used his knowledge of mineralization to help clients who were looking for mineral leases on the reservation. Senator Francis E. Warren later said that Wertz offered his clients the assurance that even if there were no minerals, the government would compensate them in case the reservation was opened to settlement. Warren said that over a period of several years, Wertz had several hundred such clients, from whom he collected a "fee or bonus", amounting to "a very profitable industry."[21]

Arapaho Chief Sharp Nose and Shoshoni Chief Washakie held a tribal conference at the Agency, and then met the Boysen group at Fort Washakie on April 1, with John C. Burnet (the Indian trader at the Fort) as interpreter. Captain Herman G. Nickerson, the Indian agent at Fort Washakie, who conducted negotiations on the government side, was a long-time resident of Fremont County, had served in the Army with President McKinley, and owed his appointment to that president. Nickerson favored leasing tribal lands for grazing and coal mining, to give the tribes revenue to replace the government annuities that were to expire in 1899 and 1900. The negotiation went well, and

---

that area. *The Clipper* (Lander) (quoting the Denver *Times*), April 28, 1899.

[21] Wertz's comment on the mineral survey was reported in Alfred K. Smith to Arima D. Smith, January 4, 1903, Interior, Appointments Division, "Charges and Protest Files," 1849-1907, RG 48, National Archives. The Cheyenne *Tribune* commented that Wertz was so familiar with the reservation land that he could accurately describe "nearly every quarter section" without referring to a map. Lander *Clipper,* quoting the *Tribune,* December 4, 1903. Regarding Wertz's fee arrangements, Warren said, "I am informed," but did not give a source. Francis E. Warren to Albert D. Lane, March 11, 1905, Francis E. Warren Collection, American Heritage Center, University of Wyoming.

we must assume Nickerson was favorable to the idea of the huge lease, perhaps in part because Boysen's political clout was truly awesome. However, Nickerson also must have been friendly to Wertz, because when Nickerson had to list three "creditable disinterested persons" who knew about the lease, he named Wertz as one such person. Nickerson's opinion of Wertz later changed drastically.[22]

The lease Boysen executed gave him the right to explore and mine coal in seven complete townships and one partial township, for a total of 178,000 acres, or about 278 square miles, located in three different places on the reservation. The westernmost township was athwart the Wind River (it included Crowheart Butte), and six miles east of that were two townships extending north of the Wind River. Finally, the remaining four full townships and one partial township were in a block in the rugged northeastern part of the reservation, lying across the Owl Creek Mountains. These townships included the watershed of Muddy Creek and of Red Canyon Creek and its tributary, Willow Creek, the latter creek's drainage being the site of the later Willow Creek copper play (of which, more later). It is at least interesting that Wertz's choice of land for the coal lease did not include any part of the "Washakie coal field" that appeared in the southeastern part of the reservation on the well-known General Land Office 1888 map of Wyoming Territory. None of Boysen's townships were in that area.

Before the meetings on April 1, Wertz wrote a syndicate agreement to take over the anticipated lease, involving sixteen members, four of whom were not named, and since Boysen was only one of the sixteen, it is most unlikely that the structure of the syndicate was his idea. The

---

[22] Noah E. Young, the Wyoming state inspector of mines, was also at the meeting, and gave some details of the negotiations, without mentioning Boysen. Young thought the negotiations were on behalf of the Burlington railroad, and volunteered the information that Thermopolis would be a "prominent" station on the extension of the Burlington line. *Wyoming Derrick* (Casper), May 4, 1899, and *The Clipper* (Lander), April 28, May 12, 1899. President McKinley, who had served with Captain Nickerson in the Civil War, appointed Nickerson as Indian Agent at Fort Washakie on April 1, 1898.

named individuals, other than Boysen, were mostly from Omaha, and although Wertz was not a named member (he signed the agreement as witness), his father-in-law and his brother were both members.

The agreement called for initial financial contributions of $2,000 by each member, but some of them (including one of the "unknowns") were excused from these contributions. One of the named members who were excused was Adam Morrell, a barber from Omaha, who was to be trustee for the syndicate, and he was to post a $20,000 bond in that position. Two other members excused from initial financial contributions were connected with the government operations on the reservation; they were Charles J. Woodhurst, an engineer from Ft. Collins, Colo., who worked with Wertz on the reservation surveys, and Josef Weis, who had been (or still was) a government employee on the reservation. Finally, Robert C. Wertz and Jacob E. House (brother and father-in-law of John Wertz) were also excused, and Jacob House was further exempted from paying "any money" in the future. Assuming the "unknowns" accepted the agreement, the initial trust fund would have been $20,000, which might have paid for some exploration, but certainly would not have paid for any development, and the agreement was silent on where additional money would come from. Morrell was to call a meeting in Omaha to elect the six-member board from among the *named* members of the syndicate, so that, in short, the syndicate was intended to be managed by John Wertz's Omaha group, with Boysen having only a single vote.[23]

Wertz had not contacted all of the prospective members to get their consent to the agreement, and a number of them never did consent. The unnamed members are a mystery, and it is possible they were added to the syndicate at Boysen's insistence. Since one of the unknowns was excused from financial contributions, the best candidate for such treatment would have been John N. Baldwin, who was acting as Boysen's attorney (and was also a key employee of the Union Pacific railroad). Obviously, Baldwin's legal work and influence with the Iowa delegation in Washington was of great benefit to Boysen,

---

[23]   Weis always spelled his name "Josef," but all of the subsequent references in the courts use the spelling "Joseph."

and worthy of suitable compensation. The other three may have been truly "unknown," and might have been intended to give Boysen the opportunity to appoint three more members to represent his interests (although they could not be directors).

The meeting to sign the syndicate agreement covering the coal lease took place at Ft. Washakie following the lease negotiation with Nickerson, but only four of the named members were present. In addition to Boysen, they were Adam Morell, the Omaha barber, Charles Woodhurst and Josef Weis. After signing the syndicate agreement, Boysen left for Omaha in the company of Wertz and Josef Weis. Haste was necessary, to intercept Harry F. Clarke, another syndicate member, to keep him from going to Wyoming to lease lands on the reservation for the benefit of his family. Although Wertz listed both Harry Clarke and his brother, John T. Clarke in the agreement, he obviously did not have their assent to all the terms.

The three men from Wyoming met Harry F. Clarke at the Omaha depot, where Boysen told Clarke that it was unnecessary for him to make the trip to Wyoming, since he had just negotiated a lease on the reservation, and he expansively assured Clarke that he would provide for "you people" (meaning the Clarke brothers). These assurances did not satisfy Harry Clarke, and the four men then went to a hotel, where they discussed the agreement that evening and the following day. At some point during these meetings, John Clarke apparently joined these four men, and in the end he signed the agreement, becoming the sixth person to accept it. But his brother Harry did not sign.[24]

---

[24]   Broatch, *et. al, vs.* Boysen, *et. al,* 175 *Federal Reporter* 702, decided January, 1910. John T. Clarke's copy of the agreement, indicating that both he and Asmus Boysen signed it, is reproduced in John T. Clarke *vs.* Wyoming Power Co., Case No. 1291, filed July 22, 1922, U. S. District Court, Cheyenne. Harry F. Clarke (born about 1861) and John T. Clarke are both listed in the agreement. John T. Clarke was the only Clarke member of the syndicate, but his younger brother, Henry Tefft Clarke, Jr. later also became involved in the controversy surrounding the agreement, as did another brother, Maurice Gordon Clarke.

Boysen now had a lease to look for coal in a huge area, but he also needed the approval of the Interior Department in Washington. Early in April, John N. Baldwin, writing on Union Pacific stationery, introduced Boysen to Congressman David Henderson of Iowa, who had been a key aide to Senator William Allison. Baldwin's introduction to Henderson produced immediate support from the key members of the Iowa power structure in Washington. At the beginning of May, letters of recommendation came from Senators Allison and Gear, Congressman McPherson and Secretary of Agriculture James Wilson. Now that he could confident of a favorable response, Boysen wrote to the Secretary of the Interior, giving copies of his letter to Gear, Allison, Henderson, McPherson and Baldwin.[25]

At the beginning of June, 1899, the Audubon *Journal* gave a fanciful account of Boysen's activity, saying that he had returned from Wyoming and Washington, DC, in connection with a "valuable silver mine" in Wyoming, that he was planning to sell to an English syndicate.[26]

Back on the reservation, Captain Nickerson steered the lease proposal through tribal councils held near the end of June, and the tribes confirmed the proposed lease. Nickerson then took five members of each of the tribes to Washington to seek approval there. On the way to Casper, one of the stages overturned, injuring an "old and lame" medicine man, and this was considered a bad omen, but the Indians finally agreed to proceed with the trip, sending their injured companion back to the reservation to recover.[27]

In Washington, Captain Nickerson had two objectives, the first to secure approval of Boysen's lease, and the second to get permission to negotiate with the tribes for the cession of surplus lands remaining after the allotting process was complete, so that those lands could be

---

[25] Congressman McPherson's letter was dated May 2, Senator Gear's letter was dated May 3, Senator Allison's letter was dated May 4, and Secretary Wilson's letter was dated May 5, 1899. Boysen's second letter to the Secretary of the Interior was dated May 10, 1899.

[26] *Audubon County Journal* (Exira, Iowa), June 1, 1899.

[27] The two tribal councils held to approve the lease proposal were held on June 26, 1899. Also, *Wyoming Derrick* (Casper), June 8, 1899.

opened for settlement by the public. Near the end of June, Nickerson and the Indian representatives returned to the reservation, and the *Clipper* noted that the Interior Department had approved the lease of the coal lands, although the newspaper account repeated the erroneous assumption that the lease was with the Burlington railroad. As to his second objective, Nickerson did not receive any encouragement on the issue of ceding the surplus lands for settlement.[28]

As a part of the approval process, Captain Nickerson certified to the Secretary of the Interior that the lease was "free from fraud or deception," and that he had no personal interest in it. He also certified that the land being leased was not needed by the tribes, and he included the supporting recommendation of three "creditable disinterested persons." The three men Nickerson named were John T. Wertz, Charles J. Woodhurst and James B. McLucas. McLucas may have been creditable and disinterested, but John T. Wertz designed Boysen's syndicate and Charles J. Woodhurst was a member of it.[29]

The final lease with Asmus Boysen was dated July 1, 1899, and it followed the proposal agreed at Fort Washakie, except for the added requirement that Boysen should only hire people who were acceptable to the tribes. Boysen accepted this amendment, and the lease was approved by the Secretary of the Interior. Josef Weis signed for Boysen as attorney in fact.[30]

Between October 28, 1899 and the end of the year, something happened to poison the relationship between Nickerson and Wertz, because at the beginning of 1900, Nickerson told the commissioner of Indian affairs that when he signed Wertz's allotment report in October, he was not aware that much of the land was unsuited for agriculture

---

[28] *The Clipper* (Lander), June 23, 1899.

[29] The Nickerson certification was provided to the House of Representatives in the minority report of January 26, 1905. *58th Congress, Third Session, House Report 3700, Part 2.*

[30] Boysen's power of attorney to Josef Weis of Omaha was dated August 21, 1899. Under the agreement, Josef Weis was authorized to borrow $250 for a year at 7% interest, but we do not know if he borrowed this money.

and that some Indians had received allotments who were not entitled to them. This criticism of Wertz was serious, but Nickerson's second letter was even more damaging.

Apparently the commissioner received a report that "certain parties" were prospecting for gold on the reservation, and in a follow-up letter on April 27, 1900, Nickerson said that the person making the report was "doubtless" a government official making $8 per day—a reference to Wertz. Nickerson then added a number of criticisms of Wertz's lack of attention to his assigned work, ending with the assertion that Wertz's "officious meddling had made him despised by every one on said reservation—even the Indians." Two weeks later, the secretary of the interior suspended Wertz, and at the beginning of July he was ordered to leave the reservation for his home in Omaha, at which point his compensation would cease. The president terminated him on April 12, 1901, and although Wertz protested directly to the president on June 26, the decision was not altered.[31]

Wertz was succeeded as allotting agent by Nickerson, so the tenor of Nickerson's letters in 1900 may not have been free of self-interest. Indeed, the government never stated an explicit reason for Wertz's termination, and he later was able to recover back pay for the period from the time he was ordered off the reservation until he was formally terminated by the president.[32]

Meanwhile, Boysen did take some steps to discover what his lease contained, and for this purpose he sent Niels C. Brorson out from Iowa. Brorson, also a Danish immigrant, was a valued employee from Audubon County, and Brorson hired Josef Weis to show him around the lease. The lease was huge, and the two men could not have

---

[31] Wertz's letter dated June 26, 1901 reached McKinley in late June or early July, just weeks before McKinley was shot on September 9 (he died September 14, 1901).

[32] Wertz collected $648 for the period before he was dismissed by the president. John Thomas Wertz *vs.* The United States, Case No. 22829 in the Court of Claims of the United States (decided May 1, 1905), *Cases Decided in the Court of Claims of the United States at the Term of 1904-05*, Vol. XL (Washington, 1905), 397.

conducted a great deal of work on it. For whatever reason, we know that Boysen's enthusiasm for the coal lease soon evaporated, probably because his railroad sponsor no longer expected to build a line through the lease area. Boysen may have been getting some feedback (or lack thereof) from the Burlington on its plan to build across Wyoming to Salt Lake City; indeed, the Burlington board did not elect to build any of the large projects being considered by its management in the years 1899-1901.[33]

Lacking any active encouragement that Wind River coal would have a large ready market, Boysen's lease was transformed from an asset to a liability, and in the spring of 1900, he offered to surrender the entire coal lease in exchange for a copper lease on two townships. If John Wertz suggested that exchange, he was leading Boysen away from the area he considered most prospective for copper (in the northeast of the lease), and since Boysen had made no move to assign the coal lease to the syndicate, he may no longer have been a "client" of Wertz, entitled to special treatment. However, Wertz could have encouraged Boysen to request the exchange, to serve as a valuable precedent for use with other clients.

By the time Secretary Hitchcock considered Boysen's request for a copper lease, he must have decided he had granted all the Boysen favors he was obligated to give, for he told Boysen that if he wanted to prospect for other minerals he would have to make a new application. The lease gave Boysen two years in which to locate coal deposits and to file a map defining his claim, and he did file a map, but it did not meet government requirements. Finally, on January 22, 1901, the government notified Boysen that his lease was terminated for failure to file the necessary map.[34]

---

[33] In his letter of April 27, 1900 to the commissioner of Indian affairs, Henry G. Nickerson disclosed the presence of Brorson and Weis on the Boysen lease, doing "assessment work." National Archives RG 75 Special Cases No. 147. Brorson later managed Boysen's affairs in his absence, both in Wyoming and later in Chicago. Also, Overton, *op. cit.,* 235

[34] Boysen's offer to exchange the coal lease for a copper lease was dated May 29, 1900, and the Secretary replied on June 4. Boysen's map was

The lease was apparently dead, and there is no indication that the syndicate partners held any other opinion at the time. Certainly, Boysen could not have been very happy with an agreement that was designed to give control of the project to John Wertz or his friends, leaving Boysen with as little as one vote. Boysen never commented on the terms of the agreement, but also he never asked the government to assign the lease to the syndicate. Consequently, Morrell never posted a bond as trustee, never called a meeting to elect a board of directors, and none of the members every made their initial financial contribution to the syndicate. However, both Charles Woodhurst, who was excused from making contributions, and John Clarke (who was not excused from contribution), did contact Boysen on several occasions for information about the project. We don't know when these contacts occurred, nor do we know if these men kept the other members informed. As to the other partners, it seemed that by common consent they thought the syndicate was also dead.[35]

We hear no more about the Boysen lease for three more years, and then it appeared that loyal Republican Boysen's efforts to assist the railroad's expansion plans were not forgotten back in Iowa party circles.

---

rejected in part because the government had not surveyed some of the land included in the lease, so that it could be described according to legal subdivisions. Boysen went to the Washington and talked to the Secretary of the Interior, and he later claimed that the Secretary had waived the requirement to file the map. On May 14, 1901, Boysen applied for a coal vein located fifteen miles from Ft. Washakie, and eight miles from Lander, which would have been outside the boundaries of his lease (which was more than eight miles from Lander), but nothing came of that application.

35 Under the terms of the agreement, the six-man board of directors was to be elected by the twelve *named* members of the syndicate, eleven of whom were selected by Wertz, and included his brother, the two fellow government employees from the reservation and his father-in-law.

3

BUILDING A FORTUNE

While Boysen's coal lease venture out in Wyoming was thus moribund, he was not idle at home in Iowa, where he turned his attentions to managing and expanding his business interests there. The means allowing him to accelerate that activity came to his wife Anna in 1896, when her father, William Leet, died, leaving a large estate. Leet's daughter, Rosa L. Thompson, was named administrator of the estate, and at the beginning of 1899, the heirs of William Leet formed a partnership in the major assets of the estate. This joint ownership lasted for several years, causing friction between Anna Boysen and her sister, but the fact remained that Anna Boysen, as one of the children of William Leet, was then wealthy. Mary Jane Leet, William's oldest daughter, married the Rev. John C. Stoughton, and after he died, Mary Jane lived for some years with her mother, Helen Leet, who was then also a widow. Mary Stoughton had no children, and she was later a long-suffering financial backer of Allan Boysen.[36]

It was the Leet family fortune that gave Asmus Boysen the backing to build his own fortune in Iowa real estate and banking. The nucleus of Boysen real estate investments in Audubon County was the 600-acre farm Anna Boysen received from her father's estate, and in 1898 and 1899, Asmus Boysen added three adjoining parcels to this farm,

---

[36] William Leet died in Aurora, Kane Co., Ill., September 5, 1896. After Leet's death, Rosa Thompson became president of the Bradford bank, where her husband, Robert Thompson, was cashier, and son Francis Leet ran the bank in Audubon County.

bringing the total acreage close to 1,000. In the 1900 census Boysen's large household included their children plus two servants and four farm laborers, and in short order, he was able to afford the life of a country squire, living on the farm in the summer, and moving to Chicago for the winter.

A significant contribution to Boysen's prominence in Audubon and Carroll counties was his close association with brother-in-law Frank M. Leet, who was involved in banking and other ventures. Soon, the two men were involved in a number of business ventures. The cornerstone of Frank Leet's banking business in Iowa was his father's bank, the Commercial Bank in Audubon County. Now, he and Boysen went on a spree adding banks to their holdings. At the end of June, 1899, they opened the German Savings Bank of Manning, Iowa, with Leet as the president. In the fall, they purchased the Farmers Exchange Bank, a private bank in Gray, Iowa, and in the summer of 1901, Leet and Boysen incorporated the First National Bank of Manila, Iowa. At the beginning of 1903, the partners purchased the Stuart Bank in Exira, Iowa, renaming it the Merchants and Farmers Bank, with Leet as president and Boysen as vice president. Boysen also owned the Bank of Templeton. While both men apparently invested in all the banks we have mentioned, they were clearly not equal shareholders, and Boysen later said that "his" four banks were the ones in Gray, Templeton, Audubon and Manning.[37]

Leet and Boysen also invested in businesses that were complementary to their other financial interests. One such business was the Leet, Boysen and Beason Loan Company, which loaned money in parallel to their several banking interests, and another was the Leet, Boysen and Beason Abstract Company in Audubon. The latter company examined land titles for real estate transactions, and would not have been a highly

---

[37] *Audubon County Journal* (Exira, Iowa), June 1, 29, July 20, 1899, November 14, 1901, August 21, 1902, January 1, 8, July 16, 1903, June 15, 1905. Boysen's testimony regarding his investments in banks is contained in Henry B. Pogson, Trustee and Augustus R. Smith, Trustee, *vs.* Big Horn Power Co, *et. al*, Case No. 1320, filed December 26, 1922 and decided March 9, 1928, U. S. District Court, Cheyenne.

profitable business, but it was a good source of information for the partners' real estate investments and speculations.[38]

Meanwhile, Boysen did not neglect his political interests, and in the summer of 1899, he again sought the nomination for Republican representative from Audubon County. This time he won on the first ballot and in November he won the seat with a margin of 406. When the legislature convened in Des Moines in January, 1900, Boysen moved his family to that city for the duration of the session, coming back to Gray from time to time to attend to business there. As further evidence of his political ascendancy, Boysen was a delegate to the Republican State Convention in Des Moines in August, 1900.[39]

In the Iowa legislature, Boysen allied himself with the Allison faction of the Republican party, and in the 1900 session he dutifully voted in accordance with the leadership instructions. He did not take any public position that reached the ears of the press, although he did sponsor a minor bill to increase the terms of school district officers. We must assume that this behavior caused him to be recognized as a loyal supporter of the Allison group, in view of the later help he received from that quarter. In the spring of 1902, Boysen went to Washington, D.C. for reasons we cannot be sure of, but we do know that he had dinner with Leslie M. Shaw, the former governor of Iowa, who was then Secretary of the Treasury.[40]

The exciting business partnership between Asmus Boysen and Frank Leet ended abruptly in the spring of 1905, when Leet died. Asmus Boysen became the administrator of Frank's estate, and he was also named guardian of Frank's son, eight-year-old William Leet. Although he did not know it at the time, the spring of 1905 was almost the last time that Asmus Boysen could be sure that he had plenty of

---

[38]   At the end of 1901, Leet and Boysen were again looking into land speculations in Nebraska, apparently first in Dixon County, then along the North Platte. *Audubon County Journal* (Exira, Iowa), April 11, July 11 (quoting the Manning *Monitor*), 1901.

[39]   Boysen's margin in 1901 was 633. *Audubon County Journal* (Exira, IA), November 23, 1899, January 18, August 2, 1900.

[40]   *Iowa State Register* (n.p.,1900).

money to finance the good life he now enjoyed. The years after his arrival in America and in partnership with Frank Leet were truly the good years.[41]

Nevertheless, the stage was set for Boysen to shift his attention back to Wyoming, this time to take advantage of an unexpected opportunity to finally realize something from the piece of paper the Interior Department summarily cancelled at the beginning of 1901. For the Wyoming congressional delegation finally succeeded in persuading Congress to reduce the tribal lands in the Wind River reservation. Captain Herman Nickerson took over the role of allotting agent in 1900, after John T. Wertz was suspended from that position, and in the spring of 1902, Congressman Mondell secured an appropriation of $10,000 to complete the allotments, so that the remaining lands could be opened for settlement under the homestead laws.[42]

---

[41] Francis Marion Leet died on April 6, 1905. His son, William A. Leet, was born February 8, 1896.

[42] *The Clipper* (Lander), April 18, 1902.

4

THE IOWA DELEGATION MAKES IT HAPPEN

Responding to political pressure, and in anticipation that the allotting process under the Dawes Act would soon be complete, the Department of the Interior sent James McLaughlin to the Wind River reservation to negotiate an agreement to open the surplus lands to settlement, and even before McLaughlin signed the formal agreement with the tribes, on March 3, 1904, Wyoming Congressman Franklin W. Mondell introduced H.R. 13481, to ratify the expected agreement with the Indians. The next day, the Interior Department (again) formally cancelled the Boysen coal lease, and since the Department had already terminated the lease back in 1901, the 1904 action could only have been an effort to "tidy" up the record. On April 22, 1904, McLaughlin signed the agreement with the tribes ceding that portion of the Wind River Reservation north of the Big Wind River.[43]

Mondell's bill opening 1.3 million acres in the northern part of the Wind River reservation to settlement under the public land laws was a major objective for the Wyoming congressional delegation, and it should have passed easily, but that was not to be. Later, Senator Warren said, ". . . [I]t was no boy's play. I had expected it would go through easily, and there was every reason why it should; but we had persistent and continuous opposition in high quarters. And besides this Boysen

---

[43]   *The Lander Clipper,* April 15, 1904.

matter had both friends and enemies and if we took sides with the one we were bound to have the enmity of the other."[44]

Nearly all of Boysen's defunct coal lease lay within the area to be opened to settlement, providing an excuse for him to argue that the lease somehow interfered with the opening of the ceded area to settlement. Support for Boysen involved the Iowa delegation in both houses of Congress, which may indicate that someone—perhaps at the Burlington railroad—felt he should be rewarded for his loyal help with the railroad's (aborted) expansion plans. In any case, the Iowa politicians and their friends were adamant in the face of strong opposition in Wyoming and elsewhere. Since former speaker David Henderson was no longer in Congress, Iowa Congressman John F. Lacey, chairman of the House Committee on Public Lands, spearheaded the case for Boysen in the House. Mondell's bill was referred to the House Committee on Indian Affairs, a subcommittee of the Committee on Public Lands, where the suggestion arose that the Boysen lease complicated the process under the bill. To be sure, some argued that the Boysen lease had already been cancelled (twice), but for a time this argument was drowned out by more powerful voices.[45]

Accordingly, in order to eliminate the supposed Boysen lease impediment, it was proposed that Boysen surrender the lease in exchange for the preferential right to select and purchase land somewhere in the ceded area. This sort of deal was not without precedent, for it had been used recently, in the Uintah reservation in northeastern Utah, where the Raven Mining Company received the right to receive patents for its claims there.[46]

---

[44] Francis E. Warren to George F. Bidwell, Manager, Chicago & North Western Railroad Company, Omaha, Nebr., March 8, 1905, in the Francis E. Warren collection, American Heritage Center, University of Wyoming.

[45] Speaker of the House David B. Henderson did not run for reelection to Congress in 1902.

[46] The Uintah reservation was opened to settlement on May 27, 1902, and the Raven Mining Company patents were authorized on March 3, 1905. 32 *Statutes at Large* 263 and 33 *Statutes at Large* 1048.

The so-called Boysen provision in the House bill gave him the right to locate not more than 640 acres of mineral or coal lands somewhere in the ceded area of the reservation. The land was to be in the form of a square, and Boysen was to pay $10 per acre for it. The provision was supported by the Iowa delegation, but it was extremely controversial. The Wyoming delegation did not like the Boysen provision, but did not openly object because they did not want to jeopardize the bill. Other members of Congress were more vocal in opposition, as was Secretary of the Interior Ethan A. Hitchcock and key government employees on the reservation. (Maj. Henry E. Wadsworth had replaced Captain Nickerson as agent.) Lacey defended the need for the Boysen provision, saying that the government failed to give Boysen the required 60-day notice of his breach of the lease, making the cancellation invalid.

Mondell did not take part in the debate, which was emotional at times, but New York Congressman John J. Fitzgerald, who led the opposition to the Boysen provision, drew Mondell into the argument by pointing out that the provision did not have Mondell's consent. Mondell then admitted that he had not requested the provision, but to avoid offending the proponents of the provision, he also said that the provision was a simple way to avoid future difficulties over the cancellation issue. He was then asked whether Boysen could use his 640-acre option to control strategic routes for railroads or highways. Here, Mondell was less than candid, for he declared that there were no such "passes" on the reservation where this was possible, although he clearly knew that the Wind River Canyon lay inside the reservation.

The acrimonious debate finally persuaded the managers of the bill that it would not pass with the Boysen provision. Senator Warren, who opposed the Boysen preference, described Mondell's dilemma, saying, "Now Mr. Mondell felt anxious enough about it [*i.e*, the bill] to accede to that [Boysen] provision as long as Mr. Lacey who was on the subcommittee, was insisting upon it, but that is what has water-logged the matter. As far as my information goes the man [*i.e*, Boysen] has never done anything on that land." To appease Lacey, Mondell promised that if the House removed the Boysen provision, it would be restored in the Senate, and the House then removed the Boysen provision by a vote of 127-47. The bill then passed the House, although emotions were running so high that Mondell could not secure unanimous consent for passage.[47]

Obviously, Mondell was in no position to guarantee that the Senate would act as he had promised, so it is obvious that he was conveying a promise from a senator, and that senator was Wyoming Senator Clarence Don Clark. Clark, who was Wyoming's first congressman, and was elected to the Senate in 1895, also had strong connections with the Iowa delegation in Congress.[48]

Clarence Clark moved to Evanston, Wyo., in 1881, where he opened a successful practice of law and developed a strong relationship to the Union Pacific railroad (his brother, Dyer O. Clark, was superintendent of mines for the company in Omaha). In Washington, Clark introduced few bills and was known as a "topnotch errand boy for his constituents." Although he was technically Wyoming's senior senator, it was Senator Francis E. Warren who led the Wyoming delegation, and Clark supported Warren on nearly every issue. The Boysen provision of 1905 was a different matter, however.[49]

On February 2, 1905, Senator Warren introduced the companion bill to the House measure to open the reservation to settlement. Warren wanted to make sure the measure could be approved before the 58th Congress expired on March 3, and as added insurance he was able

[47] Warren's remarks are from the debate in the Senate, and are quoted in *The Lander Clipper,* March 10, 1905. Debate on the Boysen provision in the House is found in the *Congressional Record,* XXXIX, February 16, 1905.

[48] Clarence Clark graduated from law school in Iowa, and when David B. Henderson ran for Congress, Clark organized Henderson clubs for his campaign; after Clark became senator from Wyoming, he supported Henderson's election as speaker of the House.

[49] The "errand boy" quote is from Taft Alfred Larson, *History of Wyoming* (Lincoln, Nebr., 1978), 318. Clark was elected to fill the vacant senate seat caused by the Wyoming senate's failure to approve Governor Osborn's candidate, and Clark took his seat on January 23, 1895; Warren's term began March 4, 1895, making him the junior senator.

to get an identical measure attached to the Indian appropriation bill. Neither bill included the Boysen preference.[50]

As Mondell had promised, the Boysen provision was far from dead, and on February 25, Clarence Clark responded to the wishes of Allison and his other Iowa friends, and restored the Boysen provision to the Senate version of the bill. This action was accepted by the Senate on a voice vote—a far cry from the contentious scene in the House. Nevertheless, Warren was very unhappy. Referring to the pressure from the Iowa senators, Warren said, "Allison and Dolliver from Iowa were exceeding insistent, and my colleague Senator Clark, who is on the Indian Affairs Committee, had promised them he would protect their wishes to the very best of his ability; so we were again 'in the midst of it.'"[51]

The House and Senate bills had to go to a conference committee to resolve the difference between them, and the membership of that committee would determine the outcome. Although Warren disliked the Boysen provision, he wanted the bill to pass, and he said he persuaded Senator William Stewart of Nevada, who was chairman of the Committee on Indian Affairs, to name Senator Clark to the conference committee for the bill. When Congressman James Sherman, who was chairman of the House Committee on Indian Affairs, appointed Iowa Congressman Lacey to the committee, passage of the Boysen provision seemed ensured.[52]

At this point, the shadow of John T. Wertz fell across the scene. Following his dismissal in 1901, Wertz continued to look for ways to make money from his knowledge of the land on the reservation. At least by the fall of 1902 he was busy contacting people in Nebraska

---

[50] After the separate measure passed the Senate, the rider on the Indian appropriation bill was then deleted.

[51] The Warren quote is from the letter of Francis E. Warren to George F. Bidwell, *op. cit.*

[52] Warren claimed responsibility for securing both the Clark and Lacey appointments to the conference committee, but it is likely that Allison was also involved in the Senate, and Lacey's appointment may not have required Warren's support in the House.

to file mineral claims on the reservation he expected to have approved through his political contacts in Washington, and the following spring he also chartered the National Mining and Development Co., a Maine corporation, to serve as the vehicle for his schemes. Thus, while he claimed that he helped Boysen get his preference tract, he was at the same time using the Boysen preference as a precedent to secure similar benefits for his other clients. In this effort, Wertz was aided by his own congressional friends, whom he never disclosed publicly.[53]

So it was, that when the reservation bill should have passed easily, an opposing group of senators appeared. It seems that some clients of John Wertz, headed by the Oyster family in Washington, D.C. (who had a thriving business in dairy products) and Edward L. Brice (who owned a laundry), also had filed applications to lease land on the reservation, which the Interior Department did not approve. This group now opposed the Boysen preference, unless they also were given 160-acre preferences. In the end, Oyster and Brice withdrew, having received promises that do not appear in the record, but Warren's description will have to suffice:

"Through the kindness of Senator Blackburn, who gave me the names, I sent for the different parties, and then got a lot of strong Washington friends after them; and by promising Oyster, Brice and a few other good men, that we would all help them to secure good places

---

[53] In November, 1902, Wertz contacted Alfred K. Smith, cashier of the Bank of Brainard, Nebr., as part of an effort to get thirty prominent men from Nebraska to file reservation claims. Alfred K. Smith to Arima D. Smith, January 4, 1903, Interior, Appointments Division, "Charges and Protests Files," 1849-1907, RG 48, National Archives. The National Mining and Development Co. was chartered May 22, 1903, with headquarters in Augusta, Me., and although it later operated in Wyoming, its shareholders were never publicly disclosed, but in 1909, Wertz gave the Washington *Herald* a list of Washington people "interested" in the National Mining Co., including Nebraska ex-senator John M. Thurston, who left the Senate on March 4, 1901.

within the reservation, giving them letters to the Indian agent, railroad people, old settlers, and others, etc, we relieved the strain there."[54]

Finally, the bill passed both houses of Congress, but then Warren had another nightmare, for he realized that Interior Secretary Hitchcock was still opposed to the bill, and might well influence President Roosevelt not to sign it. Indeed, when the Wyoming delegation went to see Roosevelt, they learned that he was inclined to reject the bill. Nevertheless, Roosevelt told Warren that he should try to gain the support of Francis E. Leupp, Commissioner of Indian Affairs, who was a friend of the President. Leupp had been friendly to the idea of selling surplus reservation lands, so Warren's task was not a difficult one, and Warren said that the Commissioner "surrendered after a short parley." On March 3, 1905, President Theodore Roosevelt signed the bill, over the objections of Secretary Hitchcock.[55]

The legislative ordeal was over, and Asmus Boysen had the right to look for valuable land, but he soon learned that making that selection was not an easy task.

---

[54] Francis E. Warren to George F. Bidwell, *op. cit.* Both Warren and Mondell identified John T. Wertz as the sponsor of the Oyster family group. *Thermopolis Record,* February 25, 1905. We also infer a connection between John T. Wertz and Edward L. Brice from a note in Wertz's papers in the Hot Springs County Museum, Thermopolis, Wyo., written on the stationary of the Star Laundry Company of Washington, D.C., listing Edward L. Brice as president. We do not know what "help" Warren promised Oyster and Brice, but in the fall of 1905, Edward L. Brice spent several weeks in Fremont County, Wyo., and a year later he was back again, prospecting for minerals on the Wind River reservation. *Wind River Mountaineer* (Lander), September 22, October 13, 1905 and October 26, 1906.

[55] Francis E. Warren to George F. Bidwell, *op. cit.*

5

BOYSEN SELECTS HIS LAND

At the beginning of March, 1905, Asmus Boysen had the legal right to select 640 acres somewhere on the ceded area of the Wind River Reservation, and there was little doubt what he hoped to find there. Five years before, he had offered to surrender his coal lease for the right to prospect for copper, and he was surely aware of the gold and copper fever running high in the Copper Mountain region, just outside the east boundary of the reservation.

Boysen did not wait until the President signed the bill before going to Wyoming, and we know he was at the Wind River canyon on the eastern edge of the reservation before February 10. That was the date when surveyors from both the Burlington and Northwestern railroads finished mapping rights of way through the canyon, and Boysen saw them there, although he did not attach any particular significance to that fact at the time. After all, this was a time when railroads were running many surveys for lines that they never built, and neither of these railroads had definite plans for a line through the canyon (the Northwestern never built there). Moreover, through his Iowa connections with the Burlington, Boysen may have learned that railroad had no immediate plans to build in the canyon.[56]

---

[56] Both railroads asked for rights of way in Thermopolis early in January, and the next week they were both surveying in the Wind River Canyon. The Burlington's map showing its right of way in the canyon was dated February 15, 1905. William J. Broatch, *et. al.*, vs. Asmus Boysen, *et. al.*,

On March 22, Boysen made a tremendous splash in Wyoming, when he incorporated the Asmus Boysen Mining Company, with authorized capitalization of $25 million and headquarters in Thermopolis. The Cheyenne *Tribune* gushed that this was "the biggest company that has ever been formed in this state," adding that the $1,250 in filing fees would "pay considerable clerk hire" for the secretary of state. Although this company later conducted the exploratory work to permit Boysen to select his land, its first work was outside the eastern reservation boundary, in the Copper Mountain play.[57]

The Copper Mountain play extended east from the Wind River reservation for a distance of ten or twelve miles, and in this district there were signs of the metal on the ground for everyone to see. Many prospectors had different ideas where the "Mother Lode" might be located, so that the Copper Mountain mining district claimed newspaper headlines for a number of years and produced some ore, before finally dying.[58]

Nis Peter Boysen, Asmus Boysen's younger brother (he was 28), who came to the U. S. two years before, arrived in Thermopolis at the end of March, 1905, to supervise his brother's prospecting on Copper Mountain, and later over on the reservation. Asmus kept his brother on a short leash, and beyond giving out his title as secretary of the Asmus Boysen Mining Company, he said little to the newspapers about the company and its plans. However, this total news blackout was partially lifted two weeks later, when the Boysen company announced that it had purchased a diamond drill, which was then on its way from Casper to Copper Mountain. The newspaper also printed a letter Asmus Boysen wrote from his Chicago office:

"Through these lines I wish to call your attention to the special act of congress which passed the house on March 2, 1905, whereby

---

Case No. 288, U. S. District Court, Cheyenne, and *Thermopolis Record,* January 7, 14, February 11, 1905.

[57] The quote from the Cheyenne *Tribune* was reprinted in *The Lander Clipper* of March 31, 1905, and the *Thermopolis Record* of March 25, 1905.

[58] *Thermopolis Record,* June 22, October 26, 1907.

I exchange my 178,000-acre coal land lease which I held with the Shoshone and Arapahoe Indians, in Wyoming, for 640 acres of mineral lands, containing copper of immense value.

"Write for my booklet giving the full history of my valuable concessions and of the ASMUS BOYSEN MINING COMPANY, incorporated in the state of Wyoming.

"Bear in mind—this is one of the greatest opportunities ever offered to the most skeptical investor. Write at once."[59]

No copies of Boysen's booklet have been found.[60]

The following week, Peter Reisgaard, who was accompanied by his lawyer, one "Louis Koch" of Omaha, took an option on four claims on Copper Mountain owned by the Basin Mining Company, posting a $150,000 bond, and depositing $10,000 as a guaranty. Reisgaard did not use Boysen's name, but in fact he was a Danish immigrant from Audubon County, Iowa, and Boysen undoubtedly supplied the wherewithal to post the bond and make the required deposit.[61]

According to the newspaper account, Reisgaard, who was described as a "practical mine operator" from Alma, Colorado, was on his way back to Colorado to make arrangements for exploring the option he had obtained when he met "an agent of the Boysen company," who purchased the option from him. N. P. Boysen, the official Boysen spokesman in Thermopolis, was at first extremely close-mouthed, but on Sunday morning he finally told the editor that the "head office" had acquired Reisgaard's option, paying that gentleman a $10,000 bonus for his trouble, and giving him a position with the Boysen company.[62]

The option transaction was real enough, but the rest of the newspaper account was fiction. Reisgaard was in fact Boysen's real estate manager in Audubon, according to the Audubon *Journal*, and the identification

---

59 *Thermopolis Record,* April 8, 22, 1905.

60 Nis Peter Boysen came to the United States from Copenhagen in the summer of 1903, and came to Thermopolis in March, 1905. *The Clipper* (Lander), March 31, 1905 and *Thermopolis Record,* April 22, 1905.

61 *Thermopolis Record,* May 20, October 21, 1905. Peter Reisgaard came to the United States in 1892.

62 *Thermopolis Record,* May 20, 1905.

of the attorney with him as "Louis Koch" was in fact a transparent disguise for Asmus Boysen's cousin, Louis Koch Boysen, then 27, who later became involved in his own Wyoming mining speculation, using his real name.[63]

. Still, there were skeptics in Wyoming, who believed that talk of Boysen's "valuable concessions" was really puffery to sell stock in his company, and that the major objective of his mining company was to prospect on the reservation in preparation for selection of the preference section of land. Even that prospecting opportunity had its doubters, for Douglas editor Bill Barlow (Merris C. Barrow) groused that the reservation had already been "as thoroughly prospected as Chicago's lake front," making any undiscovered copper or coal highly unlikely. Later, in an item written and widely reprinted around the state before Boysen made his selection, Bill Barlow opined that Boysen's tract would be worth "possibly $10 an acre [the price Boysen paid] and probably very much less." Although most readers then and for some years to come would have laughed at this harsh prediction, after more than one fortune was expended in pursuit of hoped-for value from Boysen's preference tract, Bill Barlow proved to be not far from the mark.[64]

Early in May, the Audubon *Journal* announced that Eugene Mertz, the sometime auctioneer, mayor, postmaster and druggist in the town of Gray, Iowa, was recruiting men from local farms in Audubon County for the Asmus Boysen company, and soon the company began working on the Basin Mining Co. option property with its diamond drill. Shortly after that work began, prospects for the success of the company seemed to be enhanced by news of a rich strike not far away by Pueblo "Peb" Williams, which was followed by a story of an "even richer" strike by Dudley Hale, about six miles from the Boysen Mining

---

[63] Louis Koch Boysen, the son of Asmus Boysen's uncle Adolph Boysen, was born in Milwaukee on April 22, 1878, and died in Tryon, N.C. on January 22, 1949. He was a lawyer, and lived in Chicago for a number of years.

[64] *Bill Barlow's Budget* (Douglas), May 17, December 6, 1905.

company operations. Asmus Boysen offered Hale $20 for a 2 x 2 inch sample flecked with free gold, but the latter refused the offer.[65]

Unable to buy gold from Hale, Boysen also was unable to find much of his own, and when N. P. Boysen came down from Copper Mountain in July, he was "reluctant" to say what the diamond drill was turning up—and he was not hiding any fabulous news. Indeed, the only substantive news from Boysen's Copper Mountain prospecting in the summer of 1905 was word of a seven foot rattlesnake with fourteen rattles killed on the mountain in August by Nils P. Boysen and Myron C. McGrath "after a hard fight."[66]

The news of the Williams and Hale discoveries brought a rush of prospectors to the mountain, and in the fall of 1905, a new town named Birdseye was established to serve the mining community. The furious activity on the mountain soon spawned a second town, called Depass, which by the end of 1906 had a two-story hotel, with running water piped from the creek, a general store, and "all other needed business houses." The Copper Mountain Mining District was organized in the spring of 1906, to keep a reliable record of mining claims and issue regulations for conducting annual work. By the end of April, speculative excitement was so high that the Thermopolis *Record* ran out of blanks for filing on mining locations.[67]

Despite the enthusiastic press reports, commercial quantities proved elusive, and there were no stories of rich strikes for the Boysen company. Indeed, the Thermopolis editor complained that "Sherlock Holmes would fail to get so much as a grunt" from the Boysen company regarding the "deep hole" they had drilled. Fortunately, there was something else for the company to do, and although Asmus Boysen

---

[65] *Audubon County Journal* (Exira, Iowa), May 4, 1905, *Thermopolis Record,* July 1, August 19, September 2, 1905, *The Cheyenne Daily Leader,* August 27, 1905 and *Basin Republican,* August 16, October 26, 1905.

[66] *Thermopolis Record,* July 8, 1905 and *The Cheyenne Daily Leader,* August 19, 1905.

[67] Birdseye was named for Charles E. Fogg's ranch. *Basin Republican,* November 16, 1905 and *Thermopolis Record,* October 14, 1905, March 31, April 28, December 8, 1906.

continued to participate in the play on Copper Mountain, in fact, the Boysen mining company had turned its attention elsewhere.[68]

Prospecting the ceded area of more than a million acres was a formidable task, and Boysen had to make his selection within thirty days after the government completed its survey of that area, which was expected to occur before the end of the year. These requirements raised the question as to whether Boysen could prospect anywhere that was still unsurveyed. Boysen hoped to prospect the ceded area while the surveyors were completing their work, so that he could make his land selection within the authorized time period, and at the end of July he sent John N. Baldwin to Washington to find out whether that was possible. In anticipation of a positive response, he moved the diamond drill over to the east boundary of the reservation early in September.[69]

Interior Secretary Hitchcock was never friendly to the Boysen preference, and now he refused to give Boysen permission to move the diamond drill onto the reservation. Since the law allowed only 30 days in which to make the selection, Hitchcock declared that the 30 day period in the law *included* any preliminary prospecting to gain information for the selection. Boysen was then left with the impossible task of prospecting the entire 1.3 million area within 30 days.[70]

Faced with this time constraint, Boysen got his friend, Treasury Secretary Leslie M. Shaw, to argue his side of the matter with the President, who was then on a trip in the South. Secretary Hitchcock sent

---

[68] *The Worland Grit,* September 6, December 27, 1906, April 25, 1907, and *Thermopolis Record,* March 17, April 27, 1906.

[69] Field work on the survey of the ceded area on the reservation was expected to be finished by December 1, 1905, but then the survey had to be approved. Late in November, only the strip east of the Wind River Canyon remained to be surveyed. *Wind River Mountaineer* (Lander), November 3, 1905, and *Thermopolis Record,* November 25, 1905. The Cheyenne *Tribune* gave Baldwin's title as attorney for the Union Pacific, although he was clearly in Washington on Boysen's business. *The Wyoming Tribune* (Cheyenne), July 27, 1905.

[70] *Basin Republican,* August 16, 1905 and *Thermopolis Record,* September 2, 1905.

his own recommendation to Roosevelt, as well, including anti-Boysen protests from the Wyoming congressional delegation (who were no longer constrained by the Iowans in Congress). Since Roosevelt had conflicting recommendations from his cabinet, he asked for a legal opinion.

Without waiting for the formal legal opinion, Secretary Hitchcock (perhaps acting on instructions from the President himself), did issue a permit for Boysen to prospect, *but only within the boundaries of his old coal lease.* The coal lease covered 178,000 acres, not all of which was in the ceded area, so the permit only gave Boysen access to about 13% of the ceded area. Moreover, in response to press reports that Boysen had hired 100 men, the permit limited his work force to ten men.[71]

In late October, Boysen hired Charles J. Stone, a mining engineer from Chicago, and Joseph C. Pyle, an expert from Butte, Mont., who worked for Copper King William Clark. Boysen moved the diamond drill over to the Muddy Creek area, in the northeast part of the coal lease, and the crew there apparently included Odd J. "Mid" Midthun, a Norwegian surveyor, whose knowledge of the area became significant later.

It is interesting to speculate whether John Wertz, who knew a great deal about mineral indications on the reservation, and was in the area at the time, influenced Boysen's first choice of a location to drill. It later developed that this location, on Muddy Creek, had a good deal of surface mineralization, but what later became the "hot" spot in the Willow Creek play was some four or five miles south of the Muddy Creek location (but still within the boundary of Boysen's coal lease). It therefore appears that if Wertz gave Boysen advice, it most likely was a "red herring" to keep him away from the best ground. In retrospect,

---

[71]   *The Lander Clipper,* November 3, 1905, and *Thermopolis Record,* November 11, 1905. An opinion from Solicitor General Henry M. Hoyt was dated November 3, 1905, but obviously the Secretary was aware of the substance of the opinion when he gave Boysen his permit. The formal opinion of Attorney General William H. Moody, confirming the limits in Boysen's permit, was issued in Washington on November 7, 1905. *The Cheyenne Daily Leader,* November 10, 1905.

Boysen was fortunate that did not select his square mile in the section where he was preparing to drill.[72]

Word soon got around that Boysen had a permit to prospect on the reservation, and it was rumored that he hired 100 men at $5 per day to look for signs of copper deposits on the reservation. There were many prospectors outside the reservation who wanted to prospect there, but could not do so until after the area was opened to settlement in 1906, and they were most unwilling to see Boysen have such an obvious advantage over them. The Fremont Club in Lander wired the Wyoming congressional delegation protesting Boysen's permit, and they got immediate favorable responses from all three men (notably including Wyoming Senator Clark).[73]

The terrain was very difficult, the weather was bad, and several string teams were required to move the drill, but finally, after the stormy weather cleared, drilling began. Prospecting with the drill did not proceed very long. Although the drill was supposed to be operating "night and day," on the night of November 2, the five-member crew was in camp about 100 yards away from the drill, and the drill was not guarded when two or three men apparently set off dynamite charges on the engine and drill. Newspaper accounts were not consistent, with one paper claiming the deed was the work of three masked men on horseback, while another mentioned only the tracks of two men

[72] *Thermopolis Record,* October 28, 1905. The drill was operating on Boysen's coal lease in Section 9, Township 7 North, Range 3 East of the Wind River Meridian.

[73] The Lander *Clipper* said that Boysen had hired 100 men at $5 per day, and if so, this would have been a significant increase over the 50¢ per day then being offered for work on the Big Horn Canal up in the Basin. *Basin Republican,* November 9, 1905. *The Lander Clipper,* October 20, 27, 1905. Senator Warren's protest to Secretary Hitchcock asked that Boysen be limited to prospecting on his old lease, and asked that the prospecting crew be limited to ten men, rather than the rumored "one hundred." Early in November, Senator Clark told the Cheyenne *Leader* that Boysen should have to wait until the reservation was opened, and his permit should be revoked. *Cheyenne Daily Leader,* October 31, November 4, 1905.

leading away from the scene, where a note had been left on the ground. But all accounts agreed that the engine and drill were damaged beyond repair, and several of Boysen's men were thrown to the ground by the explosions, although none was injured.[74]

Washington responded to the incident by dispatching three camps of cavalry to patrol the northern portion of the reservation. One camp was at Thermopolis, one was down on the Wind River, and the third was at Red Canyon, near where the incident occurred. Early in December, the Cheyenne *Leader,* under the headline, "Thermopolis Men Involved," reported that the U. S. Secret Service had turned up the identity of the culprits who set off the dynamite, and that one of them had confessed. According to this story, rival prospectors had secretly discovered valuable minerals in the area where the diamond drill was operating, and they had hired men to blow up Boysen's drill, to prevent him from discovering these deposits. This story was not picked up in the local papers, where there was plenty of anti-Boysen sentiment.[75]

Whatever the details may have been, Boysen was convinced that Maj. Henry E. Wadsworth, the Indian Agent on the reservation, was complicit in the effort to halt his exploration, and later a federal appellate judge flatly declared that Major Wadsworth "suffered" Boysen's drill to be destroyed. Asmus Boysen was in Thermopolis at the time of the incident, and soon after his brother received an anonymous

---

[74]   The drill was destroyed on the evening of November 2, 1905. *The Lander Clipper,* November 3, 1905, *Thermopolis Record,* October 21, November 4, 1905, *The Cheyenne Daily Leader,* November 11, 1905, and *Basin Republican,* November 30, 1905. Asmus Boysen *vs.* Harry E. Wadsworth, Case No. 286, U. S. District Court, Cheyenne. The drill was later repaired and used on the Boysen tract.

[75]   *Thermopolis Record,* November 4, 1905 and *The Cheyenne Daily Leader,* December 9, 1905. The *Leader* article was datelined Meeteetse, Wyo. on December 3, and there is no subsequent record of arrests for the crime. Most of the newspapers in Fremont and Big Horn counties were sympathetic to the effort to shut down Boysen's prospecting operation, and were not interested in learning who had brought about that result.

letter warning him and his crew to leave the reservation within 24 hours. J. A. Nixon, who operated the drill, left for Salt Lake City, and the crew moved to a location off the reservation, about 30 miles from Thermopolis. Both Boysen brothers then left the state, "fearing physical violence," and when Asmus returned to Iowa, he received a letter decorated with skull and cross bones warning him that Wyoming justice awaited him if he returned to the reservation. The threat proved unnecessary, for Wadsworth immediately ordered Boysen off the reservation.[76]

In the background of this incident, the ghosts from Boysen's meetings at Ft. Washakie and in Omaha in April of 1899 now returned to haunt him. In fact, Henry T. Clarke, Jr, John T. Clarke's younger brother, was in Thermopolis in the fall of 1905, just before Boysen lost his diamond drill, and John T. Wertz was also in Wyoming at the time. He told the newspapers he had been "enjoying a hunt in the Big Horn Mountains," but in reality he was on Willow Creek on the reservation, less than six miles south of Boysen's drill, selecting the mineral land he would file on when he could legally do so.[77]

Wertz apparently assumed that the incident would leave Boysen in a frame of mind to concede to him a share of the tract he was about to select, and perhaps Wertz even intended to offer Boysen a share in the filings he intended to make on Willow Creek. In any case, he left Wyoming for Washington the day after the drill was blown up—clearly it was not a good time to be looking for mineral lands on the reservation—and when he returned to Omaha he asked his lawyer to draw up the necessary papers for Boysen to convey a share in the preference tract to him. It is clear from a fragment of Wertz's instructions to his lawyer that he was trying to establish a position

---

[76] *The Cheyenne Daily Leader,* November 11, 1905 and *Thermopolis Record,* November 11, 1905. The government ordered Boysen off the reservation late on November 2, 1905. Judge John F. Philips made the comment regarding Wadsworth in Wadsworth *vs.* Boysen, 8th Circuit Court of Appeals, 148 *Federal Reports* 771.

[77] Edward L. Brice, one of those Senator Warren had earlier promised to help, was also on Willow Creek at this time.

somewhere between the members of the old syndicate and Boysen, keeping a foot in each camp, saying ". . . in this manner we are in a position to get a larger slice . . . ." This note makes clear that Wertz thought Boysen would not only make some settlement with him, but also would be willing to give "something" to the members of the syndicate, with "few exceptions."[78]

In order to secure his "larger slice," Wertz wanted first to make his own deal with Boysen, then broker a settlement with the syndicate members. Since he was no longer a government employee, Wertz could deal directly with Boysen, rather than using his father-in-law and brother as go-betweens. Wertz outlined his strategy as follows:

"Keep this strictly confidential and do as I suggest and I will be able to get a better settlement out of him all around. This one I know he will consent to, and when this is out of the way it is an easy matter for me to make the adjustment of the others connected in the deal. But it would not do now for me to tell him that I was back of their move as he would fly off and be as hot as a wet hen. Do as I suggest and leave it to me. I am on the ground and know the situation thoroughly and don't fear of their getting any advantage of me."[79]

Wertz's attempt to negotiate with Boysen took place at the end of 1905 and the spring of 1906, before Boysen made his selection (he received his patent in 1907). However, Wertz failed to reckon with Boysen's stubborn personality and his temper, and for whatever reasons, Boysen did not cede a share of the land to Wertz.

After the vandalism at Muddy Creek, public opinion in Thermopolis was initially sympathetic to the Boysens, and a public protest meeting

---

[78] The response to John T. Wertz's instructions is contained in a letter from his Omaha attorneys, dated December 14, 1905, enclosing the conveyances Wertz had requested. Charles E. Morgan, of the firm Wharton, Adams & Morgan (Omaha) to John T. Wertz, in Chicago, December 14, 1905. John T. Wertz papers in the Hot Springs County Museum, Thermopolis, Wyo.

[79] The quotations are from an undated postscript on Palmer House (Chicago) stationery, in the John T. Wertz papers in the Hot Springs County Museum, Thermopolis, Wyo.

was held in their support, but soon this good will dissipated. The three members of the Wyoming congressional delegation were eagerly supporting the protests against Boysen's preferential treatment in prospecting on the reservation, and of course, Secretary Hitchcock always opposed Boysen. Consequently, Boysen had no recourse but to turn to the courts, and there he found a friendlier reception.

This may have been Boysen's first lawsuit, but his journey to the U. S. District Court in Cheyenne was only the first of more than sixty cases in which he or his interests were involved directly or indirectly. This amazing tale of tenacious litigation took place in a number of courts, ranging from the justice of the peace court in Lander to the Supreme Court of the United States. The cases stretched over nearly fifty years, continuing after he died, and there were few successes and many disappointments. But in his first encounter at least, he prevailed.

John W. Lacey, who was Boysen's Wyoming attorney, was appointed chief justice of the Supreme Court of Wyoming Territory by President Chester Arthur in 1884, and he resigned two years later to enter private practice in Cheyenne, with the Union Pacific railroad as his chief client. One of his law partners was John A. Riner, who was now judge of the U. S. District Court in Cheyenne, and another law partner was Willis Van Devanter, Lacey's brother-in-law, who was now one of the judges in the U. S. Eighth Circuit Court of Appeals in St. Louis. Both judges ruled on the Boysen case.[80]

Lacey filed the case on April 23, in the U. S. District Court in Cheyenne, because he was suing Henry E. Wadsworth, the Indian Agent on the reservation, an official of the United States government. On the bench was John A. Riner, who had occasion to rule on several cases involving Boysen before he retired from the bench in 1921. Riner acted quickly, issuing an injunction on April 24, suspending Wadsworth's ejection order and giving Boysen the right to prospect not just on his coal lease, but in the entire ceded area, and setting the case for trial in Cheyenne on May 14.

---

[80] It is likely that Boysen's Omaha counsel, John N. Baldwin, suggested Lacey as Wyoming counsel, as Baldwin and Lacey would have known each other in their work for the Union Pacific.

Timothy F. Burke, the U. S. Attorney for Wyoming, entered the case to represent Wadsworth on May 9, but waited until May 14 to file a demurrer, saying Boysen did not have a cause of action. This did not convince Riner, who continued the injunction against Wadsworth and gave the government 30 days to respond. Instead of responding, Burke waited another two weeks and then asked Riner to permit him to appeal the injunction to the 8th Circuit Court of Appeals, located in St. Louis. Riner allowed the appeal the same day (May 29).[81]

Meanwhile, the surveys of the ceded area were also approved on May 29, 1906, starting the 30-day period during which Boysen had to select his land. Thus, even if the appellate court ruled for Boysen, it would be too late, and accordingly, he gave up the possibility of prospecting the entire ceded area and made use of what he had learned on Copper Mountain about mineral outcroppings just across the reservation boundary in the Wind River canyon. Boysen knew that copper mineralization was visible inside the reservation on the west wall of the canyon, and he was told to expect those copper deposits would thicken further down in the mountain to the west. Taking surveyor Cornelius Farmer with him to verify the land description, and avoiding the army patrols keeping prospective settlers from the ceded area, Boysen made his selection on June 22, 1906, squarely athwart the mouth of the Wind River canyon.[82]

The act of Congress gave Boysen the right to "not more than 640 acres in the form of a square." Boysen wanted to include the copper outcrops he found on the west wall of the Wind River canyon, and to do that he had to select parts of four sections in two townships, but he had trouble describing the land he wanted. Although the survey had been officially approved, the government surveyors were expecting settlers on the reservation who would irrigate land for farms, not

---

[81] Judge Riner's injunction was issued April 23, 1906. Case No. 286, *op. cit.*

[82] The drawings for land in the ceded area were to begin on July 16 and end in early August, after which successful applicants were to be notified by mail. Applicants for mineral lands had to wait 60 days after August 15 before entering the ceded area. *Buffalo Bulletin,* July 5, 1906.

prospectors looking for copper in the mountains. Consequently, when Boysen made his selection in June, the rugged northern portion of the tract he selected was described as "unsurveyable" on the survey plat approved for that township. Speaking of these problems twenty years later, Boysen said that he found one survey stake at the south boundary of Township 6, between Sections 32 and 33, and used that as the center of his square. He then "guessed" at the rest of the description.[83]

Of course, the government could not "guess" at the description it would have to include in Boysen's patent. In order to write a precise description of the Boysen tract, the government surveyors prepared a "protraction" of a fractional section to identify it for the patent Boysen was to receive—in case the appellate court ruled against the government. The possibility that Boysen might not get a patent arose from the fact that Burke was now challenging more than Boysen's right to prospect—he also challenged the validity of the congressional grant to Boysen.[84]

Asmus Boysen must have been very angry at his failure to get permission to prospect in the ceded area before making his selection, when he was surely aware that his cousin, Louis K. Boysen, and other Chicago partners not only located minerals, but staked mining claims in the ceded area on February 24, months before the area was opened to mining claims (such claims were not supposed to be made until 60 days after August 15, 1906). These claims were located on the south side of Owl Creek, just inside the north boundary of the ceded area of the reservation, where sulphur deposits outcropping on the surface had been known for some time. Although we were not told how those staking the claims were able to evade the Army patrols, the logical explanation was that ranchers with reservation grazing leases in the Owl Creek area permitted them to enter the ceded area on their

---

83 Boysen's comments were in testimony before the Special Master in Case No. 1291, *op. cit.*

84 In Township 6, the survey labeled all of the mountainous land on both sides of the canyon as "unsurveyable." The protraction created two lots adjacent to the canyon in this unsurveyed territory, which were included in Boysen's patent.

grazing leases. Louis Boysen and Asmus Boysen's Thermopolis attorney were each one-sixth owners of these mining claims, which were worked for a number of years by the Wyoming Sulphur Company.[85]

Now that he had made his selection, and before a patent could be issued, Boysen set his men to work, a fact that at first did not attract the attention of the cavalry detachment patrolling the eastern boundary of the reservation. Scouts working for the soldiers were looking for a trail when they reached the mouth of the canyon and found a crew of some fifty men excavating with eight drills. The 35 soldiers were able to overawe Boysen's workers, who were also armed, and the crew were given five hours to leave the reservation, which they did. The Cheyenne *Tribune* said the crew was engaged in clearing the rock for the site of a power plant—a story that would prove true more than a year later, but was certainly not true in 1906.[86]

The real reason for the presence of the crew was divulged in August by Niels C. Brorson, who was back in Wyoming as the manager of the Boysen mining company. Brorson proved to be much more accessible to the press than Boysen's brother had been, and he was most expansive in his interview with the *Wind River Mountaineer* in Lander. He said that a "large force" of men had gone to work, had already unearthed a "large pocket" of gold, that the company would immediately spend $500,000 to develop the deposit, and that the company would lay out a townsite on the Boysen tract. For good measure, Brorson also corroborated the rumor that the company had located the legendary

---

85   The five mining claims were all "discovered" on February 23, 1906, staked the following day and accepted for filing by the Fremont County Clerk in Lander on March 3, 1906. Mining Claim Book L, pages 318-326. Louis Boysen was president of the Wyoming Sulphur Company. Also, *Thermopolis Record,* May 22, 1909. Ranchers with reservation grazing leases in the Owl Creek area were ordered to remove their fences and cattle in May, but had not done so by August, thus hampering efforts of others to file on the ceded lands. *Wind River Mountaineer* (Lander), August 24, 1906 and *Thermopolis Independent,* March 19, 1907.

86   *Wyoming Tribune* (Cheyenne), July 26, 1906.

Lost Cabin mine, although he did not state whether this fabled deposit was also on the Boysen land.[87]

Meanwhile, the government had 60 days in which to appeal Boysen's lawsuit against Wadsworth, and on June 2, Acting U. S. Attorney General Henry M. Hoyt advised Burke that the appeal would not be heard in St. Louis, but before a panel of the 8th Circuit then sitting in St. Paul. Unfortunately for the government, Boysen's counsel had to consent to this change of location, and that consent was not forthcoming, so the appeal was finally heard in September in Denver. Boysen's Omaha attorney, John N. Baldwin, joined Lacey in defending the appeal, and Burke continued to represent the government. The government once again denied that Boysen had the right to go on any part of the reservation except *possibly* his old lease. The word "possibly" was used because the government now argued that Boysen's preference was totally invalid, because the tribes had not accepted it.

In Denver, the panel that heard the appeal of the Boysen case consisted of Walter H. Sanborn, presiding judge of the 8th circuit, circuit judge Willis Van Devanter (former law partner of Lacey and Riner), and district judge John F. Philips of the western district of Missouri, a former congressman from Missouri. Judge Philips wrote the unanimous opinion which was handed down late in November, 1906, affirming Riner's decision. Regarding the lack of approval of Boysen's preference by the tribes, Philips noted that the courts tried to reconcile the interests of the tribes with the intent of Congress, but if they could not do so, Congress had to prevail. The government also complained that the Boysen coal lease was defunct, and Philips responded that Congress decided Boysen had some rights under the lease, and concluded, "That consideration was legislative and is not judicial."

Philips' harshest language was reserved for Wadsworth:

"His obstruction went to the extent of suffering the destruction of the machinery so employed [in prospecting] by the appellee, and warning him, under threat of forcible ejection, from the lands included in the ceded territory outside the leased premises."

---

[87] *Wind River Mountaineer* (Lander), August 17, 1906.

Willis Van Devanter wrote a scathing concurring opinion, in which he said that Wadsworth was a "wrongdoer" who acted without justification under the duties of his office. Before the decision came down, the acting U. S. attorney general confidently advised Burke that the government would appeal to the U. S. Supreme Court, but after consideration of the 8th circuit court's opinion, the government declined to appeal. Boysen had won his right to the land.

The subdivisions included in the Boysen's tract added up to a total of 680.31 acres, which did not include the bed of the river that crossed the land. To deal with the fact that his selection was 40.31 acres in excess of the preference granted under the law, Boysen offered two alternative solutions. He offered to pay $10 an acre for the excess land, or alternatively he would give up the excess in the form of a square in the northeast corner of the block. The block he so readily proposed to give up was north of the prospective mineral area, and consisted of rugged cliffs adjoining the river. However, subtracting this block from the parcel would destroy the square shape mandated by Congress, and the Secretary of the Interior finally elected to take the extra $403.10 from Boysen and issue a patent for 680.31 acres, which he did in the spring of 1907.[88]

The river flows across the Boysen tract in the Wind River canyon, but there is no consensus as to the name of the river in that location, for there are two choices. From its headwaters the river is known by the Indian name of Wind River, and all agree that downstream from the canyon, until it reaches the Yellowstone River in Montana it becomes

---

[88] Boysen's patent was issued on May 17, 1907, covering a total of 680.31 acres, consisting of parts of Sections 4 and 5 in Township 5 North, Range 6 East of the Wind River Meridian, and parts of Sections 32 and 33 in Township 6 North, Range 6 East of the Wind River Meridian. The bed of the river occupied about 28 acres in Section 4, and was excluded from the patent. The original survey of May 1, 1905 showed the rugged portion of Section 32 as "unsurveyable." The protraction ordered by the General Land Office for the undelineated part of Section 32 was "to show fractional areas as they would appear if the necessary lines were surveyed and marked in the field."

the Big Horn River, the name given to the stream at its mouth by Lewis and Clark. But where, precisely, does it change its name?[89]

The river's name was in confusion at least as far back as 1860, when Colonel William F. Raynolds said that the river should properly change its name at the junction of the Popo-Agie and the Wind River (where Riverton is now located), but he admitted the trappers called it the Wind River all of the way to the canyon. In 1908, the Wyoming State Engineer decided that the name ought to change at the Popo-Agie junction, but the U. S. Surveyor General, relying on what he thought was local tradition, concluded it was the Wind River all the way to the canyon. To complete this confused picture, the Indians celebrate the ceremony called "Wedding of the Waters" at the *lower* end of the Wind River Canyon, a few miles south of Thermopolis. The U. S. Geological Survey has now concluded that the Wind River flows through the Wind River Canyon to the Wedding of the Waters, placing Boysen's land on the Wind River on those maps, while it is still on the Big Horn River on the State Engineer's records.

Boysen had his preferential tract, but it was a costly undertaking, involving more than $20,000 just to select the parcel and obtain the patent. According to the accounting he later presented to the court, $6,803.10 was for the $10 per acre charge specified in the statute, and $12,000 was for the diamond drill and other exploration to make the selection, and these amounts were small compared with the major exploration costs soon to follow. However, Boysen fully expected that the minerals lying deep within his portion of the mountain would richly repay those costs. And while he had a longer term vision of building a dam and power plant as well, he saw this additional investment only

---

[89] Mae Urbanek gives Big Horn as the translation by Lewis and Clark of the Indian name Ah-sah-ta, for the bighorn sheep found at the mouth of the river. Mae Urbanek, *Wyoming Place Names*, (Boulder, Colo., 1967), 23. In December 1963, the U. S. Board of Geographic Names issued a formal decision requiring federal agencies to use the spelling "Bighorn," but this usage has not enjoyed wide acceptance locally.

as a way to supply cheap power for the large mineral development he expected. He was forced to change all of these plans.[90]

Boysen achieved a dramatic win in his first lawsuit, and achieved that result in far less time than in many of the cases to follow in his legal history. While the U. S. government no longer challenged his title to the land, there were others who soon took up that task.

---

[90] Legal fees were not included in Boysen's cost summary because Baldwin received stock in the Boysen mining company with a stated value of $14,000—which subsequently became worthless.

6

THE PARTNERS SUE

Unfortunately, the legal situation created by the coal syndicate was extremely confused. Boysen had obligations under the agreement that he had never performed, and the members had obligations they had never satisfied, and John Clarke was the only member who claimed he helped secure Boysen's preference tract, even proposing that the tract be three times the size eventually granted to Boysen. John Wertz also claimed he helped Boysen obtain the preference (although he had mixed motives for doing so), and clearly he and the Clarke family felt they were entitled to a share of the new preference.[91]

Boysen contended that the agreement never came into operation, because the members had not accepted it, but those were lawyer's words. Boysen's indignation regarding the claims of his former partners stemmed from the fact that he had expended a great deal of effort and a lot of money, while they contributed nothing, and he felt they were entitled to nothing. It was a prime situation for a complicated lawsuit, which soon followed. After Boysen selected his land, seven of the named members of the syndicate filed a lawsuit against Boysen (and two other named members of the syndicate) in the U. S. District Court in Cheyenne in July, 1906.[92]

---

[91]   John Clarke's account of his lobbying for Boysen is contained in his testimony before the Special Master on October 9, 1925, in Case No. 1291, *op. cit.*

[92]   The suit asked for a conveyance of a 1/16th interest in the land to each of the plaintiffs. William J. Broatch, Harry F. Clarke, Robert C. Wertz,

This suit was filed in the U. S. District Court in Cheyenne, for a different reason than in the case of Boysen's suit against Wadsworth. In the Wadsworth case, there was a federal question involved, namely the suing of a federal agent, and the federal court was involved in the new case because none of the plaintiffs were residents of Wyoming. This so-called diversity situation permitted the federal court to hear the case, applying Wyoming law. Appeals from such a decision could still be taken to the federal circuit court of appeals, but the appellate court would also be applying Wyoming law in reaching its decision.

Only seven of the participants joined in the suit, and three were named as defendants, so that the sixteen-member syndicate was reduced to ten at this point, and it would shrink further under the scrutiny of the court. The defendants included not only Boysen himself (and his mining company), but also Josef Weis and Adam Morrell, both of whom refused to join as plaintiffs. Morrell, who was to be the trustee under the agreement, filed an affidavit in support of Boysen, arguing that the lease did not result from the efforts of the group, and also that the agreement was never executed. Boysen argued that the agreement was not to have been effective until all had signed, and that in any case there had been no performance under it.[93]

Judge Riner took the matter under advisement. It is clear that at this point Boysen didn't fear the challenge by his former partners, for he proceeded to act as though he owned 100% of the land, spending large sums of his own money to carry out the venture he had in mind. However, the legal challenge was potentially very serious, for if the other partners could make a case in the courts—as they eventually did—Boysen's interest would be diluted, and at the outset it was by no means clear how bad the dilution would be. There were originally

---

Thomas Coughlan, Charles J. Woodhurst, John T. Clarke and Mary F. House, as heir of Jacob E. House, *vs.* Asmus Boysen, The Asmus Boysen Mining Company, Adam Morrell and Joseph Weis, Case No. 288, filed July 9, 1906 in U. S. District Court, Cheyenne.

93 Curiously, although Josef Weis did not join the suit as plaintiff, he apparently never renounced the syndicate agreement, and he conveyed his interest to Maurice G. Clarke on December 1, 1920.

16 partners, so that the worst case scenario might give all but 1/16 of the land to the others, thus having Boysen spend 100% of the money for 6.25% of the benefit, plus the hope of recovering his costs from his partners. It was a long time before this uncertainty was resolved.

The lawsuit in Cheyenne was a long way from the Wind River Reservation, where excitement was in the air. Boysen's base of operations was not far from Shoshoni, a thriving new settlement that owed its vitality to the anticipated opening of the reservation, and to the arrival of the Northwestern railroad. The town was laid out in the fall of 1905, and at the beginning of 1906 it could boast of a hotel and four saloons (always a sign of vitality in western towns). The first Northwestern train arrived at the end of June, and all was in readiness for Shoshoni to be a headquarters for the land rush when the reservation was opened to settlement.[94]

Among the merchants who moved to the new town was Charles H. King, who was to be the grandfather of Gerald R. Ford, the future President of the United States. The following February, King announced that he would close his store in Casper and move his entire stock to Shoshoni. At the beginning of 1908, King became a partner in the Shoshoni lumber business owned by Peter C. Nicolaysen of Casper (another Danish immigrant), and the resulting Shoshoni Lumber Company supplied the lumber and feed requirements of the Boysen operation (although the Boysen company did not pay all of the lumber company's bills).[95]

The ceded area on the reservation was opened to settlement in August, 1906, and prospectors could file minerals claims there beginning on October 14; at midnight on the 13th there were lanterns

---

[94]   *Cheyenne Daily Leader,* October 20, 1905.

[95]   Charles Henry King was the first settler in the town that became Douglas, Wyo., where he operated his store from a tent before moving it to Casper. Margaret L. Prine, "Merris C. Barrow: Sagebrush Philosopher and Journalist," *Annals of Wyoming* Vol. 24, No. 1 (January, 1952), 76 and *Thermopolis Record,* September 9, 1905. The Shoshoni Lumber Company, which was the successor to the Nicolaysen Lumber Company, was incorporated January 25, 1908.

all around the attractive ground. The Thermopolis *Record* said, "Where the diamond drill of the Boysens was blown up seems an attractive spot, quite a large number of people waiting to drive stakes there," but it is interesting that only one well-financed group actually did file on the Muddy Creek location. That group shipped one carload of surface ore to Denver, but no further news came from that location.[96]

Among those filing on Willow Creek on the 14th was a group led by Robert McGowan, which included Odd J. Midthun, who had apparently been with Boysen's diamond drill the previous fall. This group staked their claims some four or five miles south of the Muddy Creek location, and in the fall of 1907, Asmus Boysen purchased those claims, for "a good round sum," his first purchase in that area.[97]

Some locators, including those in the Wertz group, thought that the first legal filing date was the 15th, and John Wertz and several members of his family, as well as Edward Brice (the man from Warren's Washington conversations) staked their claims on that date. The Wertz group became the largest holder of claims in the Willow Creek play, and some of their locations were directly west of the claims of the McGowan group. The Wertz group claims were assigned to Wertz's National Mining company the following summer, which soon was spending serious money, drilling shafts and erecting housing for the workers. Wertz certainly hoped that he would finally become a rich man.

Wertz did not accept the argument that October 14 was a legal filing date, and he was unwilling to cede to Boysen attractive land in the heart of "his" play. He thereupon bankrolled a lawsuit filed by Edmore Le Clair to challenge the McGowan group claims, based on Edmore Le Clair's attempt to file a claim on the land staked by the McGowan

---

[96] The Muddy Creek group, headed by John M. Roach, president of the Chicago Railways and Uriah S. Hollister, president of Continental Oil in Denver, operated through the Mac Copper Mining Co. This group was also active on Copper Mountain. *Thermopolis Record,* October 20, 1906, September 12, 1908.

[97] *Copper Mountain Miner* (Birdseye, Wyo.), August 2, 1907 and *The Miner* (Hudson, Wyo.), July 23, 1909.

group. Wertz even brought his lawyer cousin, Edwin S. Wertz, from Wooster, Ohio to give advice on the case, but unfortunately for Wertz, the McGowan group had the better legal advice. The Lander district court decided October 14 was the first legal filing date and the Wyoming Supreme Court affirmed that decision in the spring of 1909. As so often happened in this story, Boysen won the prize, but in the long run it also proved worthless.[98]

At the Wind River Canyon, Boysen moved quickly to establish his presence on his land, and he attracted others to the area who hoped to participate in the coming bonanza. At the end of January, 1907, Samuel A. Cope platted the town of Boysen on the east side of the river, only half a mile south of Boysen's tract. While Boysen must have consented to the use of his name, he had no connection with the town, which was destined to be inundated by the lake when Boysen decided to build his dam. The town was a modest undertaking of 157 lots, and apparently squatters had already erected buildings "for residence and business purposes" on the townsite when the plat was filed. Soon there was the expectation that the government would approve a postoffice. To encourage rapid development, purchasers of the lots were only given 60 days in which to commence improvements on them, a provision that soon created problems.[99]

The town of Boysen even had a newspaper, *Copper Mountain Miner,* edited by Leslie Davidson, who came to the new town from Basin. However, after only two months in that location, Davidson moved his press to the soon-to-be-platted town of Birdseye, to avoid the confused legal situation at the Boysen town, and also to be closer to the main Copper Mountain prospecting area.[100]

---

[98] Edmore Le Clair *vs.* J. B. Hawley, *et. al.,* Case No. 578, Wyoming Supreme Court, decided July 15, 1909. 18 *Wyoming Reports* 23.

[99] *Thermopolis Record,* October 21, 1905, *Copper Mountain Miner* (Boysen, Wyo.), March 22, 1907 and *Lander Clipper,* November 23, 1906, February 8, 1907.

[100] Davidson had been editor of the *Rustler* before serving as assessor of Big Horn County. The Birdseye Land Company platted the town of Birdseye on May 4, 1907, east of the reservation; the town had street names for

North of the town of Boysen, the most prominent structure on Asmus Boysen's tract was the camp building of the Asmus Boysen Mining Company on the west side of the river. In the front section of the building were the offices of Boysen's staff, and at the other end was the kitchen and dining room, presided over by the company cook. The miners had a bunkhouse, and there was a two-room house for Scott Hazen, the foreman. A blacksmith shop and a warm barn completed the camp.

Boysen brought two men from Iowa to head his staff, Charles E. Breniman and Niels C. Brorson. Breniman, who had been county treasurer and an investor in Boysen's bank in Audubon County, first came west with Boysen in 1905, and later managed both the mining company and the power company. Niels Brorson had scouted the coal lease for Boysen in 1900; he later moved back to Chicago to run Boysen's office here. These men had the task of looking after Boysen's operations in Wyoming and keeping him informed when he was absent in Chicago and other parts east.[101]

We have noted that before he selected his tract, Boysen had seen the rich copper outcropping high on the west canyon wall. This vein was 4-16 feet wide, exposing ore that assayed at $70-123 per ton and Boysen later estimated that 1,000 tons of commercial quality ore was exposed in that position. After he took possession of the land, he mounted a serious effort to find that vein deep in the mountain, where his experts told him it would be.

By the end of March, 1907, a crew of about twenty men were at work exploring the Boysen tract. The next month stage traffic to the bustling camp was so heavy that the owner of the stage line was contemplating placing 6-horse Concord coaches on the line, and in June he did order two 11-passenger wagons for that service. The mining company needed to operate on both sides of the river, and even considered building a steel bridge to give access to the east side. When

---

Copper, Silver and Gold. *Copper Mountain Miner* (Birdseye, Wyo.), April 26, 1907.

[101] *Copper Mountain Miner* (Boysen, Wyo.), March 1, (Birdseye, Wyo.), 29, 1907 and *Riverton Republican,* February 13, 1909.

that idea proved impracticable, the company purchased a ferry, and placed it in operation at the Boysen camp.[102]

The ferry was the scene of a potentially serious accident in June. Boysen and Breniman were riding in a buggy, and when Breniman drove the buggy on the ferry the spirited team became excited and backed the rig into the river. Fortunately, the two men were only badly soaked, but the raging river, which was swollen by spring runoff, swept the unfortunate team and buggy down the canyon. The carcass of a horse later found in the river at Thermopolis bore mute testimony to this near-disaster.[103]

The Boysen miners drove a 375-foot tunnel into the canyon wall, and the newspaper claimed the tunnel had cut a 4-5 foot vein of galena (lead), assaying at $12 per ton, as well as an 8-foot vein of fine quality graphite. The mining company reported copper deposits running from 3% to 15%, and also four veins of "free gold," and it was hoped that a dredge in the river would find gold in paying quantities in the gravel. Unfortunately, all these reports were only newspaper puffery. The real story was far less encouraging.[104]

Brorson was quoted as saying this first tunnel would be driven 900-1,000 feet into the mountain. Yet, at the beginning of May, when that tunnel had reached only 420 feet, the crews were pulled out and transferred to a crosscut tunnel. The crosscut tunnel, which entered the mountain from the gulch running in from the west, was then 250 feet long, and it was expected to cut the large copper vein at 375 feet. The pace of work was stepped up, with a second shift added by the beginning of August, and to assist with the work, the boiler and the

---

[102] The ferry was formerly used on the road from Shoshoni to Lander. *Copper Mountain Miner* (Birdseye, Wyo.), April 26, June 7, 1907.

[103] The report of the accident was given in the *Copper Mountain Miner* (Birdseye, Wyo), June 14, 1907, but curiously without identifying the men. The names of the men were given in the *Cheyenne Daily Leader* under a June 12 dateline, and this item was then reprinted in the *Audubon County Journal* (Exira, Iowa), June 27, 1907.

[104] *Copper Mountain Miner* (Birdseye, Wyo), March 29, May 4, 1907.

remains of the diamond drill from Muddy Creek were also brought to the new camp.[105]

Evidence of paying quantities of minerals continued to be elusive. Boysen later recalled that the crosscut tunnel did find the vein some 700 feet into the mountain, and followed it west another 500 feet. Instead of the increased richness they expected, the vein was a poor shadow of their expectations, and to quote Boysen, they "did not find anything."[106]

Still, for public consumption, Boysen said he was not discouraged. When he was interviewed by the *Copper Mountain Miner* in June, 1907, the editor waxed lyrical, under the heading "Was Satisfied," (perhaps in the need to fill up the column in the paper):

"Mr. Boysen is an enthusiast when referring to the undeveloped resources of Wyoming, he being one of those who can see, with the eye of faith, the sky of the future black with the smoke from a hundred smelters and lurid with the flames from ceaseless fires in our manufactories, while trunk lines of railroad give us an outlet to all points with the products of our fertile plains and valleys and our inexhaustible veins of coal, backed by thousands of oil wells, these all outside of the greatest mining district that the west has ever known, Copper Mountain."

Boysen's enthusiasm made good press relations, but it didn't put any money in his pocket. In fact, he spent nearly $78,000 just for the two main tunnels. Although he sold $39,000 worth of stock in the mining company, the rest of the money came from his own resources and that of his wife, putting a great financial strain on him. Now, he

---

[105] *Copper Mountain Miner (*Hudson, Wyo*)*, June 21, August 2, 1907.

[106] False rumors of paying quantities of ore on the Boysen property continued to circulate as late as the fall of 1908. A news item headlined "Strike at Boysen" told of a 14-foot vein with "altogether satisfactory" mineralization. *Thermopolis Record*, August 8, 1908. Boysen's recollections are in his testimony before the Special Master in Case No. 1291, *op. cit.*

turned to other ways to recover the money he had spent, and even make a profit.[107]

In the meantime, the suit by the syndicate partners was still pending before Judge Riner, but there was still no sign that Boysen was worried about that. While both sides awaited the answer, John Clarke decided to make a public record of his claim to Boysen's land, by giving a mortgage on the interest he hoped to acquire in the property to the Clarke Land & Loan Co, a corporation owned by members of the Clarke family. This filing seems to have been a way of advertising the fact that the Clarkes were very involved in Boysen's operations, whether he liked it or not.[108]

---

[107] Broatch, *et. al, vs.* Boysen, *et. al,* 8th Circuit Court of Appeals, 236 *Federal Reports* 516, *op. cit.*

[108] The mortgage from John T. Clarke to Clarke Land & Loan Co. was filed in the Fremont County Clerk's office on June 7, 1907.

7

FROM COPPER TO ELECTRICITY

Boysen later claimed that he did not intend to build a dam when he located the land, although he did admit that when he selected his land he saw that there was a power site, "in there some place." After the search for minerals proved unfruitful, his next venture to recover value from his Wyoming land involved building a dam and power plant as a source of cheap power for the expected mining activities in the area. His first application for a dam was filed in the fall of 1906, for a 35-foot dam, expected to cost (only) $50,000.[109]

The State Engineer reviewed the application, and the following month returned it for corrections. While Boysen's people were still correcting the first application, he filed a second application at the end of March, 1907, asking permission to build a power line. But a month later this application was also returned for corrections. Meanwhile, trouble was brewing with the railroad.[110]

---

[109] Boysen's quotation is from his testimony before the Special Master in Case No. 1291, *op. cit.* The history of Boysen's application for the dam is given in Big Horn Power Co. *vs.* State of Wyoming, 23 *Wyoming Reports* 281-86.

[110] The first application was returned for corrections on September 21, 1906, and the power line application was filed March 27, 1907, and returned for correction on April 13, 1907. Big Horn Power Co. *vs.* State of Wyoming, 23 *Wyoming Reports* 271, decided June 1, 1915.

Back when the House of Representatives was debating the Boysen preference, the question was raised whether he might do something to obstruct railroads or highways, and Congressman Mondell assured the House this was not possible. Indeed, other informed observers also thought the canyon itself was a barrier to transportation and most people who came to the canyon simply went around it. In the spring of 1860, the Army tried to find a "practicable" route through the canyon, and they could not even find a pathway for horses and mules, and had to proceed through the rough country east of the defile. In his formal report, Capt. William F. Raynolds described the country through which the detachment traveled as "repelling in all its characteristics, and can only be traversed with the greatest difficulty."[111]

The Wind River canyon had defeated the topographical engineers, and for a long time no one believed that a route through the canyon was feasible. Indeed, when Boysen was asked whether he had examined the canyon, he said, "You could not get through the cañon then." Unfortunately, it was Boysen's bad luck that both a railroad and a highway later were built through the canyon, even though the effort cost much money and more than a few lives.[112]

Numerous dams had been built on streams in the West (those in Wyoming were constructed in support of various irrigation projects) and in 1897 the Corps of Engineers prepared a detailed report on the feasibility of building more such dams. Of course, Boysen was planning a dam and a power plant, not an irrigation project (although he later added irrigation as one of his objectives), but two of the observations in the government study are relevant to Boysen's scheme.[113]

---

[111] *Report on the Exploration of the Yellowstone River, by Bvt. Brig. Gen. W. F. Raynolds* (Washington, DC, 1868), 30.

[112] Boysen's quote is from his testimony before the Special Master in Case No. 1291, *op. cit.*

[113] The River and Harbor Act of June 3, 1896 authorized a study of the practicability and desirability of constructing reservoirs for the storage and utilization of water in Colorado and Wyoming, and the report was dated November 13, 1897. *Preliminary Examination of Reservoir Sites in*

The study noted that a serious condition affecting reservoir construction in the West was rapid deposition of sediment in some of the streams, and this problem was to prove significant in the case of Boysen's site. The mouth of Badwater Creek entered the river less than five miles (perhaps twice that distance along the river) south of the location Boysen selected for his dam. Badwater Creek has a large drainage area, nearly a third of the total area feeding the river at this point, but in normal times it supplies only a tiny fraction of the flow of the river. However, when storms strike the large dry Badwater drainage the creek develops a significant flow of water, laden with silt, as well as debris. The government report noted, ". . . the amount of material carried in flood is so great that it would rapidly destroy the largest of artificial reservoirs . . . ." The close proximity of Badwater's mouth to the dam meant that much of the material carried in the flooded stream would collect at the dam site, rather than being deposited along the river above. In the spring of 1906, not long after the town of Shoshoni was established, Badwater flooded nearby railroad grading camps, and drove at least one family from their home, as a preview of the performance this aptly-named stream was capable of.[114]

The government report also addressed the question of the best entity to build a dam. Regarding the possibility of construction by an individual, the report said, "Even if the financial resources of the individual would permit the construction, the use he would make of it afterwards would probably not require as large a reservoir as could be built, and he certainly could not be expected to build for the benefit of others . . . . *[I]t is wholly improbable that works so built, looking only to immediate returns upon investments, would be of that permanent and enduring character which it is greatly to be desired that they should possess."* [emphasis supplied] The italicized quotation is a remarkable prediction of the future of the Boysen dam.

Wyoming and Colorado, Document No. 141, House of Representatives, 55th Congress, Second Session.

[114] *Ibid.*

In addition to the caveats raised in the government reports, there was also the very real possibility that Boysen's location would interfere with other potential use of the site. Boysen himself admitted that before he made his selection he saw two railroad survey teams busy in the Wind River Canyon, but at the time dismissed the thought they might build a railroad in the canyon, because—as he later said—he had been told that the Burlington railroad was not going to build its line there. There is no reason to doubt that statement. Yet, as early as March of 1907, Niels Brorson said that the railroad was insisting the dam be no higher than ten feet, and in a letter at the beginning of August, Boysen was already complaining to the State Engineer that the Burlington railroad was interfering with his plans to build the dam.[115]

Obviously not worried about the railroad's opinion, in October, 1907, Boysen filed yet another application, this one for a 60-foot dam. He also gave the project its own corporate organization the following month, when the mining company transferred an 88-acre parcel to the Big Horn Power Co., in exchange for half of the authorized stock in the power company. This parcel included the land on either side of the river at the head of the Wind River Canyon, where the dam was to be constructed, together with the tract directly to the north, bordering on the west wall of the canyon.[116]

---

[115] *Copper Mountain Miner* (Birdseye, Wyo), March 29, 1907 and Asmus Boysen to the State Engineer, written from Boysen's Chicago office, August 7, 1907.

[116] The parcel transferred to the power company on November 16, 1907, consisted of 88.16 acres, and excluded the bed of the river, which had not been conveyed to Asmus Boysen, and remained in government ownership. The Big Horn Power Company was incorporated on October 16, 1907, with a total authorized capital of $700,000, of which 3,500 shares with a stated value of $350,000 were transferred to the mining company. The first board of directors of the Big Horn Power Co. were Asmus Boysen, Niels C. Brorson, Charles E. Breniman, John N. Baldwin and William A. Conover. Brorson and Breniman came to Shoshoni to join the active management of the Boysen projects, Baldwin was Boysen's lawyer in Omaha, and Conover was Boysen's Illinois lawyer.

The Boysen mining company continued to do some exploratory work in the area, but the land transfer to the Big Horn Power Co. signaled a new priority for the Boysen operations in the area. Charles Breniman, who headed both Boysen companies, halted all minerals exploration work on November 15, and transferred the entire workforce to the power company for dam construction. Breniman also took over the task of dealing with the newspapers, which was formerly the province of Boysen's brother and Brorson.[117]

Without waiting for the necessary permit from the State Engineer, at the end of September, 1907, Boysen announced that he would start work on the dam on or before November 1, and to mark the beginnings of this project, John N. Baldwin, Boysen's attorney and fellow director, came from Omaha in his private Union Pacific railway car, which was hauled to Shoshoni over the Northwestern lines.[118]

Building without a permit not only risked incurring the wrath of the State of Wyoming, but launching the project at this time was also financially risky, considering the fact it would consume a good deal of money, and at a time when the country was in the midst of the panic of 1907. We have noted that since Boysen came to the United States as a young man in 1886, he had enjoyed a remarkable good fortune. He married the daughter of a rich man, and as the country was recovering from the panic of 1893, made a string of investments in land and banking that gave him considerable wealth. From this foundation, he entered Iowa politics and against formidable odds got the Congress to give him a section of land in Wyoming, where he expected to make even more money. But by 1907 the Boysen string of successes had ended, and his fortunes began to turn down.

The first bit of bad luck for Boysen began in March of 1907, when the stock market crashed at the onset of the panic of 1907, starting the latest in the series of financial panics that plagued the country beginning in the nineteenth century. In Audubon County, Iowa, the first public

---

[117] Wyoming accounts no longer mention Nis Peter Boysen, that mostly uncommunicative spokesman, and by 1910 he was back in Iowa, attending college.

[118] *Copper Mountain Miner (Birdseye, Wyo),* November 15, 1907.

sign of financial strain for Boysen and his brother-in-law came in April, when the firm of Leet, Boysen & Beason stopped running their weekly advertisement offering to lend money.[119]

In October, just days after Boysen declared his intention to begin dam construction, the New York Clearing House refused to honor the checks of the Knickerbocker Trust, which precipitated a run on nearly every trust company in New York. Local Iowa newspaper accounts concentrated on the troubles in far-off New York and Washington, and at the end of October a headline reported the crisis was over. (The Audubon paper did carry the story of the suicide of an Iowa banker who was caught in the market crash, perhaps because that problem was in Lucas County, half a state away.)[120]

But the unreported ripples were at work in Iowa, and Asmus Boysen's assets in Audubon and Carroll counties were caught up in the storm. He sold the Iowa farms in the declining market of that terrible year, and the change of ownership of Boysen's home farm only was inferred when Mr. and Mrs. Ribley, who lived there, announced that they were returning to Illinois. The Boysen banks were also caught up in the panic. Again, little news of these troubles reached the newspapers, but Boysen supplied that information for us in later testimony, saying that he had to sell the banks to pay off depositors. The shrunken proceeds from all these sales were swallowed up by the construction in Wyoming—construction that was far from complete.[121]

---

[119] *Audubon County Journal* (Exira, Iowa), January 17, 1907. The issue of April 11 no longer carried this advertisement.

[120] *Ibid.*

[121] The panic did not cause the failure of a large number of banks in Iowa, as only one national and four state banks failed. Howard H. Preston, *History of Banking in Iowa* (Iowa City, IA, 1922), 178-79. The panic of 1907 provided the impetus for the creation of the Federal Reserve System, to regulate the financial flows that gave rise to a number of the panics. The Farmers Exchange Bank in Gray, which Boysen and Frank Leet purchased in 1899 was purchased by Lida Leet and Helen Leet, the sister and mother, respectively, of Anna Leet Boysen, in 1907. At the beginning of 1908, the Leet, Boysen & Beason Company bought Boysen's

On Boysen's tract in Wyoming, it seemed that no one paid much attention to all of this bad news from the East. Indeed, the State of Wyoming was relatively unscathed by the panic, as no banks failed, although some had to issue cashier's checks to deal with the currency shortage. Boysen also moved forward with construction, for although his own search for copper was a failure, he still expected the Copper Mountain play to produce commercial quantities of ore, and that he would be well-placed to benefit from that development by supplying power for the exploratory activity. Looking further ahead, he also wanted to build a smelter to handle the ores coming off the mountain, and he hired a Boston engineer to design a smelter to be located at the upper end of the lake to be formed by the new dam.[122]

When Boysen filed an application for a 60-foot dam, the Burlington railroad became very concerned. Boysen dismissed this objection, as he still did not believe the Burlington would extend its line south from the Big Horn Basin through the canyon. While James J. Hill, who controlled the Burlington, did have the dream of a connection between the Pacific Northwest and the Gulf coast, he also had two different ideas to achieve that; while one alternative did involve extending the Burlington line that now ended in the Basin at Kirby, south through the canyon, the other, which didn't require the costly canyon route, involved extensions to other Hill lines. Moreover, Baldwin, whose Union Pacific connections would have told Boysen something about the cost of building a rail line through a canyon, undoubtedly reassured Boysen of the impracticability of that project.

To be sure, the Burlington had laid out a route through the canyon, at least on paper, and this could be joined to the southern end of the line at Kirby, in the Big Horn Basin. However, all of that was on paper, and in fact, the railroad had not been particularly forthcoming about its plans, so that even the State Engineer was dubious whether the railroad would build in the canyon. Indeed, Boysen's assumption that

---

Templeton bank. *Gray Community History, 1881-1981* (n.p, 1980), 18. Also, *Audubon County Journal* (Exira, Iowa), August 22, November 7, December 6, 1907, February 13, 1908 and Case No. 1320, *op. cit.*

[122] *Riverton Republican,* January 25, 1908.

the line would not be built might well have been correct, had not the Burlington's decision to build through the canyon been directed by new events outside Wyoming.[123]

The event that decided the issue was the Burlington's acquisition of the Colorado & Southern railroad, which had service to Orin Junction in central Wyoming, and that possibility was not one of the pieces of James Hill's original plans for the Burlington's access to the Gulf coast. Filling the gap between Orin Junction and Kirby by building through the canyon to give the Burlington a through route from the Gulf of Mexico to the Pacific Northwest would be expensive, but it would be worth the cost.[124]

Negotiations to acquire the Colorado and Southern actually commenced late in 1907, and continued through nearly all of 1908, so that in the meantime the Burlington needed to keep Boysen from interfering with their plans. Accordingly, the Burlington sued Boysen in the Cheyenne federal district court at the end of January, 1908, to restrain dam construction. Like the suit by the syndicate members two years earlier, this case was filed in federal court because of diversity of residence. Hoping to resolve the opposing views, Governor Brooks called a meeting of the Union Pacific, Burlington and the Chicago and North Western railroads to discuss the matter.[125]

The state officials were suspicious of Boysen, because they thought his plans were influenced by the Union Pacific, as a way to keep the Burlington from building through the canyon, but they were also annoyed at the Burlington and Northwestern, because both refused

---

[123] In the summer of 1905, the Northwestern announced that it would extend its line northward from Shoshoni to Thermopolis, but that line was never built. *The Lander Clipper,* July 7, 1905.

[124] However, even when Hill was trying to acquire the C & S, one possible connection he contemplated in northern Wyoming was with the line from Alliance, Nebr. to Billings, Mont., not the line southward from Kirby. Overton, *op. cit.*, 273-274.

[125] The Burlington's action was Big Horn Railroad Company *vs.* Asmus Boysen, U. S. District Court, Cheyenne, Case No. 363. This case never did come to trial, as we shall later see.

to say definitely when or *whether* they were going to build through the Wind River Canyon. After hearing the conflicting views aired at the Governor's meeting, the State Engineer decided that the Boysen's proposed dam should not be higher than 35 feet, saying the higher dam would "threaten to prove detrimental to the public good."[126]

Immediately after the State Engineer announced his decision, Charles Breniman went back to Shoshoni to circulate a petition to have the decision modified. Public opinion had been wary of Boysen when he seemed to have an unfair advantage in prospecting on the reservation, but once it became apparent that he was going to spend a great deal of money on his property, the public mood turned favorable. A delegation from Thermopolis, Birdseye and Shoshoni (including prospectors who had formerly opposed Boysen) went to Cheyenne to protest the State decision. Members of the delegation emphasized that they did not want to support either the dam or the railroad to the exclusion of the other, but wanted both to succeed. In defense of Boysen, they contended that the railroad grade over the dam would be little more than the grade would be if the dam were not built, and it would be less than the maximum contemplated for a line built all the way from Frannie to Guernsey.

Responding to the community protest, the Governor sent a telegram to George W. Holdredge, general manager of the Burlington, on January 31, 1908, noting that Boysen had reduced his request from a 60-foot dam to a 50-foot dam. He asked the railroad to withdraw its objections, saying, ". . . I greatly desire that their wishes as to height of dam be allowed." The next day, Holdredge took a hard line in response, repeating the railroad's opposition to the dam, saying, ". . . [T]he increased cost would probably be fatal to the construction of the line for

---

[126] In the fall of 1905, George W. Holdredge, who was general manager of the Burlington west of the Missouri River, "literally confirmed" that the Burlington would build from Guernsey to Salt Lake City, a move which never came to pass. *Cheyenne Daily Leader,* October 25, 1905 and *Riverton Republican,* February 1, 1908. The State Engineer's opinion was dated January 27, 1908.

many years." Following this exchange of telegrams, the State Engineer scheduled a formal hearing on the matter.[127]

The formal hearing before the State Engineer was held on February 7, in the Supreme Court room in the capitol building, where "every seat was filled," and there were lawyers aplenty. Boysen hired John W. Lacey (and Lacey's son Herbert), the Northwestern had its lawyer, and the Burlington was represented by three, while the local communities surrounding the dam site hired Charles W. Burdick, of Cheyenne. Burdick's clients told him to negotiate a compromise that would permit both the railroad and Boysen to go forward with construction.[128]

Boysen was there, as was the engineer from the Ambursen Hydraulic Construction Company, who had the contract to construct the dam. John Lacey elicited from Boysen a description of his plans for the dam and power plant to serve the mining operation on Copper Mountain. The Ambursen engineer said that a 50-foot dam costing $90-100,000 could generate 4,500 horsepower, while a 35-foot dam, which would cost $85,000, would only generate 1,500-1800 horsepower.[129]

The railroad lawyers tried to show that there were no working mines near the dam site that would be potential purchasers of power, and the Wyoming State Geologist said that although the Copper Mountain

---

[127] *Copper Mountain Miner* (Birdseye, Wyo.), February 7, 1908. More than thirty years after the fact, Governor Brooks wrote a very different account of his involvement with the Boysen matter. He said that Boysen had asked for permission to build a 90-foot dam, saying "I questioned the advisability of granting Boysen permission for his proposed construction." Bryant Butler Brooks, *Memoirs of Bryant B. Brooks: Cowboy, Trapper, Lumberman, Stockman, Oilman, Banker, and Governor of Wyoming* (Glendale, Calif., 1939), 215-16.

[128] The detailed report of the hearing in Cheyenne is from the *Copper Mountain Miner* (Birdseye, Wyo.), February 14, 1908.

[129] When the Ambursen engineer mentioned as an aside that his design was cheaper to build than the design for the Shoshone River dam then under construction near Cody, there was an extended diversionary cross examination on that point. The Buffalo Bill dam, which was completed soon after the Boysen dam, was 316 feet high.

mining district was richly mineralized, he knew of no properties where there was "ore in sight." To demonstrate that there was no economic justification for Boysen's power plant, the railroad lawyers asked Boysen where he expected to sell the amount of power he proposed to generate, and how much he was going to charge. Boysen gave no specific answers to any of these questions, stubbornly insisting "the ore is there, and if we have cheap power we can get it out."[130]

To counter the negative testimony, Dudley N. Hale, superintendent of the Wind River Mining & Milling Company, testified that his company had 40,000 tons of ore "in sight." Hale emphasized the need for cheap electric power, citing the high cost of gasoline-powered alternatives, and debunking the possibility of using coal as fuel.

The railroad attorneys then asked Boysen how this ambitious project could be financed. Boysen responded that except for $14,000 of stock purchased by his friends, he owned all of the stock of the Boysen Mining Company. The attorneys then scoffed at the idea that Boysen expected to pay for the construction with $14,000, which sparked his indignant reply that his payroll was then running $10,000 per month.[131]

The high point of the hearing was the testimony of George W. Holdredge. Holdrege was general manager of the Burlington railroad, and his presence gave the state officials a rare opportunity to press the railroad on the specifics of its plans. Holdredge gave a fairly long summary, starting with the Burlington's first plans to enter the Big Horn Basin in 1896, and ending with the current concept of building a trunk line from the Burlington line in Nebraska, through the Wind River Canyon to connect with the Northern Pacific at Billings. Although he stressed the value to the railroad of a line through the canyon, he never

---

[130] The railroad lawyers also asked Boysen how much his own mining claims were worth.

[131] Lacey elaborated on the source of the $14,000 investment, saying that the stock was issued to John N. Baldwin for legal services, again emphasizing that the Union Pacific had no interest in the project, but that Baldwin was acting in his personal capacity as Boysen's attorney.

gave a hint whether the extension would be built anytime soon. Then, he dropped his bombshell on the hearing:

"[W]e have made many surveys, and we find our best outlet by far is through the canyon. It is the way nature made it and it seems to me a crime, commercially speaking, to shut it up with a dam, for if we got out of the Big Horn basin in any other way, we must go over a mountain, which will compel grades and curves which will ruin our plans and hopes for a level first class line through this state."

Holdredge went on to assert that to increase the grade to accommodate the dam would add $750,000 to the cost of the line.

This statement was shocking, because the state officials expected that the Burlington would accept a 35-foot dam, and Holdredge seemed to be saying he opposed any dam. When John Lacey's turn came to cross examine Holdredge, he put the question directly, saying, "But you do not oppose a 35-foot dam?" to which the witness replied, "Yes, I do." Soon, it developed that the Holdredge had not been briefed on the company position, for the Burlington attorneys later admitted that the railroad was, in fact, prepared to accept a 35-foot dam.

There was other testimony from the acting mayor of Shoshoni and from others in the area, as well as affidavits from Lander people who did not attend the hearing. All of this testimony was generally to the effect that the local communities wanted both the dam and the railroad. Although the railroads objected to some of this testimony, the State Engineer accepted all of it, reserving for the future the question of what would appear in his final report.

In the record of the hearing there is a letter (which may have been instigated by Boysen) from Odd J. Midthun, a civil engineer who had been in a charge of one of the railroad survey parties in the canyon in 1905. He declared that the Burlington could keep its line "high" from Thermopolis south to the location of the Boysen dam at "very little additional expense." Moreover, he claimed that building the line in the canyon ten feet above high water would be "practically the same" as building sixty feet above high water. This surprising conclusion apparently received no consideration at the time.[132]

When the hearing was over, the State Engineer wrote his final report, which was dated March 2. Johnston was fully aware that his decision would likely not be the final word on the matter, and he was clearly irritated with all of those who had appeared before him. First, he criticized the Burlington for its secrecy (which he darkly hinted might prove detrimental to them), and suggested that they might be motivated by a desire to give the Lincoln Land Company the opportunity to buy up townsites at low cost.[133]

Johnston was also clearly frustrated by those urging him to decide whether the Copper Mountain play would be successful enough to justify the power plant, but he reserved his harshest language for Asmus Boysen, who built his dam before receiving the necessary permit. He said, "Never in the history of the State Engineer's office has an investor shown greater disregard for the law relating to permits . . .," and then accused Boysen of treating the law as "a matter of convenience and pleasure." Having vented his irritation and frustration, Johnston concluded that Boysen could generate sufficient power from a 35-foot dam, and confirmed the permit he had previously issued on that basis. The reservoir contemplated by the permit was expected to cover 1,715 acres to a mean depth of 35 feet. The dam, which was to be 35 feet above mean low water, was expected to cost $150,000 and require two years to construct. So it was that Boysen received a permit to build a dam, although he did not come close to completing it within the

---

[132] Midthun apparently was with Boysen's diamond drill crew in the Muddy Creek area in the fall of 1905. Midthun's letter was dated February 4, 1908, and may have been received by the State Engineer after the hearing. State Engineer's files, Wyoming State Archives.

[133] The Burlington railroad submitted a 24-page supplement to its oral testimony, dealing with questions raised at the hearing, generally in a scornful tone. On the question of the railroad's plans, the supplement said Holdrege's testimony "speaks for itself." Boysen Dam Hearing 1908, in the State Engineer's files, Wyoming State Archives. The Lincoln Land Company was an affiliate of the Burlington railroad.

estimated cost, nor did the finished dam conform to the specifications the State approved.[134]

In the spring of 1908, Boysen lost a friend who had given him much political, legal and financial help. John N. Baldwin, the general solicitor of the Union Pacific, who handled Boysen's appeal in the Federal courts (and invested the legal fees he earned for this work in mining company stock), died in Omaha on April 19, 1908. Baldwin was only 50 years old, and his death must have been a great shock to Boysen. Unfortunately, there were many other disappointments for Boysen in that year.[135]

---

[134] *Ibid.*

[135] *Audubon County Journal* (Exira, Iowa), April 23, 1908.

8

BOYSEN'S DAM

Boysen let the contract to construct the dam before the state engineer issued a permit to him, and also before the extended wrangling in Cheyenne over whether he should get a permit at all. When the state engineer finally did issue Boysen's permit in March, 1908, the crew had been working up in Fremont County since the previous November.

The location chosen for the dam was not readily accessible for the heavy construction work required, and it was necessary to build a road to carry heavy traffic to the site, carved out of the mountain on both sides of the river, it was a thoroughfare "second to none in the state" for durability and smoothness. At the beginning of December, plans were also afoot for a telephone line from Shoshoni to the dam site, and sagebrush had to be cleared to make way for buildings to house a 100-man workforce, seventy of whom were already at work in early January. The work was heavy and dangerous, and Boysen hired Dr. Charles E. Lane, a young physician from Riverton, to run the "hospital" at the dam site. To complete the management team, Boysen's eighteen-year-old son Allan moved to Shoshoni in 1908 to help supervise construction.[136]

Boysen used the latest dam architecture in his project, for the Ambursen Hydraulic Construction Company of Boston, which had the contract to build the dam and power plant, used a hollow dam,

---

[136] *Riverton Republican,* January 18, September 26, 1908. Breniman said the grade of the road would not exceed 4 per cent. *Copper Mountain Miner* (Birdseye), May 22, 1908.

requiring far less concrete than conventional construction. Boysen's objectives as announced to the press were grand, indeed. The *Riverton Republican* hailed the project as "the biggest power dam in Wyoming," saying that it was to generate 10,000 horsepower. Electric power from the dam was expected to supply the Copper Mountain mining district, as well as the towns of Riverton, Arapahoe, Hudson, Lander, Shoshoni, Birdseye and Thermopolis. The lake to be created by the dam was to be stocked with black bass, and orders "now in" for water craft would make the place a "conveniently located summer resort.[137]

By Christmas, 1907, carpenters were building "cribs" in the cofferdam to divert the river, so the foundations of the dam could be laid in the streambed, as the company rushed to complete the foundation before high water came in the river. At the beginning of January, 1908, the newspaper editor visited the dam site and met with Verne Kellogg, foreman of the construction project, who showed him the plans, "and explained the intricate technical points." By the end of February, excavation for the foundations was complete so that concrete could be poured, and a dynamo was rigged up to provide light, turning night "into day."[138]

Labor was scarce, and Boysen hired many foreign workers, beginning with 50 Italians, who were thought to be "skilled rock men," followed by 21 Austrians in December, and in April, 75 Greeks nearly doubled the workforce to about 150, allowing both a day and night shift. There were also a number of Bulgarians, and it is interesting that their presence in Wyoming received very little attention in the contemporary press.[139]

---

[137] *The Cheyenne Daily Leader*, November 12, 1907 and *Riverton Republican*, November 16, 1907, January 18, 1908.

[138] *Copper Mountain Miner*, (Birdseye, Wyo.), January 10, 1908.

[139] In the fall of 1908, talk of war between Serbia and Austria made the Bulgarian workers restive, raising concerns they might leave the job to "take part in the scrap," and apparently many of them did go back to Bulgaria at the time of the Balkan Wars of 1912-13. *Wyoming Tribune* (Cheyenne), December 12, 1907 and *Riverton Republican*, March 7, April 4, 1908. After the dam was completed, many of the Greek immigrants

The foundation work was completed by the end of May, 1908, and construction was then suspended, to be resumed in the fall when the river was lower. The Ambursen managers then moved the entire workforce (except for 50 Bulgarians) to Douglas to work on the 136-foot dam they were building for the La Prele project, and the Bulgarians were set to work building the road from the camp to Shoshoni.[140]

The Ambursen workforce did not return to the Boysen dam, and Breniman went East at the beginning of August to hire men so that construction could commence again. He was obviously not successful in this effort, for when work finally resumed late in September, it was with workers recruited by Denver agencies. It was also necessary for the Boysen company to run its own string of freight wagons, and a carload of 24 Missouri mules ("superior to anything ever seen in Fremont county") joined the freight outfit. To manage the project, Boysen hired Fred W. Hart, an electrical engineer from Littleton, Colo., and construction could then resume. In early October, 75 men were at work, and at the end of the month there were 100 at the site. Dr. Lane, who had been vacationing in Riverton during the work stoppage, returned to Boysen to look after the hospital there. A month later, Fred Hart predicted that water would be running over the top of the dam by February of the following year.[141]

The Ambursen Hydraulic Company continued to run concrete on the dam during the 1908-09 winter, by heating the buttresses to keep the concrete from freezing. Boysen came back from the East in February, hoping to see a completed dam, but the foundations had not risen above water level. Nevertheless, he was told that future progress would be favorable, and he was assured that an additional $40,000

---

employed there went to work on railroad construction. *The Wyoming State Journal* (Lander), October 16, 1908.

[140] *Riverton Republican,* August 8, September 26, 1908 and *Copper Mountain Miner* (Birdseye, Wyo.), November 15, 1907, May 22, 1908. The Ambursen company took the contract for the much larger La Prele dam in the expectation of beginning work in May, using the Boysen workforce. *The Laramie Republican,* April 28, 1908.

[141] *Riverton Republican,* September, 26, 1908.

would complete the job. Unfortunately, when he visited the site again six months later, the dam was only a few feet higher than before.[142]

Hart's prediction for completion of the dam proved optimistic, although only by a few months, but the job was more difficult, took longer and cost a lot more than was originally estimated. High water in the river halted construction in the spring of 1909, but the dam finally was complete in May, 1909. The Boysen dam was a hollow concrete structure extending across the river, the entire top of the dam serving as the spillway. The power house floor inside the dam was about four feet above the high water level of the unobstructed river. Sluices to feed the turbines were located above the powerhouse floor, and they were opened all the time. Extending under the dam from below the floor of the powerhouse were three underflow gates, each 10 x 12 feet. These gates remained open during construction but were then blocked with heavy timbers in April, 1911, after the dam was complete.[143]

"Central Wyoming's Greatest Completed Enterprise" was the headline in the Lander *Journal* for May 21, 1909. Asmus Boysen later testified that the dam cost a little over $386,000 and we do not know what items were included in that total, but the number is clearly more than double the $150,000 original estimate, and it was a figure that constituted a financial disaster of colossal proportions for the Boysens. We do not know the details of money spent, but it is possible to sketch the broad financial situation.[144]

---

[142]   Boysen's story of the dam construction was related by him to Dave Johnston in 1921. Also, *Riverton Republican,* February 13, 1909.

[143]   The description of the dam was contained in testimony by Charles E. Breniman in Frank Martin *vs.* Big Horn Power Co., Case No. 1548, Fremont County District Court. The dimensions of the underflow gates are given in Chicago, Burlington & Quincy Railroad Co. *vs.* John T. Clarke, *et. al,* Case No. 1513, filed December 9, 1924, U. S. District Court, Cheyenne. Although there were apparently seven gates in the original plans, Asmus Boysen testified in 1925 that only three were installed. One of the gates was permanently obstructed because machinery was installed behind it.

[144]   Boysen testified to the cost of the dam in Case No. 288, *op. cit.*

While Boysen's acquisition costs for the land and the cost of his unsuccessful search for minerals were not a part of the dam and power plant project, they amounted to over $102,000, and were a major charge against his fortune, limiting his ability to finance the several ideas he had to earn more money from the dam.

The dam itself was a relative bargain at a bit more than the $85,000 the Ambursen representative estimated in 1908 (which certainly did not include the generating equipment, and probably did not include the superstructure), but just getting to the location to do the work involved a lot of work and a large outlay of money. The road to the construction site was a major project by itself, costing thousands of dollars, and more money was spent to build the buildings housing the men and equipment. Once the dam was built, generating equipment ($6,500) and other amenities were needed to support an operating power company. Even then, customers for power could not be served before spending $35,000 just to supply the small town of Shoshoni, and more than $42,000 to reach Riverton. The $60,000 or so it would cost to build a line north through the canyon to serve Thermopolis was clearly beyond the realm of possibility. Whatever the monetary details may have been, it is obvious that even with optimistic projections of the customer base in the two towns, there was no hope of generating enough revenue from the plant to pay current expenses (including interest on borrowed money) and generate a profit to recover the investment, so the fortunes of Asmus and Anna Boysen were lost beyond recovery.

Boysen had exhausted his own fortune by May, 1908, and had to look elsewhere to raise the money to complete the dam. At the beginning of 1908, the Big Horn Power Co. issued $350,000 worth of 5% gold bonds, secured by a deed of the land and the water rights. Asmus and his wife bought some of the bonds, and some of the bondholders also purchased stock in the power company. We do not know who all of the original bondholders were, but most of the bonds must have been sold to investors in Iowa, and to a few suppliers of materials for the project.

Two Iowa banks formerly controlled by Boysen and Frank Leet were also bondholders.[145]

We do not know how much money Boysen raised from the bond issue, but it was certainly not as much as $350,000, although the Lander newspaper quoted Boysen as saying the company was expected to earn a fantastic $350,000 per year, and at first, he only offered $200,000 worth of bonds for sale. However the cash needs of the project soon consumed the proceeds of the entire issue, and more. At the end of 1908, Anna Boysen made a large financial contribution to the Wyoming project, selling her Audubon County farm to her sister-in-law, Lida Leet, and loaning $150,000 to the Big Horn Power Co. While Breniman ran the company affairs in Wyoming, Boysen was soon back East, trying to find money to pay the bills.[146]

The power company managed to meet its $5,400 monthly payroll for the construction laborers, but many other bills went unpaid. Anna Boysen was able to lend nearly $25,000 more to the company in the last half of 1909, but with that effort her own financial resources were exhausted. The Boysen dam was finished, for all the world to see, but there was no money to buy generating equipment, so that the power plant could begin paying for itself.[147]

---

[145] The Commercial Savings Bank of Audubon, Iowa, was listed as trustee for bondholders, and the German Savings Bank of Manning, Iowa was listed as a bondholder. We learn from John T. Clarke's affidavit of June 26, 1917 in the case of Joseph Weis and Maurice Gordon Clarke *vs.* Asmus Boysen, *et. al,* in the Fremont District Court that Boysen had owned bonds with a face of at least $12,000, and in Case No. 1320, *op. cit,* Asmus Boysen said that his wife had owned $25-30,000 of the bonds.

[146] The Lander paper said that each purchaser of a bond received an equivalent value of company stock (*i.e,* five shares for each $500 bond), but this cannot have been the case to any significant extent. *The Wyoming State Journal* (Lander), November 29, 1907. Anna Boysen's $150,000 note from the Big Horn Power Co. was dated December 3, 1908 and was due 10 years later with interest at 7%. Case No. 1320, *op. cit.*

[147] From the premiums for workmen's compensation we can estimate that the payroll for the year ended January 28, 1909 was $64,659.67 and was

There were many unpaid bills, one of which was from the Shoshoni Lumber Company, owned by Peter C. Nicolaysen and his new partner, Charles H. King. This account was destined to play a significant role in the fortunes of the Boysens, as well as all of the other parties contending with them. The Shoshoni Lumber Company supplied lumber, fuel and coal for the dam construction project, and the account was supposed to be settled at the end of each month. Soon after construction started, payments began to lag, the bill for March, 1908 was not paid until May, and the record got steadily worse after that, until the matter ended up in court.[148]

Unpaid bills were not the only obstacle to be overcome, for Boysen's permit limited his dam to 35 feet, which would limit his power output, and he did not tell the newspapers how he was going to deal with that problem. Consequently, rumors flew. One story was that the State's contention had failed in court, another claimed the railroad had become reconciled to 60 feet, and a third said the railroad was actively assisting Boysen with his project. In fact, none of those stories was true, and final construction simply did not conform to the permit on two points.[149]

One of the features of the completed dam that deviated from the permit was the seven concrete piers (each measuring two feet on the side), which were authorized by the permit, but only extended to the top of the dam in the plans. Boysen extended the piers upward an

---

$43,422.00 for the year ended January 28, 1910. London Guarantee & Accident Co. *vs.* Big Horn Power Co., Case No. 1317, filed October 7, 1910 and decided June 30, 1911, Fremont Count District Court. Also, *The Miner* (Hudson, Wyo.), November 27, 1908, February 19, 1909. Anna Boysen loaned $23,177.22 to the Big Horn Power Co. on July 1, 1909, and $1,629.09 on December 1, 1909, both notes due January 1, 1918, with interest at 7%. Case No. 1320, *op. cit.*

[148] The account of Big Horn Power Co. with the Shoshoni Lumber Company is reproduced in Shoshoni Lumber Co. *vs.* Big Horn Power Co, in Case No. 1372, filed March 3, 1911 and decided September 11, 1915, Fremont County District Court.

[149] *Riverton Republican,* September 26, October 4, 31, 1908.

additional 29 feet above the top of the dam, to support a wagon bridge across the dam. Boysen altered the plans in this fashion because he was making the footings of the dam strong enough to accommodate a taller dam, in case he later got permission to build it higher. In that event, the wagon bridge would be just above the new spillway of the dam, and the extended piers would provide the internal support for the future extension of the buttresses.

The dam authorized by his permit did not have the generating potential Boysen needed, and he needed to try to overcome that problem. Since his permit limited him to a 35-foot dam, Boysen appears foolhardy in spending the money on footings and extended piers to accommodate a taller dam, but he actually had some justification for doing so. Under pressure from unnamed constituents in Fremont County, State Engineer Clarence Johnston informally modified his decision somewhat, as he explained some eighteen months after the permit was issued. Johnston said, "I told Boysen that if the railroad did not build through the canon he would be allowed to build his dam 50 feet high instead of 35." In a letter written to Governor Bryant B. Brooks on the same day, Johnston vented his frustration with the Burlington, saying, "We have no assurance in any form from the railroad that the canon route was to be followed." Although Johnston's comments help to explain Boysen's decision to build his dam differently than the permit authorized, the permit was never modified, and it was the only authority he could legally rely on, as he found out later.[150]

The top of the dam functioned as the spillway, and another important deviation from the permit was the width of that spillway. Boysen planned a 143-foot spillway for a 60-foot dam, but when the State Engineer reduced the height to 35 feet, he did not also change the width of the spillway, so as to be consistent with the narrower opening between the canyon walls at the 35-foot level. Moreover, in the light of Johnston's comments, we should not assume that his engineers "forgot" to reduce the spillway length, if they, too, anticipated that the dam

---

[150] Johnston's first letter dated July 2, 1909 was to Justin Kingdon, an engineer in Casper. Both letters are in the State Engineer correspondence in Governor Brooks' records in the Wyoming State Archives.

might later be built up to a height where the canyon walls were 124 feet apart.

Nevertheless the permit clearly called for a 35-foot dam with a 143-foot spillway, even though the canyon was only 125 feet wide at the 35-foot level. To create room for a 143-foot spillway would require a large and expensive cut into the canyon walls, and Boysen therefore ignored the spillway length requirement, building a dam with a spillway 110 feet long. In spite of evidence that the State Engineer would have authorized this deviation, he had not done so, and that caused trouble for Boysen in the subsequent lawsuits.[151]

The spillway was further reduced on either side of the dam, as the space between the end piers and the canyon wall was taken up by a stairway on one side, and a machine hoistway on the other. When the displacement of the seven piers plus the side panels was subtracted from the length of the spillway, the unobstructed portion of the spillway was further reduced from 110 feet to only 89.25 feet. These factors considerably reduced the capacity of the spillway to deal with high water in the river. Moreover, Boysen used the piers to support wooden panels that further obstructed the flow of water, and raised the effective height of the dam considerably, so as to increase the generating capacity of the plant.[152]

Although Boysen should have had his hands full building a dam in the Wind River Canyon, he still had time to consider other ways to

---

[151] In an affidavit sworn by Clarence T. Johnston on May 22, 1913, he stated that Boysen never asked him to reduce the length of the spillway from the 143 feet in his original application for a 60-foot dam, and that had Boysen asked for an adjustment, Johnston would have done so. Case No. 1513, *op. cit.*

[152] When the State Engineer gave Boysen his permit, he reduced the height of the dam from 60 feet to 35, without changing the other dimensions. The federal appellate court agreed that the State Engineer would not have required as wide a spillway with a 35-foot dam as with a 60-foot dam. The dimensions of the roadway and open spillway are slightly different in Clarke, *et. al, vs.* Boysen, *et. al,* 39 *Federal Reporter Second Series,* 800, at 817. We have used the testimony in Case No. 1513, *op. cit.*

spend money—money he did not have. In the summer of 1908, he went over to the Big Popo Agie River above Lander to survey the possibility of building a dam and power plant on that stream. His engineer from the Boysen dam project had already surveyed the project, and on his inspection tour Boysen brought high-powered visitors from the East, including William J. "Fingy" Connors, the legendary Democratic boss from Buffalo, N. Y., and Robert Murphy, a New York City hotel proprietor. According to the newspaper account, Murphy had "many" interests in Wyoming, including coal mines at Big Muddy (in association with Governor Brooks and John D. Woodruff). These men certainly could have accomplished a great deal politically in New York, but Boysen needed money, and none was forthcoming from them.[153]

While Boysen was thus occupied with business affairs in Wyoming, he was suddenly interrupted by the eruption of family troubles in Chicago. We know that Asmus not only managed Anna's extensive property, but he was also the administrator of the estate of Anna's brother, Frank Leet, and he was the guardian of Frank's minor son. This sort of financial control might have implied harmony with Anna and her family, particularly since much of Anna's money was devoted to Boysen enterprises, but harmony was not the word to describe the Boysen/Leet relationship—at least not by the fall of 1908. Moreover, the relationship between Asmus and Anna began to seriously unravel in the summer of 1908, when the Boysens were living in Chicago.

Chicago was then entering the phase when the use of opiates and cocaine was expanding rapidly, and Anna became involved in this trend. The real crisis in the Boysen family came when Anna introduced Rudolph Hough, a tall young red-headed skating instructor, into the Boysen family circle, causing Asmus to leave the family home, taking Allan with him to live in Shoshoni. He continued to manage Anna's property, and Niels Brorson, who was then managing Boysen's affairs in his Chicago office, had the task of sending "big" monthly allowances to Anna. (Boysen later claimed that he was unaware that Hough was being supported from these allowances.) Three months after Boysen's departure, Anna closed down their home in Chicago, sent her daughters

---

[153] *The Wyoming State Journal* (Lander), July 24, 1908.

to boarding school in Cheyenne, and moved in with her sister, Rosa Thompson, in the Thompson house in Chicago.[154]

Anna's brother-in-law, Robert Thompson, said that Anna was "mentally unbalanced," that Asmus Boysen was a "grasping and indifferent husband," and accused him of abandoning his wife. He said, "Her domestic troubles, desertion by her husband and his abuse have affected her brain . . . ." For whatever reason, it is clear that Anna Boysen was associating with a bad group, and in November, 1908, she moved from her sister's house to a Chicago rooming house, where she was joined by Rudolph Hough. Anna was 37, and young Hough was then about a month short of his 17th birthday.[155]

Anna's mother and Rosa Thompson were very disturbed by Anna's move to the rooming house, and Helen Leet took the extreme action of having both Anna and Hough arrested. From this point on, each of the parties hired a lawyer, and Anna's choice of Clarence S. Darrow as her attorney brought the case to newspaper headlines across the country. Darrow, who was 51, was nationally known since his defense of Eugene V. Debs in 1895, and in 1907 he won the acquittal of an Idaho union leader on a murder charge. After that trial, he returned to a lucrative practice in Chicago, where he was turning down many requests for his services. Darrow said, "I have stood for the weak and the poor. I have stood for the men who toil." Anna Boysen was neither poor nor a toiler, but she was obviously weak, and perhaps that would have qualified her as a client, although Darrow did not need an excuse to help a beautiful woman.[156]

---

[154] Joseph Spillane, "The Making of an Underground Market: Drug Selling in Chicago, 1900-1940," in *Journal of Social History* (Fall, 1998). *The Chicago Daily Tribune,* November 12, 1908.

[155] Coincidentally with Anna's move from the Thompson house, Rosa Thompson and her husband also moved from the Chicago house to the Auditorium Hotel. *Ibid.* Newspaper accounts do not say why the Thompsons also left their Chicago house, which may indicate that there was more trouble afoot than Anna's departure from the home.

[156] William Haywood was charged with the assassination of Idaho Governor Steuneberg, and Darrow obtained an acquittal of him on June 28, 1907.

Darrow at once secured the release of Anna and Hough on bail, whereupon Anna collapsed and went to recover at the Sherman House, while Darrow set about putting the best face on the facts. He said that Hough was actually Anna's employee, assisting her in obtaining her share of property from her father's estate then being held by her sister Rosa. He also said that Anna and Hough occupied separate rooms at the rooming house, and that the criminal charges were "absurd," part of a scheme to deprive Anna of her property, which he valued at some $300,000.[157]

The Chicago *Tribune* carried fulsome details of the unsavory story, complete with a large studio photograph of Anna Boysen, obviously taken in happier days. To counter Darrow's attack on their motives, Helen Leet, her son Keller Leet and Thompson issued their own statement to the press. Thompson flatly denied that there had been a family quarrel, saying, "We intend to save her if we can and not persecute her, as stated by her attorney."[158]

Family quarrel, or no, there were plenty of Leet family stories to interest the press. The reporters remembered that back in 1898, Helen Leet, whose wealth was estimated at $2 million, eloped with Matthew T. Chapman, president of American Well Works, then divorced him and sued to void their prenuptial agreement. Daughter Rosa Thompson had her own interesting difficulties. She was president of her father's bank in Bradford, Ill., and she was soon to be sued on a charge of looting a coal company where she was the principal shareholder. (She responded that the suit was "spite work.")[159]

Charles Yale Harrison, *Clarence Darrow* (New York, 1931), dedication page (quote above), 78, 121, 141, 142.

[157] Asmus Boysen hired William A. Conover, and Helen Leet hired Richard J. Cooney (her son-in-law, Robert Thompson, was also a lawyer). *The Chicago Daily Tribune*, November 13, 1908.

[158] *Ibid.*

[159] After Helen Leet sued Chapman for divorce, he refused to move from her house, until Robert Thompson hired some pugilistic toughs to evict him. *Ibid.* Rosa Thompson was the treasurer and principal stockholder of the Clark City and Wilmington Coal Company, which was capitalized

The newspapers reported that there had been a family conference at the Auditorium Hotel. However, Anna was still suffering from "nervous prostration" at the Sherman House (then a favorite gathering place for Chicago's high society), her sister was confined to her bed at the Auditorium Hotel, and Asmus Boysen was still in Wyoming. Consequently, the "family conference" at the Auditorium Hotel was really a lawyer's conference. Darrow said that Anna trusted Asmus more than she trusted her relatives, and at this meeting, Boysen's lawyer said that Asmus would take Anna back on condition she get rid of Hough. Helen Leet then agreed to drop the criminal charges, apparently on the same condition. The *Tribune* intoned that poor Hough "is now being made to bear the brunt of the family difficulty . . . ." Unfortunately, poor befuddled Anna's health continued to decline, and she lived less than two years after these troubles.[160]

Although Asmus Boysen's reputation fared better than that of the Leets in the public press, Robert Thompson's criticism of Asmus' marriage with Anna was not without foundation, for Asmus' extensive travels made his wife very lonely, and, in fact, Asmus had another relationship in the background, with Kathryne Fanning. Asmus and Kathryne married in 1914.[161]

The year 1909 marked the physical completion of Boysen's dam, but it also was the year in which the Burlington railroad decided on its expansion strategy in Wyoming. While the Burlington consistently opposed Boysen's dam construction, at the same time it stubbornly refused to state definitely whether it was going to build a line on its right of way through the Wind River Canyon. We now know that this reticence arose from conflicting alternative expansion plans the railroad was juggling at the time. At first, the Burlington's expansion into the Big Horn Basin was intended to open areas where development was slow

---

at $260,000, and employed about 100 men, but suddenly shut down in 1909. *Fort Wayne News,* December 22, 1909.

[160] *The Chicago Daily Tribune,* November 13, 1908. In 1910, Rudolph Frank Hough was working on his father's farm in Lenawee County, Mich.

[161] Kathryne called herself "Kathryne Boysen" in the 1910 census, when Anna was still alive.

because of the lack of transportation, and the Burlington completed the Toluca line to Cody in 1901, serving the north end of the Basin. In 1904 the Burlington built south through the Basin, to Worland in the summer of 1906, and then to Kirby, where spurs were run to serve the coal mines at the new town of Gebo. At this point railroad construction paused for a time. This was the situation when Boysen commenced construction on his dam.[162]

The Burlington's plans for the Big Horn Basin changed dramatically in December, 1908, when the Burlington purchased the Colorado and Southern Railway Company. The new Burlington strategy was not just to fill in spur lines in the region, but also to build the connection to the C & S at Orin Junction, in central Wyoming, so as to give the Hill lines a through system from the Pacific Northwest to the Gulf Coast. To execute that strategy it was necessary to build through the Wind River Canyon, over the right of way the Burlington had obtained back in 1905. Losing no time, at the end of January, 1909, the railroad sent a crew to each end of the canyon to complete the final detailed survey of the canyon route before the ice broke up in the river, and at the beginning of February the railroad paid $1,400 for the right of way.[163]

As a first step in the new strategy, in the summer of 1909, the Burlington let a contract to MacArthur Brothers Company of New York to extend the Burlington line. The extension began at Kirby, ran south to Thermopolis and then through the canyon to a connection with the Northwestern at Shoshoni. The canyon portion of the project was a major undertaking, and the contract contemplated building ten tunnels in the canyon, including one 900 feet long; three tunnels were to be located in whole or in part on the Boysen tract.[164]

Removing rock to make way for the roadbed involved a great deal of blasting, followed by a large crew of men with picks and shovels. The job was expected to employ 1,000-1,500 men, and a commissary

---

[162]   The line opened to Kirby on September 3, 1907. Richard C. Overton, *op. cit,* 269.

[163]   *Riverton Republican,* February 6, 1909.

[164]   *Thermopolis Record,* July 10, 1909. The location of tunnels on the Boysen tract is contained in testimony in Case No. 1513, *op. cit.*

building to serve the crews was built at the north end of the canyon. The work was dangerous, and two hospitals with two doctors, one on each end of the canyon, testified both to the size of the work force, and the risks the workers faced.[165]

Blasting powder and food for the crews had to be carried by a herd of 100 burros from the end of track at Kirby, so a trail had to be constructed to carry these materials to the construction site. The trail for this traffic could not be built on the west side of the canyon without interfering with rail construction, and in any case there was no room for the trail, as sheer canyon walls (later pierced by tunnels) blocked the way. Consequently, an expensive solution involved building a trail southward (upstream) from the mouth of the canyon, on the east side. Men and burros carrying powder and other supplies from Kirby came up the west side of the river to the mouth of the canyon, where they were ferried across the river to take the trail south. Boats in the canyon ferried these men and 10-15 burros across the river to the work sites on the west side, and at one location a bridge was built to carry burros across. From the south end of the canyon, a narrow wagon road similarly afforded access on the east side of the canyon, to the place where boats crossed the river.[166]

Railroad construction in the canyon continued in 1912, but progress was slow. Tunnel construction took nearly two years, the most difficult being tunnel No. 5, the so-called Black tunnel adjacent to the Boysen dam, where the rock was particularly hard. The railroad tracks from the north finally reached the Boysen dam by February, 1912, and

---

[165] Each man moved an average of eight or nine yards of rock per day, although the Swedish workers could remove eleven or twelve yards, and the Japanese workers lost their jobs when they only moved a yard or two.

[166] Information regarding the railroad construction was given by Harry N. Schafer, who was a young axeman on the project. *Greybull Standard,* June 4, 1959.

the following month, crews were busy rip-rapping the line downstream in the canyon.[167]

In preparation for the opening of its line through the Wind River Canyon, the railroad announced the location of three new stations, both north and south of the Boysen dam. The northernmost was located at the mouth of the canyon, and was named Minnesala, apparently from a Sioux word meaning red waters. The second, named Dornick, was in the canyon, near several springs, where one of the railroad construction camps was located. "Dornick" is a Gaelic word meaning small stone, a considerable understatement for the rock at this location. The third station, located south of the Boysen dam, was initially named Emery, but its name was later changed to Boysen.[168]

The Burlington line through the Wind River canyon officially opened to traffic in October, 1913. Initially, the schedule did not provide though service on the line, for the run from Thermopolis to Casper required 11 hours. Through passengers from the north had to remain overnight in Thermopolis, but their leisurely journey through the canyon included a stop at the Dornick station, to let passengers view the scenery there.[169]

The Burlington now needed to deal seriously with the problem created by the dam Boysen had built at the head of the canyon. In the summer of 1909, the Burlington revived its 1908 opposition to Boysen's dam in a second lawsuit filed in the Cheyenne federal court. In this second lawsuit, the railroad also asked the court to declare that the title to its 1905 right of way was superior to all the contesting claims from Boysen's former partners. Soon, the newspaper reported

---

[167] *Thermopolis Record,* January 11, February 15, 1912, February 20, March 13, 1913. The Black tunnel was 740 feet long, but was apparently later shortened by removing additional rock. Testimony regarding tunnel construction is from Case No. 1513, *op. cit.*

[168] *Natrona County Tribune,* April 12, 1911.

[169] At first, the Burlington announced that it would lease the Northwestern line from Powder River to Orin Junction, but this deal fell through, and early in 1913, the Burlington let a contract to build its own line to Orin Junction. *Thermopolis Record,* May 1, 1913.

that the railroad suit had been "settled." However, the settlement was no comfort to Boysen, for the railroad merely withdrew to let the State of Wyoming pursue the matter with its own lawsuit in the Fremont County district court.[170]

The entry of the State of Wyoming in the legal fray against Boysen was the most serious threat to his plans. We have already noted that the piers and wagon road atop the dam obstructed part of the spillway, and in its case, the State asked the court to order Boysen to remove them; in July, Judge Charles Carpenter in Lander issued a temporary injunction requiring him to do so. Boysen had already completed work on the dam in May, so this injunction represented a major potential disaster if it were allowed to stand.

To demonstrate the economic hardship the injunction would entail, Boysen first noted that he was spending $18,000 a year just for coal for his own operations. Then he listed the customers for power who would be deprived of service. A major consumer would be the 2,000 horsepower pumping plant to irrigate the 30,000-acre reclamation project he was planning. He would have to build a 25-mile transmission line to this location, and there was another customer on that line wanting to run a 250 horsepower dredge in the river. Moreover, the Williams-Luman company on Copper Mountain wanted power 14 miles east of the dam, while people in Thermopolis would be customers for irrigation and other uses. He did not say what it would cost to build

---

[170] Case No. 363, *op. cit,* and C. B. & Q. Railroad *vs.* Big Horn Power Co. and Asmus Boysen, Case No. 485, filed July 27, 1909 in the U. S. District Court in Cheyenne. *The Miner* of September 3, 1909 noted that the railroad case was set for trial on the 8th, and on September 17 the paper reported the settlement between the parties, but erroneously said that Boysen could build the dam to a height of 50 feet. The State filed its action against the Big Horn Power Co. and Asmus Boysen in Fremont County district court on July 24, 1909 (Case No. 1154), and the pendency of this action apparently brought about the resolution of the railroad case. State of Wyoming *vs.* Big Horn Power Co., Case No. 1154, Fremont County District Court.

the transmission lines to serve these customers, or how he proposed to pay for them.[171]

In order to avoid hardship to him and his potential customers, Boysen asked the State to permit him to install machinery in the dam and to begin operations while he waited for the trial to determine whether the injunction should be made permanent. At the end of November, the State agreed to let Boysen install the generating equipment and begin operating the plant, pending the resolution of the case. The case was then continued until the following summer, with nothing resolved, so there was no good news for Boysen, but there was no bad news, either. Indeed, more often than not, *delay* proved to be the most important friend Boysen had in the course of his many legal conflicts.[172]

---

[171] *Riverton Republican,* August 14, 1909.

[172] Judge Charles E. Carpenter granted the temporary injunction on July 24, 1909, and following the agreement of the parties, the injunction was modified on November 24, 1909. Case No. 1154, State of Wyoming *vs.* Big Horn Power Co., District Court of Fremont Co., Wyo.

THE POWER PLANT *VS.* THE RIVER

9

GETTING READY
TO DELIVER POWER

We break off the chronological narrative at this point to trace Boysen's operation of the power plant, and continue the story of Boysen's legal war in the next section. This separation of the story of the operation of the plant from that of the legal hassles makes sense because it mirrors the actual separation of events up in Fremont County from the wrangling in the courts at more distant points. For it is true that the little power plant seemed almost to be in a different world from that inhabited by lawyers and judges, as there was only one very short interval when the plant's operation was at serious risk of disruption by the courts.

That is not to say that the plant avoided disruptions, for there were many, but they were caused by the river, which paid no attention to lawyers and judges as it waged its own war on the dam. Boysen was introduced to the river's tantrums in 1907 and 1909, before the dam was completed, and in June, 1911, when the railroad was at work on its line in the canyon, the river put on quite a display. Driftwood and trees came down the river to lodge against the Boysen dam, where the water level rose 16.7 feet over the top of the structure. The grade of the railroad was flooded, and a torrent surged through the recently completed tunnel alongside the dam. Burlington General Manager Holdredge headed a high-level railroad delegation that came to the canyon construction site late in June to inspect the damage. The railroad said that construction could resume by July 15, 1911, but that proved optimistic, as the railroad had to raise the grade a further two feet so that construction trains could run over it, and crews were still repairing washouts in the canyon at the beginning of September. And the river had even more dramatic shows in store for both the Boysen dam and the railroad.[173]

Once the dam was completed, albeit without generating equipment, newspapers began carrying stories speculating on customers for the new power plant. At the end of February, 1910, the Riverton *Republican* headlined "Electric Lights for Riverton," a story in which Breniman assured the reporter that the generating equipment would be installed as soon as weather permitted. He also pointed out that Shoshoni and Thermopolis were "in the market for lights," and that Copper Mountain was asking for power, but the question of how large those markets might be was not discussed.[174]

There was plenty of activity to talk about in the Riverton area, but signs of solid success there were few. Settlement on the ceded portion of the reservation was opened with great fanfare, but about 1 million acres were not taken up initially, and then the government tried to sell the remaining acreage to the highest bidder. For those who did try to establish farms, legal, financial and physical difficulties interfered with construction of the "Big Ditch" that was to carry irrigation water to the fields, so that the Riverton irrigation project did not begin to prosper until the 1920s—too late to boost Boysen's financial prospects.

Boysen's desperate financial straits and legal maneuvers were largely unknown to the newspapers, and when the Wyoming Press Association held its meeting at Shoshoni in June, 1910, a trip to view the new Boysen dam was on the agenda for the editors. By then, the lake reached seven miles upstream, inundating the former town of Boysen (which

---

[173] The river averaged a flow of 649-738 feet per second at Thermopolis in the early months of 1911, but peaked at 18,100 feet per second on June 19. *Eleventh Biennial Report of the State Engineer of Wyoming to the Governor of Wyoming, 1911-1912* (Laramie, Wyo., 1913), 67. The railroad delegation arrived at the canyon on June 26, 1911. *Thermopolis Record,* June 29, August 3, September 7, 1911, and *Riverton Republican,* June 23, 1911.

[174] *Riverton Republican,* February 25, March 18, 1910.

disappeared without comment from the editors). The superstructure on the dam carried a road over the river, and the *Miner* editor reported this bridge was 75 feet above the water. He also said the sound of water flowing out of the gates could be heard for "miles." At the nearby Boysen camp, Charles Breniman, "that prince of entertainers," served a banquet to the visiting editors, and then led a tour of the power plant, which, of course, was still "under construction," which is to say the company still had no money to buy generating equipment.[175]

Boysen had exhausted his personal fortune, but incredibly, even before the dam and power plant were completed, he spent (borrowed) money to launch another mammoth project, to pump water from the river to irrigate a huge tract of land to be taken up under the Carey Act. In the fall of 1908, he hired an engineer to investigate the feasibility of this new idea, and yet another Boysen company came into being in the fall of 1910, this one bearing the name of Riverside Irrigation Company. This company was to have the task of carrying out what Boysen had called a 30,000-acre venture, but which had grown to 40,000 acres on the east side of the river, upstream from the dam. The company, which was capitalized at a fanciful $800,000, was to build the transmission line from the dam, the pump station, and about twenty miles of canals.

Boysen always could attract knowledgeable people to advise him on his projects, and in this case he chose Dr. James M. Wilson, a physician and sheep man from Douglas, who was involved in a large agricultural development in Colorado, as well as the La Prele irrigation project in Wyoming. Boysen did not say where the money to develop the project would come from, although the general assumption was that French investors were behind the deal. Boysen and Dr. Wilson brought an inspector from the Department of the Interior to look over the project, so that the land could be segregated under the Carey Act, and Boysen assured the newspaper that if the inspection report from Washington was favorable, the entire project would be completed during 1911.[176]

---

175   *The Miner* (Hudson, Wyo.), June 10, 1910.
176   *The Wyoming State Journal* (Lander), October 28, 1910. The Riverside Irrigation Company was incorporated on September 20, 1910. Dr.

In November, 1911, Boysen returned from the East, accompanied by Sophus F. Neble, editor of the Danish newspaper, *Den Danske Pioneer,* and Fred Brodegaard, a jeweler from Omaha. The visitors were in Wyoming on a hunting trip, but Boysen took advantage of their presence to acquaint them with his irrigation project. He expected to use the pages of the *Pioneer* to promote his project among Danish settlers in the U. S. Boysen told the Riverton newspaper that he would have water on his Shoshoni project by May 1, 1912. He hired an engineer to lay out the canals for the project and later announced that the Carey lands had been released, making it possible for crews to be in the field by February 1.[177]

Since Boysen lacked the funds to do little more than promote the project, Dr. Wilson chartered a new $3 million dollar corporation, the Shoshoni Power and Irrigation Company, to finance the irrigation project and associated power line. This company apparently took the place of Boysen's Riverside company, which does not appear again in the records. The representative of a French bank visited the Wyoming Central project on the reservation in April, and while the visit apparently had nothing to do with the Boysen and Wilson project, the mere mention of French money was a favorable sign for Boysen. The summer passed without further mention of the irrigation project, but early in 1912, Boysen told the Riverton *Republican* that he and Dr. Wilson had raised the necessary money for his irrigation project. He

---

Wilson and De Forrest Richards were in the sheep business in Converse County, and in Pueblo County, Colo., Dr. Wilson was president of a company developing 100,000 acres adjacent to the new town of Wilson, Colo. (named for the doctor). In August, 1908, "Shoshoni capital" (later revealed as Boysen) hired George J. Schenk of Basin to investigate a project to irrigate 40,000 acres from the river. *Riverton Republican,* August 15, 1908.

[177] *Riverton Republican,* October 13, 27, November 10, 17, December 1, 29, 1911.

didn't say where the money was coming from, but Boysen said he had hired William H. Rosecrans of Chicago to begin work.[178]

In the midst of these promotional efforts, another man moved to capitalize on the expected boom the Boysen project would bring. Nathaniel Shipton platted the new town of Wahaba in the area Boysen expected to develop, and lots were advertised for sale beginning in June. By the end of June, a general store was under construction at Wahaba, and a livery stable was soon to follow. There is no indication that Boysen and Wilson were involved in the Wahaba townsite at the outset, but at the end of 1911, Boysen organized the Dannebrog Investments Company to take over the townsite of Wahaba, which was renamed Dannebrog, using the Danish word for the flag of Denmark.[179]

The town was expected to be the staging point for the anticipated influx of settlers on Boysen's new irrigation project, and the acquisition was a friendly affair, as Nathaniel Shipton was a "large" shareholder of the Dannebrog company, and Boysen's friend, Bernard H. "Barney" Aronson, was also a shareholder (Aronson was also the secretary of the Big Horn Power Co.). The Dannebrog company also platted a nearby town, named Neble, for the Omaha publisher.[180]

In March, Boysen began promoting his irrigation project in the pages of *Den Danske Pioneer*. The advertisements in the *Pioneer* told of the availability of 10,000 acres. The project was open only to Danish settlers at the outset, and sales to Wyoming farmers would only be made if Danes did not take up all the land. Settlers were to pay $75 per acre for the water rights, with the first payment of $10 per acre, followed by two years with no payment, and the remainder in eight

---

[178] The visitors to the Wyoming Central project were George E. Roberts of the U. S. Mint and Herman C. Huffer, a 26-year-old junior partner of the French banking house of Huffer & Co. *The Wyoming State Journal* (Lander), April 21, 1911. Rosencrans was formerly in charge of the Wyoming Central project on the reservation. Also, *Riverton Republican*, December 1, 1911, February 9, 1912.

[179] *Riverton Republican*, January 20, May 26, June 2, 30, 1911.

[180] The town of Neble had streets named for Aronson, Breniman, Boysen and Boysen's daughter Helena.

years. As a protection against crop failure, the settler would have the option of paying half the crop rather than the specified annual payment. Finally, as a further guarantee, those taking up 80 acres would also be given a pledge from "responsible people" to purchase the land from the settler for $125 per acre when the farm is paid for and the water rights secured. Boysen added some puffery about the Riverton project, saying that land reclaimed in that project only three years before was already worth $150 per acre. To demonstrate his own confidence in the project, Boysen promised to build his own house in the new colony. A single rail excursion trip to visit the area departed from Omaha on June 12, with a round trip fare to Shoshoni of $23.75. (The fare was to be refunded to those who purchased land.)[181]

The excursion party of prospective Danish settlers from the Midwest and Canada arrived at Shoshoni on June 13, and Boysen took them first to the dam and power plant (the ad said it cost $750,000), and then they went up the river to Neble to look at the lands in the irrigation project. The Riverton newspaper carried the announcement that Boysen expected to start work on the ditches for his project on July 1, predicting that sixteen miles of ditches would be completed before September. This date was soon extended, but a later story reported that Boysen had actually signed contracts with the William Kenefick Company of Kansas City, calling for commencement of construction in mid-October, and completion of fifteen miles of ditches by December 1.[182]

The impetus for these stories stemmed from Boysen's discussions with another promoter, Arthur F. Day. Day and his father-in-law, William Kenefick, were in conversations with a Franco-Belgian syndicate to supply funds for the Wyoming Central irrigation project on the ceded area of the Wind River Reservation. Day, a young man

---

[181] *Den Danske Pioneer,* April 4, 1912, translated by Dr. Tim Jensen. Boysen ran a total of seven quarter-page advertisements in the *Pioneer.*

[182] *Riverton Republican,* June 14, 21, October 11, 1912. William Kenefick was president of three Kansas City contracting companies, one of which was involved in building the Missouri, Oklahoma & Gulf Railway, where he was also president.

of 29, lived in New York, where he was the vice president of a French bank, and although he was clearly a promoter, he did have credentials, for he had just completed two years as receiver of the Denver Reservoir Irrigation Company, involving the Standley Lake project northwest of Denver. While his chief interest in Wyoming was the large Wyoming Central project, he was also trying to raise money for Boysen.[183]

In the light of Boysen's embarrassed financial condition, it is doubtful that he contributed much more than promotional efforts and Danish names to either the irrigation project or the towns, and neither project proved to be economically viable. The irrigation project was to reclaim land by pumping water from the river, and the power line from the Boysen dam to the pump site would also be favorably located to supply electricity to a gold dredging operation along the river. The public reports did not address the question of how the project could afford to pay to pump the water some fifty feet above the river, while other irrigation projects were conveying river water by gravity in ditches taken from the river upstream from the farms. While power from the Boysen facility might be reasonably low cost, it could not compete with free delivery of water—but that point was not recognized for a long time.

Back at the dam, the new structure in the river continued to draw attention. A group from Thermopolis took a handcar trip south from Thermopolis through the canyon to the Boysen dam, and brought back the prediction that ". . . the only chance they can see for it to go out is for the solid rock walls to spread asunder." The *Thermopolis Record* also optimistically denied that the dam would interfere with the

---

[183] The Boysen project was much the smaller of the two areas of interest for the French capitalists. The larger project consisted of the unbuilt portion of the Central Wyoming Irrigation Co. project, which was then embroiled in litigation. In May, the Governor announced that the French interest had guaranteed 75% of the cost of the Wyoming Central project, and the remaining 25% was guaranteed by "American capital." *Riverton Republican,* May 31, 1912.

railroad, thus failing to recognize the very real risk to the dam from that source.[184]

Boysen's top priority was to buy generating equipment so that the plant could start earning money to pay off the many obligations, but he needed a new source for this money, since he had worn out his welcome with his Iowa friends. Fortunately, Boysen knew some people working nearby who could help find him the money. His connection with the men we shall refer to as the Akron group came about as the result of negotiations to sell power to the dredge being set up to look for placer gold along the river bed south of Shoshoni. It is likely that Bernard H. "Barney" Aronson, Boysen's business associate and friendly bartender in Shoshoni, was the one who introduced Boysen to the owners of the dredge, since the Aronson family were members of that group.

The owners of the dredge were looking for gold in the sands in the riverbed, and they were operating on a grand scale, with 46 placer claims covering several thousand acres in the riverbed. The mining engineer for this group was Arthur U. Marsh, of Indianapolis and Akron, Ohio, who was active in the area at the end of 1908. Arthur Marsh's associates did not invest in the Boysen operation, but Marsh could introduce Boysen to other moneyed people in Akron.[185]

In the summer of 1911, the Akron group organized the Fremont Power Company, with an authorized capital of $50,000. Asmus Boysen was a director of the new company, but admitted he was only a token shareholder. Four members of the group were directors of the company, but the man who supplied 40% of the capital was not a director. He was Frank A. Seiberling, the president of the Goodyear Tire and Rubber Company.[186]

---

[184] *Thermopolis Record,* February 15, 1912.

[185] In November, 1908, Arthur Marsh spoke to the editor of the Riverton *Republican,* estimating that some of the gravel in the riverbed would contain gold worth $1.50 per yard. *Riverton Republican,* November 14, December 5, 1908.

[186] Boysen does not appear on the shareholder list of the Fremont Power Company, which was submitted to the Wyoming Public Service Commission. The first board of directors of the Fremont Power Company,

The Big Horn Power Co. leased its entire operation to the Fremont company at an annual rental of $10,500 per year, and the newspapers were told that the Fremont Power Company would build power lines and distribute power from the dam. First, however, the most important task for the new company was to buy the generating equipment, and to install it. The Akron group owned the Fremont company, but apparently operations in Wyoming continued under Boysen control for a time, with Allan Boysen in charge. Later, that situation changed.[187]

Using money supplied by the Akron group, the generating equipment was purchased and installed by the middle of October, at a cost of about $6,500. The newspaper description of the facility, probably taken from old applications, was mostly fanciful, saying the dam was 50 feet high, with a 124-foot spillway (as built, the dam was 35 feet high with an unobstructed spillway of less than 90 feet). The lake was expected to be fourteen miles long and up to two and a half miles wide, reaching to within five miles of Shoshoni.[188]

In anticipation of power plant completion, the underflow gates through the dam were plugged in April, 1911, bringing the lake up to its full extent, and increasing the water flow through the turbines. Then on November 7, 1911, the Fremont company began delivering power to customers, initially power to the Boysen mining company, which was still doing some prospecting on the mountain, and in late 1911, the transmission line was completed to the large dredge located

---

which was incorporated July 19, 1911, consisted of Asmus Boysen, Samuel F. Ziliox, president of Commercial Printing Co, Fred A. Lane, treasurer of Commercial Printing, Raymond C. Ellsworth, secretary of Akron Cultivator Works, and William T. Tobin, a director of M. O'Neil Co, a wholesale and retail dry goods company. There were eight original shareholders, including Raymond Ellsworth's mother (the Ellsworths owned 15% of the company). Ziliox was president of the company and Ellsworth was the secretary and treasurer.

[187] Case No. 1320, *op. cit,* and Shoshoni *Gazette,* quoted in *The Miner,* May 20, 1910. The Fremont Power Company was in possession of the dam and power plant until November, 1917.

[188] *Thermopolis Record,* October 12, 1911.

on the river, some 20 miles south of the dam. Sales to the dredge were minimal, for after it was satisfactorily tested in November, the operation was shut down for the winter. The plant also supplied power to the railroad for its construction in the canyon, but unfortunately, having the railroad as a customer for power did not keep it from being a persistent enemy of the Boysen project.[189]

The next urgent construction project was to build the transmission lines to supply Shoshoni, the first municipal customer, and in anticipation of that move, members of the Akron group came out to see the dam in May, 1912. They reportedly saw that everything was "progressing," and after they returned to Akron arrangements were made to finance the line.[190]

The prospect of significant additional income for the power plant also seemed bright for awhile early in 1912, as the Lander town council granted a franchise to the Western Light, Heat & Power Company to distribute power in the town, and it was expected that the Boysen dam would supply the electricity. In June, the town of Bonneville actually signed a contract to obtain power from the Boysen dam. Before either town could receive power, transmission lines had to be built, and we hear no more about these customers.[191]

Asmus Boysen suffered a personal loss near the end of 1910, when Anna Boysen died on November 10. She was only 39. Anna had been living with her sister in Bradford, Ill, but she spent the last ten days of her life in the Baptist Hospital in St. Louis, Mo. Her own fortune was exhausted in the support of the dreams of her husband and her son, and when she died there was no sign of the $300,000 fortune Clarence

---

[189] By May, 1912, the dredge operating on the river became a favorite site for the curious. *Riverton Republican,* May 3, 1912.

[190] *Riverton Republican,* June 14, 1912.

[191] *Riverton Republican,* February 9, April 26, May 3, June 14, 1912 and *Thermopolis Record,* October 24, 1908, and *The Wyoming State Journal* (Lander), February 9, 16, 1912. The town of Bonneville was laid out on the Burlington railroad by the Lincoln Land Company, an affiliate of the railroad. On March 1, 1919, Allan Boysen said the Bonneville line was never built. Docket No. 104, Public Service Commission files.

Darrow spoke of back in 1908, for her only remaining assets were a few of the power company bonds, which were in default. At this time, Asmus Boysen closed his Chicago office, and while he was often in Shoshoni, he continued to live most of the time in a Chicago hotel.[192]

Boysen's two older daughters married in 1911 and 1912. The girls married two young men who were partners in a sheep ranch on Owl Creek, in the northern part of the ceded area on the reservation. In the fall of 1911, Anna Marie Boysen married William Kyne, and the next year Helena Boysen married Fred Aishton, son of the superintendent (later president) of the Northwestern railroad. Aishton soon left the sheep ranching business and moved to Casper, where he served as Natrona County treasurer in 1915-16, and by 1920 he was in Milwaukee, running a grain store. William Kyne was still a sheep trader in 1922, when the Worland *Grit* claimed that he had accumulated a "large fortune" in the sheep business. However, the sheep business declined during the agricultural depression of the 1920s, and William Kyne then moved to Casper for a time, before returning to the sheep business in the Big Horn Basin.[193]

[192] Anna Boysen did not even retain the three notes signed by the Big Horn Power Co., because she had assigned them to her son, Allan Boysen. Case No. 1320, *op. cit.*

[193] *Worland Grit,* April 6, 1922. Anna Marie Boysen and William H. Kyne were married in Casper, September 12, 1911, and Helena Boysen and Fred Aishton were married September 12, 1912 in Evanston, IL Also, *Thermopolis Record,* October 10 (quoting the Shoshoni *Gazette*), December 12, 1912.

10

THE AKRON GROUP
TAKES OVER

The power plant at the dam could now generate electricity, but there were few customers, and the company continued to lose money. By the end of 1912, the Fremont company ran out of its initial capital and raising new money became a laborious process. A small infusion of capital came in the form of a $2,600 one-year loan from some members of the Akron group. Beginning in the following summer, seven members of the Akron group loaned varying sums to the Fremont company on short term notes, some for as little as $14. Eventually, 69 of these notes were issued in the years 1912-14, for a total of $13,800, none of which were ever paid by the company.[194]

At the end of 1912, the Akron group sent their own man out to take over operations at the Boysen dam, using the newly-chartered Shoshoni Light and Power Company, with an authorized capital of $20,000 as the operating company. The Shoshoni company was to lease the generating equipment and to build transmission lines and sell power in Fremont County. The first board of directors of this company were five Akron businessmen who were also shareholders of

---

[194]   Fred A. Lane *vs.* Fremont Power Company, Case No. 1904, filed October 19, 1914 and decided November 20, 1914, Fremont County District Court.

the Fremont Power Company, and the president was Ray Ellsworth, who came to Shoshoni to manage the company.[195]

Raymond Ellsworth, whose family owned 15% of the Fremont company, was 35 when he came to Wyoming to run the power plant. In Akron, he was secretary of the Akron Cultivator Co., (maker of wheelbarrows), and he was also a director of the Midland Continental Railroad, a Frank Seiberling project. After he left Wyoming, Ellsworth became private secretary to Seiberling, which was undoubtedly a more pleasant job than he had at the Boysen dam.[196]

With a fresh injection of capital from Akron, the Shoshoni Light & Power Company built the 20.5 mile transmission line to Shoshoni, and installed the distribution system in the town, at a total cost of $35,000. In January, 1913, the company issued its first rate schedule for Shoshoni and began selling power in April.[197]

The town's plant on the river pumped water into a pipeline for distribution in the town. When the Boysen plant brought electricity and water to the town, Nell Morrison, who lived there at the time, said, "What luxury it was to have running water." Unfortunately, the supply of both light and water was sometimes interrupted. A sheepman, who

---

[195] The Shoshoni Light and Power Company, incorporated on December 12, 1912 with an authorized capital of $20,000, had a board consisting of the four Ohio investors in the Fremont company, plus Gilbert C. Marsh, a partner in Wagoner & Marsh, shoe dealers in Akron. The six of the seven shareholders each owned 10% of the company, and Seiberling's position was again 40%.

[196] The Midland Continental Railroad, which was eventually wholly-owned by Frank Seiberling, was initially a grand plan to build a railroad from Winnipeg through North Dakota to the Gulf Coast, but the company only built 71 miles of track extending north and south of Jamestown, No. Dak.

[197] The description of the lines to Shoshoni is given in the Bill of Sale dated August 29, 1928, whereby Mary J. Stoughton released her mortgage on these properties to Mountain States Power Company. Public Service Commission files. The cost of the Shoshoni investments is given in Allan Boysen's filing with the Wyoming Public Service Commission, June 18, 1924. Public Service Commission files.

was familiar with "dry" camps in the hills, said, "We have an eighty thousand dollar water system, but are on a dry camp a good part of the time."[198]

The revenue from the Shoshoni account was modest. We do not know the details for 1913, but ten years later there were only 86 residential and 38 business customers, paying a *total* of only $350 per month. The 50-hp town pump used more electricity than the residential customers, paying $318 per month. Total revenue from Shoshoni in May 1924, including street lighting, was only a little over $750 a month, just over $9,000 per year.[199]

In hopes that he could regain control of the Boysen power plant, Allan Boysen now entered into an instalment agreement with the Akron group to buy stock in both the Fremont Power Company and the Shoshoni Light and Power Company. He agreed to invest $35,000, for a 50% interest in each of those companies. The agreement called for payments of $3,600 per year, and the stock was to be escrowed until paid for. Allan Boysen did not make the payments under this agreement, but his widowed aunt, Mrs. Mary J. Stoughton, made at least some of them.[200]

The passing of power plant management to the Akron group meant that Asmus Boysen would lose his best manager, for Charles Breniman had to turn his eyes elsewhere to make a living. He ran for the office of Fremont county clerk in the fall of 1910, but was overwhelmed by the Democratic surge of that year, and in the spring of 1912, he unsuccessfully sought the position as Indian Agent on the reservation. Although he passed the civil service examination, he did not receive the appointment, which is understandable, considering the history of Boysen conflicts with the Indian Bureau. In the fall of 1912, a cryptic announcement in the Riverton *Republican* noted that

---

198 The quotations are from Nell Morrison's manuscript, in Bob Edgar & Jack Turnell, *Lady of a Legend* (Cody, Way, 1979), 102-03.

199 Allen Boysen to Wyoming Public Service Commission, September 20, 1940, June 27, 1924. Public Service Commission files.

200 The share purchase agreement provided for semiannual payments of $1,812.50. Case No. 288, *op. cit.*

Breniman had accepted appointment for "special duty" in the south, a task expected to require him to be gone several weeks. While nothing further was reported on this assignment, it obviously was the precursor to Breniman's employment with the Bureau of Investigation (later the Federal Bureau of Investigation).[201]

Despite all the chatter in the newspapers, the town of Shoshoni was actually the only significant customer for the Boysen plant—everything else was speculation on the future. Plans to run lines through Riverton and Hudson to Lander hadn't got off the ground, and the Riverton town council was considering buying its own power plant, that would operate around the clock, pumping water during the day, and delivering electricity for lighting at night.[202]

The Boysen irrigation project was a casualty of efforts to secure French financing for the Wyoming Central lands on the reservations. In June, 1913, Arthur Day once again showed up on the Wyoming Central lands, this time accompanied by another of Boysen's Iowa politician friends, George E. Roberts, director of the U. S. Mint, who was trying to secure the support of French capital for this project. Roberts was interested in agriculture, and his attempts to secure financing for irrigation projects was a part of that interest. These efforts seemed to be bearing fruit, when Day and his assistant in the French-American Bank organized a $3 million corporation to take over the development of 210,000 acres on the Wyoming Central project, but once again, the project did not get off the ground.[203]

---

[201] *The Wyoming State Journal* (Lander), May 17, 1912 and *Riverton Republican,* October 31, November 8, 1908, February 13, 1909, August 30, 1912.

[202] *The Wyoming State Journal* (Lander), April 25, 1913 and *Riverton Republican,* May 2, 1913.

[203] Roberts also brought Herman C. Huffer, of the Paris bank Leopold Huffer & Sons, to the Wyoming Central project in April, 1911. *The Wyoming State Journal* (Lander), April 21, 1911, October 4, 1912, June 6, 1913. Although Boysen's promotional efforts for his huge irrigation project did not attract the necessary money to get the project underway, the Burlington railroad was sufficiently impressed to make sure it could share

The State Land Commissioner announced that Day and Kenefick were not able to raise the money for the Wyoming Central project, and although Boysen's project was not mentioned, it was obvious that the French had lost their appetite for large irrigation projects in Wyoming, and we hear no more about the Boysen project. In the fall of 1925, Asmus Boysen explained that the cost of raising the irrigation water 50 feet above the river, to reach the land to be irrigated was more than the land was worth. Boysen's town of Neble was also a casualty of this unrealized dream, but a few residents remained, and the town had its own post office until 1926 when the Post Office department closed it down.[204]

Another surprising rumor surfaced in October, 1913, to the effect that Lucien L. Nunn and his brother Paul, who were installing an electric light plant in Casper, had an option to buy the Boysen dam and power plant for $400,000. The newspaper optimistically mused that the deal might mean power lines to Riverton, Hudson and Lander, as well as down the Northwestern tracks to Casper. However, the paper also noted that Boysen's lawsuit(s) in Cheyenne would "probably" have to be settled before the property could be sold. The Nunn brothers had a strong reputation, and for them to take an option from Boysen was not far-fetched, but they were also astute businessmen, and when they became aware of the complications of Boysen's legal situation, the Boysen dam option certainly would not have looked attractive.[205]

Ray Ellsworth worked hard to bring new customers to the power plant, and in November, 1913, the Riverton town council granted him a 50-year franchise to supply power to the town. The franchise

---

in the boom, if there was one. Early in February, 1914, the newspaper learned that the railroad had filed a right of way from the Boysen dam south to Neble (still being called Wahaba), and then southeast off the reservation. This line was never built.

[204] *The Riverton Review,* February 6, 1914. The 1919 Wyoming business directory gave the population of Neble as 20, and the 1921 directory gave the count as 25, and both of these round numbers were probably estimates.

[205] *The Wyoming State Journal* (Lander), October 21, 1913.

authorized Ellsworth to provide the poles and other equipment necessary to supply power for lighting, heating and power, but the stumbling block that remained—and it was formidable—was to find the money to build the transmission line.[206]

Several towns in Fremont County would have welcomed electricity, but the Boysen companies lacked the money to connect them to the dam and build the transmission line and distribution facilities. Meanwhile, other generating projects arose to compete with the Boysen alternative. In the spring of 1914, Peter Dykeman of Riverton proposed to build a power system for Lander, fed by a plant to be built on the Popo Agie River, ten miles upstream from the town. Dykeman was said to have access to $100,000 of eastern capital, contingent on raising $7,500 from local subscribers. In April, Dykeman got a franchise to distribute electricity in Riverton from a gasoline-powered plant, thus competing with the unbuilt Ellsworth/Boysen franchise. In the middle of May, Dykeman gave assurances that he would begin work within 30 days, so that the town could be lighted by the 4th of July. This forecast proved optimistic, but Dykeman did complete the project in December, when the *Riverton Review* ran its triumphant headline, "Riverton in Darkest Night is Now as Light as Day." Unfortunately for the Boysens, Riverton's light was not Boysen light.[207]

Dykeman also continued his efforts to build a power plant on the Popo Agie River, some nine miles southwest of Lander, and he announced in June, 1915, that he had secured the support of Chicago capital to build this plant, at an estimated cost of $156,000. This plant would supply the power needs of Lander's power plant, which only operated at night, and charged rates considerably higher than Dykeman

---

[206] Ellsworth was clearly acting for the Shoshoni Light & Power Company, but the franchise was granted to him personally. *The Riverton Review,* October 10, November 7, 1913.

[207] The newspaper noted that $6,000 had already been raised locally. *Riverton Review,* March 20, April 17, May 15, December 11, 1914. Dykeman was president of the Popo Agie Light and Power Company.

expected to charge. The town of Hudson would be on the power line to Lander, and would also buy power from Dykeman.[208]

Property taxes on the dam and power plant (as well as the rest of the Boysen tract) had not been paid, and in the summer of 1911, the treasurer of Fremont County sold the dam and power plant for taxes. The certificate was purchased by the bondholder committee of the Big Horn Power Co. Since the property could be redeemed at any time in the three years before a deed issued, the Boysens did not immediately respond, for the county was one of the few places they could borrow money, although the interest rate was high. In the fall of 1914 the county was ready to issue a tax deed for the property, a deed that would give the bondholders a quick and inexpensive title to the power company's assets. To deal with this crisis, the Big Horn Power Co. borrowed almost $3,900 from Anna Boysen's sister, Rosa L. Thompson, and redeemed the property from the country treasurer. This action left the power company with its original 11/16 interest in the tract, and although the company also had an additional debt that it could not pay, at least that obligation was in the family.[209]

The $3,900 loan was the only one Rosa Thompson made to the Boysen interests, although her sister, Mary Jane Stoughton, continued to back Allan Boysen's hopes for a number of years. Since Rosa had been called "one of the shrewdest business women in the country," it is surprising that she made this loan to the Boysen company, which was hardly a good credit risk. If the loan was made as a favor, she extended that favor to Allan Boysen, rather than his father, whom the Thompsons sharply criticized at the time of Anna's Chicago episode.

---

[208] The Lander plant expected to begin "day service" in September, 1915. *The Wyoming State Journal* (Lander), June 11, 1915.

[209] Part of the 88-acre tract (Lots 1 and 7) was sold for taxes on July 13, 1911. Section 2428 of the 1910 *Wyoming Compiled Statutes* permitted redemption of the property in the three years after date of sale, on payment of a 15% penalty, plus 10% interest per annum on all unpaid taxes. Allan Boysen redeemed the property for $3,892.72 on July 13, 1914. Rosa L. Thompson later assigned her note to Allan Boysen. Case No. 1320, *op. cit.* See Chapter 13 for explanation of the 11/16 fraction.

Allan assumed responsibility for the loan, and at the same time he purchased the tax certificates on the remainder of the Boysen tract (the taxes there were minimal).[210]

The prospect for new customers for the power plant was far from encouraging, for Boysen's irrigation project was dead, and the Wyoming Central irrigation project on the ceded part of the reservation was only partially built. Instead of attracting new settlers, Fremont County was actually losing people, and more than 2,000 people (18.5%) left in the five years after 1910. (Shoshoni, which boasted a population of 750 in 1908-09, only counted 278 people in 1915.) At the same time, there was now competition for the Boysen plant, as both Lander and Riverton had their own power plants, and in the fall of 1916, a new dam on the Popo Agie River was planned to supply electricity to replace the Lander plant and to supply Hudson. The outlook for adding electricity customers was not good.[211]

Reliability was a problem for the Boysen plant throughout its operating life, mostly because of the river, but an unexpected shutdown at the end of 1914 also interrupted all its customers, including the town of Shoshoni. The press report speculated that one of the underflow gates had failed, causing the water level at the dam to fall below the intake pipe.[212]

The river didn't listen to judges and lawyers, nor did it cooperate to make Boysen's life easier. The spring runoff in June, 1912 brought debris, including brush and logs down the river to lodge against the

---

[210] The quote is from the *Fort Wayne News,* December 22, 1909, quoting a Chicago dateline.

[211] The 1925 census total for Fremont County was 9,633, as compared with 11,822 in 1910. *The Wyoming State Journal* (Lander), August 6, 27, 1915. The 1908-09 population estimate for Shoshoni is from *R. L. Polk's Wyoming State Gazetteer and Business Directory for 1908-1909,* which would have reflected the presence of mining exploration operations and construction workers, plus an unknown amount of promotional estimation. Also, *Wyoming State Journal* (Lander), December 15, 1916.

[212] *Thermopolis Independent,* quoted in *The Riverton Review,* January 1, 1915.

superstructure of the dam, but that fact did not reach the newspapers. Beginning at the middle of June and continuing for two or three weeks, water ran through the railroad tunnel next to the dam to a depth of 15-24 inches in the ditch alongside the tracks. The railroad continued to operate, but the flooding made it necessary to send a crew on foot ahead of each train, to remove debris from the tracks and to check the integrity of the ballast under the rails. The river was relatively quiet in 1913, peaking almost 25% below the level of the previous year.[213]

These "normal" June floods became an annual event at the Boysen dam, causing the railroad delays and increased repair costs to remove silt and debris and to restore ballast. In some years the water was high enough to reach the journal boxes on the cars and engines, flushing out the lubrication. To avoid so-called "hot boxes," the journal boxes on all of the cars had to be repacked within 20-50 miles after leaving the flooded area. On at least one occasion, the flood waters rose high enough to extinguish the fire in an engine.[214]

The year 1914 was a dry one in which the river gave Boysen a respite from seasonal flooding. The peak flow in the river was 10% below the moderate level of 1913, and 35% below 1912. Unfortunately, no one could—or would—take advantage of the quiet time to do anything substantive to reduce the risk of more floods in the future.[215]

---

[213] The river flow peaked at 20,000 feet per second at Thermopolis on June 11, 1912, or 10% above the level of the 1911 flood. *Eleventh Biennial Report of the State Engineer of Wyoming, op. cit,* 68. John F. Phelan, who was trainmaster for the Burlington railroad, testified regarding flooding conditions at the dam in the years 1912-18 and Bruce M. Campbell, roadmaster of the railroad, also testified about the 1912 flood. Case No. 1513, *op. cit.* The river peaked early in 1913, reaching 15,400 feet per second on May 31, 1913. *Twelfth Biennial Report of the State Engineer to the Governor of Wyoming* (Laramie, 1914), 77.

[214] F. H. Warner, a conductor on the railroad, testified regarding the effect of flooding on the journal boxes. Case No. 1513, *op. cit.*

[215] The peak flow in the river for the year 1914 was reached on June 5, at 13,000 feet per second. *Twelfth Biennial Report of the State Engineer, op. cit,* 78.

The river once again flexed its muscle in 1915. A storm in the mountains above Badwater Creek sent trees and other debris down the creek, wiping out the Burlington railroad bridge. The railroad placed an engine on the bridge, hoping to hold it down, but the flood dumped the engine and a refrigerator car in the creek. In total, the flood took out 14 bridges and culverts, washed out four miles of track, and damaged over twenty miles of track so severely that it was rendered unsafe until repairs could be made. Downstream at the dam, the flood covered more of the rails than in 1912 and extended upstream about a mile, inundating both the main line and the sidetrack at the Boysen station.

It is not clear why this flood was so damaging near the dam, because the peak flow in the river (as distinguished from that of Badwater Creek) was actually only 84% of the previous year and 55% of the high experienced in 1912. Perhaps the accumulation of silt behind the dam seriously reduced the lake's capacity, or perhaps debris in front of the dam restricted the spillway even more than normally. Trains could only operate in the flooded area during daylight hours, and a three or four man crew met each train and checked the track. After the train passed, the crew prepared for the next train by replacing ballast on the track washed away by the flood. The June flood of 1916 was about 14% above the year before, but there seem not to have been any abnormal problems on the railroad[216]

Perhaps the high point of Ray Ellsworth's tenure as manager of the power plant was when he got the town of Riverton to grant him a franchise to supply electricity to the town, because it was all downhill after that. There was no money to build the necessary transmission line, so the franchise became worthless, money from power sales was never enough to pay operating expenses, and the river was troublesome

---

[216] Testimony about the 1915 flood was by B. Campbell, roadmaster for the Burlington railroad. Case No. 1513, *op. cit.* The peak stream flow at Thermopolis in 1915 was 10,900 feet per second on June 3. *Thirteenth Biennial Report of the State Engineer to the Governor of Wyoming, 1915-1916* (Laramie, 1916), 182. Also, *Riverton Review,* June 11, 1915, and *The Wyoming State Journal* (Lander), June 11, 1915.

at least once a year, and sometimes more often, and finally, some of the folks in Akron who sent him out to this place added their lawsuit to the blizzard of cases assailing the Big Horn Power Co. and the Boysens. It was time for Ellsworth to go home.

Ray Ellsworth finally gave up the thankless job of managing the power plant at the Boysen dam as of November 1, 1916, and went back to Akron. On November 4, 1916, Allan Boysen signed an agreement with Ellsworth, whereby the Fremont Power Company and the Shoshoni Light & Power Company turned over their business to Boysen. The property and business assigned to Allan Boysen consisted of the interests of the two corporations in the Boysen power plant, the transmission line to Shoshoni and to the Shoshoni town pump, as well as the distribution system in the town of Shoshoni. The consideration was $35,000, payable over time, and Allan Boysen—and his Iowa aunt—made sure this obligation was paid.

Asmus Boysen's business affairs were in shambles, but he chose this time to regularize his personal life. Poor Anna was gone, his two older daughters were married, and only Allan and Darlene were still at home. In the spring of 1914, in Fort Wayne, Ind., Asmus married Kathryne Fanning, who had been calling herself Kathryne Boysen for at least four years. Kathryne's son Raymond Boysen was then eight years old, and although his father may not have been Asmus, in every other significant respect he was the son of Asmus Boysen. When they were married, Kathryne was 35 and Asmus was 46.[217]

In the fall of 1916, after Ellsworth turned the operation of the Boysen plant back to Allan Boysen, his father borrowed $20,000 from

---

[217] The marriage license, which was filed in Fort Wayne, Ind. On April 2, 1914, contained a great deal of fiction. She was actually born Kathryne Cecilia Fanning in Mississippi on August 19, 1879, the daughter of William F. Fanning (an Irish immigrant) and Elizabeth Cullen. From the evidence we have, Kathryne was in Europe when her son was conceived, for she landed in Liverpool on the *Teutonic* on August 11, 1904, and returned from Cherbourg to New York on the *New York* on February 11, 1905; Raymond Michael Boysen was born July 30, 1905 in Ft. Worth, Tex.

his new wife, and promptly enjoined Allan to assume the responsibility to repay it. In a letter from Chicago on November 17, 1916, he wrote:

"I owe Aunt Kathryne $20,000.00 and I have executed a note to her for this amount . . ., due in five years . . ., interest at the rate of six per cent per annum . . . on the 17th of every month.

"I ask you to assume this debt and keep the indebtedness secret to yourself, and pay it when you can, and the interest till you can pay the note.

"It is an honest and secretive debt, which you will keep more than any other debt, to be cared for by you, should anything happen to me, so that I should be unable to remain on earth to pay it.

"You will do this in respect to me.

Your loving father

Asmus Boysen"

We do not know where Kathryne laid her hands on $20,000, but perhaps it came from Asmus in easier times. But despite the stern injunction, this note was never paid, either.[218]

---

[218] The note and letter are in possession of William Boysen, of San Pedro, Calif.

11

IT'S ALLAN BOYSEN'S TURN

After Ellsworth left, managing the power plant became Allan Boysen's responsibility, and the transition was not orderly, as Ellsworth did not leave much of a paper trail. Allan Boysen found that he did not even have copies of rate filings Ellsworth made with the Public Service Commission. We know that Allan Boysen left the day-to-day operations at the plant in the hands of James Rodgers, the lead electrician, as Allan later said that he was only at the dam for two months in 1916 and 1917.

The Public Service Commission regulated the Boysen power plant beginning in 1915, but aside from a few rate filings, the commission had little knowledge about the operation. However, Commission Secretary Henry A. Floyd came to Shoshoni in the spring of 1917, and while he was there he talked with the mayor, who told him that a company called the "Fremont Light and Power Company" (rather than the Shoshoni company) was supplying electricity to the town, and that the rate recently had changed. Floyd had to catch the train back to Cheyenne before he had a chance to discuss this startling fact with Allan Boysen, but when he got back to Cheyenne, Floyd wrote Allan a letter, scolding him for changing companies and changing rates without approval of the commission.[219]

---

[219] Ellsworth apparently made a total of six filings with the Public Service Commission. H. Allen Floyd to Allan Boysen, May 8, October 4, 1917, Public Service Commission files.

Allan Boysen replied to Floyd's letter, explaining away the confusion caused by the mayor. When Ellsworth left, he took the Shoshoni company bank account with him (there could not have been much money in it), and Allan then opened a new account, in the name of the Fremont Power Company. However, he followed Ellsworth's former practice of depositing both company's receipts in the Fremont company bank account, which caused the confusion in the mayor's mind. He admitted that he had reduced rates, but he thought the Commission would not be "interested" in reductions. In a particularly unfortunate sentence, Allan said he had assumed that the Public Service Commission was only charged with settling "disputes." That statement received a stern response.[220]

Floyd tartly corrected Allan's idea of the Commission's duties, but quickly assured him that the Commission never tried to be "meddlesome or technical" in carrying out its responsibilities. Soon the correspondence became cordial, with Floyd offering to come up to Shoshoni to help straighten out the paper work, and the folks at the plant offering him "fine" fishing at the dam.[221]

Allan Boysen continued to use the name Fremont Power Company and James Rodgers continued submitting rate schedules to the Public Service Commission in the name of the Shoshoni Light and Power Company as late as October, 1918. Using these companies was obviously awkward, because both the Fremont company and the Shoshoni company had a lot of shareholders other than Allan Boysen. It was time to organize yet another Boysen corporation.[222]

---

[220] H. A. Floyd, May 9, 1917, Public Service Commission files.

[221] James W. Rodgers, the electrician at the plant wrote on September 8, "The fishing is fine at the dam now and if you like to fish there is no reason why we cannot fish and talk rates at the same time." H. A. Floyd to Allan Boysen, May 19, 26, 1917, Allan Boysen to H. A. Floyd, May 24, 1917 and J. W. Rodgers to H. A. Floyd, September 8, 1917. Public Service Commission files.

[222] James W. Rodgers took over the filing of schedules for the Shoshoni Light and Power Company with the September 17, 1918 filing, and the

In November, 1917, Allan Boysen and his brother-in-law, Fred Aishton, organized the Wyoming Power Co. This company took over the lease on the dam and power plant, and purchased the assets of the Fremont Power Company and the Shoshoni Light and Power Company. These assets consisted of the transmission lines to Shoshoni, and the Shoshoni distribution system. The Wyoming Power Co. paid $25,375.50 for these assets, giving its note for the full amount, secured by 50,000 shares of Wyoming Power Co. stock. However, the town of Shoshoni continued to pay the rates filed by the Shoshoni Light and Power Company until 1920, when the Wyoming Power Co.'s rate schedule was approved by the Public Service Commission.[223]

At this point, world events intervened to add to the legal confusion of the Boysen projects. The United States entered World War I on April 6, 1917, and the following month Congress instituted a military draft, requiring men between 21 and 31 to register. One of those men was Allan Boysen, who served in the U. S. Army from the spring of 1918 until the spring of 1919.

This was an awkward time for Allan to be absent from the power plant management, because he had launched a new company to operate the plant, and he also wanted to do something about his problem with the railroad, by building structures to relieve flooding at the dam. While he was in the Army, Ben Bowman managed Wyoming Power Co. from Lander, while James Rodgers handled day-to-day operations

---

last one recorded is the one approved October 7, 1918. Public Service Commission files.

[223] The Wyoming Power Company was incorporated on November 30, 1917, with headquarters in Lander and an initial authorized capital of $5 million, later reduced to $500,000. The bill of sale was dated October 22, 1919. Allan Boysen said that he was president of the Wyoming Power Co. and owned all the stock. Case No. 288, *op. cit.* and Clarke *vs.* Boysen, 39 *Federal Reporter Second Series* 800, at 808. Information regarding the purchase from Fremont Power Company and Shoshoni Light & Power Company was provided to the Wyoming Public Service Commission by B. F. Bowman on March 27, 1919. Public Service Commission files.

at the plant. Obviously, Bowman had no authority to deal with strategic questions, so the important issues remained in limbo.

We have only fragmentary information about the finances of the Boysen companies before the Wyoming Power Co. filed a financial statement with the Public Service Commission for the year 1918, the first year of that company's operations. The company had net income of $860 on revenues of $9,200, but its cash position was perilous, with only $7.10 in the Shoshoni bank. One piece of positive information was that the obligation to the Akron group had been reduced by $9,625, using money advanced by Allan's aunt, Mary Jane Stoughton.[224]

Nevertheless, the Boysen power plant continued to deliver electricity, and the Wyoming Power Co. even tried to extend its limited service territory to the town of Thermopolis. At the beginning of 1919, Ben Bowman tried to persuade the town of Thermopolis to grant the Boysen company a franchise to supply electric power to the town. The timing seemed propitious, since the town fathers were unhappy with their local electric company, and had already asked the Public Utilities Commission for permission to operate their own power plant. However, Bowman was told that Wyoming Power Co. had to prove it could construct the necessary power line to the town and also guarantee uninterrupted service, and these were impossible conditions.[225]

When he came back from the Army in 1919, Allan Boysen decided to apply directly to the Wyoming Public Service Commission for the Thermopolis franchise. Thermopolis was then receiving electricity from the Hot Springs Light & Power Company, which had its own plant, located by a rock dam in the river south of town. Of course, the Hot Springs company opposed the Boysen application and the Commission held a hearing on the matter in Cheyenne on March 10, 1919.[226]

---

[224] Wyoming Power Co. financial statement for 1918. Public Service Commission files.

[225] *Thermopolis Independent,* February 21, 1919. In 1920, Bowman was the assessor for Fremont County.

[226] The Thermopolis town council opposed the Hot Spring company's request for a small rate increase, until the company "render a proper and

Allan Boysen was not well prepared for the hearing and he was vague in his answers about the financial situation of Wyoming Power, for good reason. Floyd elicited the fact that there was an outstanding note to the Akron group for the purchase of assets from the Fremont and Shoshoni companies, and asked whether Wyoming Power could pay the balance of the note when it fell due. Boysen replied, "As far as I know. My relatives in the east have taken care of my affairs."[227]

Without mentioning the State demand that the superstructure be removed, Allan's attorney tried to minimize concern on that score. In response to his questions, Allan blandly said that the dam had 35 feet of head providing "abundant" water to supply the plant "at all times," and he also noted that the plant was using only about a quarter of the available horsepower. However, it soon became apparent that there was a rock just below the dam, which backed up water, and therefore reduced the "head" of the power plant, limiting its capacity. When questioned about limitations on the plant's head, Allan declared the rock could easily be removed, and if that didn't suffice, he grandly added, "I can build a new dam below ours down there . . . . We can do a lot of other things, you know."[228]

In a similar vein, when pressed on the question as to whether he could supply Thermopolis using existing equipment, Boysen was dismissive, saying he could install more equipment, if it were needed. When Bowman testified, he was no more realistic than Boysen, saying the company would like to expand to Worland and Gebo and "possibly" Casper.[229]

Since the pending litigation with the Clarke group could have a significant effect on Wyoming Power's title to the dam and power plant, Allan Boysen tried to put the best face on that situation. When

satisfactory service." *Thermopolis Independent,* January 24, 1919. Also, *Thermopolis Record,* March 28, 1908, and Dorothy Buchanan Milek, *Hot Springs: A Wyoming County History* (n.p., 1986), 155.

[227] Docket No. 104, Public Service Commission files.
[228] Ben Bowman said the rock could be removed at a cost of about $250. *Ibid.*
[229] *Ibid.*

asked how he got title to the dam, Allan responded, "The easiest way would be to look up the abstract." However, Harlan Thompson, of Billings, who was the majority owner of the Hot Springs company, had his own source of information about the Clarke group litigation from John T. Clarke, himself.[230]

John Clarke knew Thompson from earlier discussions with the Hot Springs company, and Clarke gave Thompson a mostly fanciful update on the pending lawsuits, which Thompson used to give a scornful response to the claims made by Allan Boysen and Bowman. Thompson said that Clarke told him "he has deeds" from the U.S. court for a 15/18 interest in the "power plant and land." Moreover, Clarke assured Thompson that there were two more judgments pending that he thought would coming down "in the next year or two," giving him the entire title to the power plant. As to Allan Boysen's title from the lumber company foreclosure, Thompson said, ". . . I don't think Mr. Boysen's title to that land is worth more than $2,800."[231]

When Floyd asked whether the transmission line to Thermopolis would be built in the canyon, or up on the mountain, Allan Boysen became testy, asking, "Why do you ask that?" After Floyd replied, "Because its my right to ask that," Boysen finally decided the line would be built through the canyon, without any comment on the difficulties and cost that project would face.

Allan Boysen gave Bowman the chore of estimating the cost of the Thermopolis project. Bowman estimated that the transmission line would cost nearly $29,000, but admitted that replacing the Hot Springs company's distribution system in the town would add another $50,000 to the cost of the project. The Commission expected to hear what rates would be charged in Thermopolis, and what rate of return would be earned on these rates, but Boysen and Bowman gave no definitive

---

230 *Ibid.*

231 *Ibid.* Harlan J. Thompson was the older brother of Merrill W. Thompson, who managed the Hot Springs company. Harlan Thompson owned 82% of the company, and Merrill Thompson owned 18% of it.

answers to either question. On April 5, 1919, the Commission denied Boysen's application.[232]

The Wyoming Power Co. was finally able to sign up the town of Riverton as a new customer for power in the summer of 1919. The franchise Ray Ellsworth received from Riverton had never been taken up, because there was no money to build the transmission line to the Boysen dam. In the meantime, Riverton generated its power from its local steam plant, but that source of power was unreliable, and by 1919, the town was ready to sign an agreement with the Wyoming Power Co. to supply electricity over a new transmission line from the dam.

The power line from Shoshoni to Riverton cost a lot of money—more than $42,000, and of course this was money Wyoming Power did not have. Accordingly, the line was built with more borrowed money, and a $50,000 line of credit that was to be repaid from the revenue for the Riverton service. Work immediately began on the 23-mile line, from the substation south of Shoshoni, then passing by Neble, and from there direct to Riverton. Riverton began using Boysen power in November, 1919, but the monthly debt service made the Riverton account a net cash drain for the company.[233]

The increase in demand from the Riverton account justified installing the second 450 KW generator in the Boysen plant, but unfortunately, the added load did little for the Wyoming Power's financial condition. Revenues for 1919 increased $3,600 to $12,800 as the result of adding the Riverton account, but the carrying cost of

---

[232] *Ibid,* and *Third Biennial Report of the Public Service Commission of Wyoming 1919-1920,* 34-41.

[233] The arrangement for the construction of the transmission line to Riverton was detailed in Allan Boysen's testimony before Commissioner Maurice Groshon at Riverton on September 25, 1926. Docket No. 532, Public Service Commission files. The cost of the power line to Riverton was $42,098.37, and the remaining balance on the mortgage at the end of 1923 was $39,797.51. In addition, the company purchased lots in Riverton for a substation, at a cost of $245.50. Allan Boysen to Wyoming Public Service Commission, June 18, 17, 1924. Public Service Commission files.

the expansion overwhelmed the financial statements. Mary Stoughton advanced an additional $9,000, to pay the Akron group instalment, and to install the additional capacity in the power plant. All of this resulted in a loss of $10,000, according to Allan Boysen's system of accounting.[234]

Another potential competitor for the Boysen plant appeared in the spring of 1919, when the Lander newspaper headlined, "River to Furnish Power for Lander." Lander had its own diesel-powered plant, but the town wanted a lower-cost, reliable source of electricity. The Lander power company contracted with the Sinks Canyon Hydro Power Company, which was building a dam at a favorable site in the Sinks Canyon on the Popo Agie River, southwest of Lander. The dam was only nine feet high and 60 feet across the top, to hold back the water for a 36" pipeline two and a half miles long, to the power plant located over 900 feet below the dam. Power lines were built to the South Pass mining area and to Lander and Hudson, and soon the Riverton light company was negotiating for a connection, as well. The Sinks Canyon plant began operation late in January, 1920, supplying Lander, as well as some of the oil and mining companies in the area. Although the plant was much smaller than the Boysen facility, it drained away customers Boysen that needed to reach a profitable level of operation.[235]

---

[234] The Popo Agie Light & Power Company owned the distribution system serving Riverton. *The Riverton Review,* June 11, November 12, 1919, April 21, 1920. The net for the year included an unspecified "loss" of $11,776.77, which probably included items that should have been capitalized as assets. The statements for the years 1918-21 do not contain any charge for depreciation on depreciable assets, which would have increased the annual losses by about $1,800 per year (using the 2% depreciation rate later adopted). Wyoming Power Co. financial statements. Public Service Commission files.

[235] In September, 1922, the Sinks Canyon company modified its dam to increase the head, and thus the capacity of its plant. *The Wyoming State Journal* (Lander), December 15, 1916, April 25, May 9, June 20, July 25, 1919, January 16, February 13, September 8, 1920.

The 1920s were the time of the agricultural depression in Wyoming following World War I. The easy money times of wartime were gone, and the twenties brought down more than 100 Wyoming banks, striking all except a handful of towns. It was a poor time to try to establish an economically viable electric generating business.[236]

The year 1920 was the first full year of service to Riverton, and Wyoming Power's revenues for that year were $24,200, an increase of $1,400 over the year before. However, the entire increase in revenue was consumed by the doubling of salaries and wages from $4,100 in 1919 to $8,300 in 1920. There were three electricians and a helper on the plant payroll, plus Ben Bowman in Lander and Allan Boysen himself. Interest expense to carry all the new debt also skyrocketed, rising from $2,700 to nearly $8,100. After deducting other expenses, the loss for the year was $5,500. On the balance sheet, additional costs on the transmission line to Riverton and the regular payment of $3,625 to the Akron group swelled Wyoming Power's liabilities and further increased the deficit. Increased business definitely did not make the company healthier.[237]

We have noted that the Wyoming Power company did not get the Thermopolis franchise in 1919, because the town had its own local utility. However, by the spring of 1921, the town had outgrown its local plant's capacity. The Thermopolis Chamber of Commerce then asked the Hot Springs Light Company to consider buying power from the Boysen dam. Unfortunately, neither party could raise $60,000 for the transmission line and distribution system.[238]

---

[236] Wyoming banks failed in every year of the twenties, peaking with 40 in 1924, for a total of 108 in the decade. L. Milton Woods, *Sometimes the Books Froze: Wyoming's Economy and Its Banks* (Boulder, Colo., 1985), 118.

[237] Included in expenses for 1920 was a commission of $7,455 that was not explained. Public Service Commission files.

[238] It will be recalled that Allan Boysen proposed to build the transmission line to Thermopolis for less than $29,000, so the $60,000 total quoted here must include purchase of the Hot Springs company's Thermopolis distribution system, as well.

The most important current problem was the financing on the Riverton transmission line, which did not generate enough revenue to cover the debt service. The cost of the line was refinanced in the spring of 1922 with a new 8% note with Bankers Mortgage Company of Des Moines, Iowa. The note was for $38,000, a reduction of $8,000 from the previous financing, and it called for $700 monthly payments—which was just about equal to the revenue produced by the line. To free up cash for the most pressing requirements, Allan Boysen didn't pay some of his own salary, borrowed about $3,300 from brother-in-law William Kyne, and increased his aunt's notes by $6,200.[239]

Wyoming Power Co. continued to limp along financially in 1921, reporting revenues of $21,900 and a profit of $1,800. As we have noted, these early statements of the company do not charge earnings with depreciation, which would have eliminated the small profit shown. Consequently, the most we can say about this report is that the company's dismal financial picture did not become worse in 1921.[240]

Revenues for Wyoming Power Co. were a bit better in 1922 than in the year before, and the company again reported a profit of $1,700, which this time reflected a charge of $1,800 for depreciation. However, the cash situation actually worsened, because of the drain imposed by refinancing the transmission line loans. Moreover, Boysen's hopes of attracting new customers were seriously threatened by the prospect of another hydroelectric plant in Fremont County, this one financed by the government.[241]

Near the end of 1922, the Bureau of Reclamation decided to build a plant about 27 miles upstream from Riverton, using water from the main irrigation canal, where it dropped into Pilot Butte Reservoir. This plant was smaller than the Boysen plant, with only two 1,200-horsepower turbines, of which only one was installed at the outset. The

---

[239] The note was dated March 1, 1922. William Kyne *vs.* Wyoming Power Co., Case No. 4218, filed on July 9, 1928 and decided May 13, 1929, Fremont County District Court.

[240] Wyoming Power Co. financial statements. Public Service Commission files.

[241] Wyoming Power Co. financial statements.

plant was originally built to supply power for the draglines constructing irrigation works on the Riverton project, and for some commercial sales. The plant was expected to be built in 1923, and come onstream in 1924, providing a well-financed competitor for the Boysen plant.[242]

If the financial picture for the Boysen power plant was dismal, the plant's relationship with the river was no better. With the spring runoff in 1917, the river ended its truce with the railroad and the Boysens, as the river rose to the levels not known "since white men settled the valley." The power plant was shut down from the middle of June to the middle of August, cutting off power for Shoshoni. High water endangered nearly all the bridges in Fremont County and damaged the railroad bridge between the Wind River Canyon and Thermopolis so badly that rail traffic was halted for a time. A large number of mine timbers, saw logs and driftwood lodged against the superstructure of the Boysen dam, backing water over the tracks half a mile to the south and sending water 16-18 inches deep through the railroad tunnel. There were even fears that the Boysen dam would fail.[243]

Nor did the river take a holiday while Allan Boysen was in the Army. The June flood of 1918 was almost as high as that of the previous year, and carried away one span of the large Northwestern railroad bridge near Neble (between Shoshoni to Riverton), and other Fremont County bridges were damaged, as well. However, there must

---

[242] *Riverton Review,* November 29, 1922.

[243] *Thermopolis Record,* May 24, June 28, 1917 and *The Wyoming State Journal,* (Lander), June 22, 29, 1917. F. T. Kiser, who supervised the wrecking crew for the railroad, gave testimony regarding water depth through the tunnel in 1917. Case No. 1513, *op. cit.* Despite the dramatic language, the peak flow of the river in 1917, at 19,400 feet per second on June 24 and 27, was actually about 3% below the peak of 1912, but the flood season was much longer than usual, beginning on June 18 and extending through July 10. *Fourteenth Biennial Report of the State Engineer to the Governor of Wyoming, 1917-1918* (Laramie, 1918), 109. Information regarding the power outage of 1917 is given in *Third Biennial Report of the Public Service Commission of Wyoming 1919-1920,* 40 (Docket No. 104).

not have been as much obstruction at the dam, because the plant did not shut down, although "some grass and stuff" got into the water wheel. The powerhouse was flooded because the rock just in front of the discharge backed up the water into the powerhouse windows. A temporary solution to this problem was to concrete the lower part of the windows, leaving openings of only two or three feet. Allan Boysen implied that the rock needed to be blasted out, but we do not know if that was done. The good news was that the year 1918 was not one when the railroad complained about obstructions at the dam.[244]

High water returned in 1920, and the river again ran through the railroad tunnels at the Boysen dam, although it did not cover the rails. Also in that year, there was more bad luck, this time not the fault of the river or the lawsuits. A Baptist pastor from Riverton was electrocuted while fishing from the top of the dam and accidentally let his steel fishing rod touch a 33,000-volt transmission line.[245]

The onset of the June, 1921 high water in the river struck first near Neble, where poles of the Riverton transmission line were washed out, halting power delivery to that town until the local plant could be started up again. The following week, the highway bridge three miles southwest of Shoshoni became impassable from flood damage, and had to be replaced. Later in the month, the flood was a record in Thermopolis. At the Boysen dam the river ran through the railroad tunnel for six days, thirty inches over the rails, covering 4,500 feet of track. Logs, trees, brush and other debris piled up against the top of

---

[244] *The Wyoming State Journal* (Lander), June 14, 21, July 12, 1918. The peak flow at Thermopolis in 1918 was 19,000 feet per second on June 17, some 2% below the peak of 1917. *Fourteenth Biennial Report of the State Engineer, op. cit,* 109. Information regarding the power outage at Boysen is contained in *Third Biennial Report of the Public Service Commission of Wyoming 1919-1920,* 40 (Docket No. 104).

[245] *Thermopolis Independent, September 17, 1920.* Apparently both 1919 and 1920 were dry years, with no flooding at all in 1919. The 1920 peak flow at Thermopolis reached 13,800 feet per second in June, only 71% of the 1917 peak. *Fifteenth Biennial Report of the State Engineer to the Governor of Wyoming, 1919-1920* (Laramie, 1921), 13.

the dam, raising the water level, so that some of the logs that floated down the river actually passed through the railroad tunnel. The section crew stationed at the Black tunnel next to the dam had to walk in hip-deep water through the tunnel to check the track, and on one occasion a man stepped off into the ditch alongside the track, in the water up to his neck. The flood completely washed out the sidetrack at the Boysen station, and the water behind the dam was high enough to cause timbers to lodge against the railroad bridge a mile and a half upstream from the dam.[246]

A major design deficiency of the Boysen dam was the failure to anticipate the amount of silt that would be deposited above the dam, particularly from Badwater Creek. In the fall of 1921, Allan Boysen said that the silt behind the dam was high enough to cover the underflow gates, so that they could not be opened to let high water through the dam. He was undoubtedly truthful when he said the silt covered the underflow gates, but it was disingenuous of him to suggest that otherwise they might have been opened. In fact, the underflow gates were permanently plugged with timbers when the dam was completed, so opening them required more than removal of the silt. The real problem was that that the reservoir behind the dam was filled with a lot of mud, which reduced the capacity of the lake, and eventually threatened the power plant itself.[247]

---

[246] *Riverton Review,* June 1, 8, July 13, 1921. *Thermopolis Independent,* April 15, June 17, July 16, November 18, 1921. Testimony regarding the logs in the railroad tunnel was given by Bruce M. Campbell, roadmaster of the railroad, and testimony regarding the section crew was given by C. E. Walker, who was then section foreman at the dam. Normally, the railroad bridge south of the dam had a clearance of about 16 feet above the water level, but in June of 1921 the water was so high the logs in the river couldn't pass under the bridge. Case No. 1513, *op. cit.* According to the official gauging at Thermopolis, the 1921 flood level was a record flow rate of 20,800 feet per second, 51% above the previous year and about 4% above the previous peak in 1912. *Sixteenth Biennial Report of the State Engineer to the Governor of Wyoming, 1921-1922* (Casper), 15.

[247] Allan Boysen's testimony of October 19, 1921 is given in Case No. 1154, *op. cit.* In his 1912 testimony in Case No. 1548, Charles Breniman said

12

A VERY BAD RIVER

In 1922, it became likely that there would be new construction in the Wind River canyon alongside the Boysen dam, in response to public pressure to build a highway through the canyon. Back in 1911, when the legislature formalized the system of highways in Wyoming, the Yellowstone Highway from Cheyenne north to Cody was given a route entering the Big Horn Basin via the Birdseye Pass over the mountains, rather than through the Wind River canyon, and that highway over the mountain opened in the summer of 1916. However, the Birdseye Pass route gained a "fearful reputation" among tourists, and after the Wyoming Highway Commission was organized in 1917, the possibility of building a highway through the canyon project received serious consideration.[248]

Leroy E. Laird of Worland was appointed to the highway commission in 1919, and he became highway superintendent in 1921. With a Big Horn Basin advocate of the canyon road in charge, the commission awarded the contract for the road to the Utah Construction Company

---

that the underflow gates were plugged with concrete, although other sources say that timbers were used to plug them.

[248] Before the highway commission was organized, the State Engineer was responsible for the location of state highways. *Eleventh Biennial Report of the State Engineer, op. cit,* 53. The Yellowstone Highway was finally routed up Buffalo Creek, in preference to the steep grades of the Birdseye road. The new highway opened on July 13, 1916. *Thermopolis Record,* January 12, 1912, April 29, 1915, July 12, 1916, July 23, 1923.

in 1922. The initial contract total was more than $294,000, with a completion deadline of April 1, 1923, and both provisions proved optimistic. Moreover, while no one said so at the time, this action raised the possibility that a bad flood at the Boysen dam might send the river through a highway tunnel, as well as a railroad tunnel.[249]

The railroad had preempted the best route through the canyon when it selected its right of way in 1905, and the highway route along the east wall was a more difficult one. Three tunnels had to be bored through the canyon wall to accommodate the roadway, and the longest was alongside the dam and across the river from the so-called Black Tunnel, which had given the railroad so much trouble. Although at first the construction company did not foresee "any trouble" completing the job on time, the Wind River Canyon soon conquered that optimism.[250]

In July, 1922, the contractor began mobilizing its construction crews, which were distributed throughout the canyon to minimize delays on the project. The company moved its steam shovels on the railroad, and then built sidetracks and bridges to reach the work sites across the river. The task was difficult, and in December, 1922, a rock slide nearly buried one of the shovels under 500 yards of rock. The longest tunnel, alongside the dam, which was 368 feet long, was drilled using power from the Boysen dam to operate compressors for the work, and this tunnel broke through in January, 1923. In the summer of 1923, before the highway opened, highway engineers around the country were marveling at the phenomenon of a highway costing as much as $97,000 per mile in a state with fewer than 200,000 people. The financial cost of the highway project was over $500,000, more than double the original contract amount (the one-mile section that included the tunnels cost $101,000), and there was a considerable cost in human life as well. To make a difficult job even worse, construction

---

[249] The U. S. government approved the canyon project in May, 1922. *Worland Grit,* May 16, 1922.

[250] *Thermopolis Independent,* October 1, 1920, November 11, 1921. The interview with the Utah Construction Company was quoted from the Powell *Tribune,* in *The Riverton Review,* July 19, 1922.

also commenced in time for the contractor to experience one of the worst flood summers.[251]

For the Burlington railroad, the flooding problem at the dam became a more serious problem as rail traffic increased. The Casper division of the railroad, which included the line through the Wind River canyon, handled a lot of traffic, and considerable traffic was also diverted there from the Sheridan division. To maintain this traffic volume, the railroad had to be able to offer reliable schedules, and the periodic floods delayed trains, and raised maintenance costs.[252]

When the tracks in the canyon were flooded, each passenger train was delayed for half an hour, each freight train was delayed for up to two hours, and no trains could run at night, creating a twelve-hour delay for them. Flooding increased maintenance costs, as when the railroad had to send a massive wrecking machine with an 8-man crew to Boysen to deal with derailments, entailing a cost of about $100 per day. Section crews who guided trains over flooded tracks and repaired flood damage incurred additional costs for payroll and ballasting materials.

For the Boysen plant, it was also fateful that 1923 was the year when it seemed as though the town of Hudson might be added to the plant service area. The Riverton power company signed a contract in April of 1923 to furnish power to the town of Hudson, through a line to be constructed from Riverton. When completed, there would be a single circuit connected to the Boysen plant, consisting of the towns of Shoshoni, Riverton and Hudson. The Riverton paper declared that when Hudson was connected it would enjoy the same "excellent electrical service" that Riverton was receiving. It seemed too good to be true, and the river soon offered proof that it was.[253]

---

[251] *Thermopolis Independent,* December 8, 1922, July 6, 1923. Also, *Thermopolis Record,* quoted in *The Wyoming State Journal* (Lander), January 12, 1923. In 1928, the Utah Construction Co. sued the State because it was only paid $423,000 of its $511.953 cost on the project. *The Riverton Review,* July 26, 1928.

[252] The regular daily schedule on the Casper division consisted of two passenger trains and six freight trains.

[253] *Riverton Review,* April 18, 1923.

The year 1923 was a bad one along the river. When the ice broke up in the spring, it took out two of the highway contractor's piling bridges and four of its suspension bridges in the canyon. To resume work, the contractor put a ferry in the river, but the ferryboat broke its cable and washed downstream, nearly drowning four men. Upstream, a heavy rain storm in the Riverton area at the beginning of June covered fields with two feet of water, and damaged ditches, the highway and the railroad. The river's first peak was in June at some 26% over the low level of the previous year, but still below that of 1921. But there was much worse to come.[254]

A heavy rain storm in July brought more high water and caused a great deal more damage. On the railroad between Thermopolis and Casper, five bridges were destroyed, and much of the damage was caused by the rampaging Badwater Creek. In the neighborhood of Bonneville, that creek carried away a steel bridge on the railroad's main line, wiped out 1,200 feet of new fill on the Burlington railroad and buried several rail cars (they were never recovered from the creek bed). At Bonneville, the residents fled to the hills for safety, as the town was almost totally destroyed. The Badwater flood raised the river to levels not seen before, nearly 30% above the previous high in 1921. At the Boysen dam, the July flood ran four feet deep over the railroad tracks in the tunnel for four or five days. Since the rails were 15 feet above the crest of the dam, this means the flood was at least 19 feet over the top of the structure.[255]

---

[254] *Riverton Review,* June 6, 1923. The June peak flow at Thermopolis on June 14 was 15,300 feet per second, only 74% of the 1921 high and 26% over 1922.

[255] *Worland Grit,* July 19, 1923. The timber company at Dubois lost more than a thousand ties in the river, which undoubtedly contributed to the debris down at the Boysen dam. *Riverton Review,* July 25, August 29, 1923. The July peak flow in the river was on July 25, at 27,000 feet per second. *Seventeenth Biennial Report of the State Engineer to the Governor of Wyoming, 1923-1924,* 15. The town of Bonneville was home to about 300 people in 1923. *Wyoming State Business Directory, 1924* (Denver, 1924), 117.

Two years later, an engineer for the railroad gave a precise evaluation of the July flood as it affected the Burlington. He estimated the flow over the dam at 28-29,000 cu. ft. per sec., and he calculated that the spillway would have had to be 160 feet wide—as compared with the actual width of less than 90 feet—to avoid flooding the railroad tracks. A crew of 250 men worked three shifts to restore service on the railroad, and it was the middle of August before even a work train could pass "cautiously" through the canyon again.[256]

The Boysen operation was hard hit. The powerhouse at the Boysen plant was flooded on July 23, and the intakes were filled with silt, halting power production. Power lines across five streams went down, and although they were repaired by July 28, the plant could not be restarted. The Popo Agie Light & Power plant in Riverton started up its local plant and supplied the Boysen customers in Riverton and in Shoshoni until August 19, when the Boysen plant came back on stream. The town of Hudson was left without power, for although the government was building its new plant at Pilot Butte, that plant was still a year away from completion.[257]

Damage from the storm continued downstream in the Big Horn Basin. In Thermopolis, the lower part of town was under four to five feet of water, and flooded cars had to be towed to higher ground by horses. The town was without water for a few hours, the light plant was not operating "most of the time," and there was no gas. At least two men were drowned. Between Thermopolis and Worland, Cottonwood Creek wiped out the highway bridge and weakened the railroad bridge enough to require repairs before traffic could resume.[258]

---

[256] Case No. 1513, *op. cit.*

[257] Ray Purdum, the manager of the Popo Agie Light & Power Company in Riverton, announced that purchase of power from the Pilot Butte plant was expected to commence on August 1, 1924, and at that time, Shoshoni would also be served from that plant. *Riverton Review,* July 18, 1923, July 24, 1924.

[258] *Thermopolis Independent,* July 27, August 17, 1923 and *Worland Grit,* July 26, 1923.

Incredibly, the July storm, which occurred in the traditional high water season, was not the worst of that bad year for storms. At the end of September, a storm that struck the eastern half of Wyoming raised torrents in normally dry or modest watercourses, bringing widespread flooding, with considerable damage and the loss of more than a few lives. In the region around the Boysen dam, railroad crews were still working on repairs following the July flood when a week of heavy rain raised the river to flood stage again on September 27. The temporary bridge the railroad built near Bonneville was washed away, as was 1,200 feet of new fill, sending the trains from the south back to Casper. For the next eleven days water flowed over the tracks in the tunnel alongside the dam and for six or seven days it was 52 inches deep over the rails. This information implies that a major collection of debris was obstructing the flow of water over the dam debris, because the peak flow in the river only lasted three of those seven days. The flood on the tracks extended for more than a mile down the river from the dam, stripping ballast under the rails and depositing silt and refuse eight inches deep on the tracks.[259]

At the Salt Creek field, north of Casper, there was seven feet of water in the gas plant, bridges were washed out and at the baseball diamond water was "up in the tree tops." In the Powder River Basin, many hay stacks were swept away, "all grain along the river" was lost, and sheds and wagon boxes, chickens and livestock could be seen floating down the Powder River. In Sheridan, Goose Creek took away most of the wooden paving blocks on the streets, and basements of 300 homes

---

[259]   At Riverton on September 27-28, the first day of the five-day storm, 3.75 inches of rain fell, and the total for the five days was 4.33 inches. At Shoshoni, stranded travelers consumed all the food in the town. *Riverton Review,* October 4, 1923. The gauging records at Thermopolis show that the river reached 18,900 feet per second on September 28, which is consistent with the testimony of a September 27 onset of the flood at the dam. The highest flow rate was 20,400 feet per second on the 29th, and the river dropped to 11,100 on the 30th, and only 5,370 on October 1. *Seventeenth Biennial Report of the State Engineer, op. cit,* 15. Also, *Greybull Standard,* June 4, 1959.

were flooded. In the Big Horn Mountains, work on the road to the Big Horn Basin had to be halted because of the heavy snowfall.[260]

In the Big Horn Basin, Manderson was "all flooded," and 300 feet of Burlington railroad track was washed out. The farms along the river were all under water, houses were flooded with two to six feet of water, and at least one dairy herd and several hogs were carried away. Nearly all the bridges in the northern part of the Basin were either washed out or badly damaged.[261]

The wreck causing the greatest loss of life occurred where the Burlington line east of Casper crossed Cole Creek, ordinarily an insignificant stream. Even though a Burlington track man checked on the condition of the bridge before the passenger train's arrival, a sudden wave of water swept down Cole Creek and took out the bridge, dumping the entire train in the creek, where several of the cars were buried in the sand carried down by the stream. Although we can never know for certain how many died, there were 26 known dead and two others whose bodies were never recovered and were presumed dead. At least two bodies in the Platte River were only recovered in 1924.

The railroad had to bring 10-15 carloads of rock to repair the damage from the September storm to its roadbed in the Boysen area. We know that the grade of the railroad in the canyon past the dam was raised from the level anticipated in the original specifications, and it is likely that this was done after the 1923 flood. The railroad was out of commission for three months and eight days, at a cost "near" a million dollars. The interruptions were so frequent that the Thermopolis *Independent* wryly remarked that the town was back to using stagecoaches to communicate with the outside world.[262]

---

[260] *The Buffalo Bulletin,* October 4, 1923.

[261] *The Buffalo Bulletin,* October 4, 1923, *The Cody Enterprise,* October 3, 1923 and *The Basin Republican,* October 4, 1923.

[262] *Thermopolis Independent,* August 17, September 28, October 5, 12, November 2, 1923. J. C. Brown, who was assigned as station agent at Boysen the month before the September, 1923 flood, testified as to the conditions during and after the flood. Case No. 1513, *op. cit.* In 1925, an engineer for the railroad testified that the grade of the line past the dam

The Boysen plant came back onstream in August after repairing the damage from the July floods, supplying Shoshoni with power for a time, but the September storm again tore out transmission lines from the Boysen plant across three streams, and the town of Shoshoni was out of power from September 28 to October 31, when the plant began operating again.[263]

The 1923 financial statements for Wyoming Power did not portray the disaster one would expect to result from the trials of the summer and fall. Indeed, the output from the plant, including the Hudson business, was 45.5% over the number for the previous year. The company reported revenues of $21,600, only a little under the previous year, but increased labor and other expenses produced a loss of about $2,100. Money continued scarce, as Allan's Aunt Mary continued to fund the deficiencies in the bank account.[264]

The name of a new employee appeared on the statements for the first time in 1923, as Asmus Boysen, who had conceived the idea of this remarkable project, became a paid employee, receiving a salary of $125 per month, except for the times when he wasn't paid at all. As noted earlier, he closed his office in Chicago at the beginning of 1910, the year his wife died, and later he said of those years, ". . . I really had no home. My home was in Wyoming [*i.e.,* Shoshoni) that I called my home, but I was seldom there."[265]

---

was raised from the original specifications, which were based on a 35-foot dam with a 143-foot unobstructed spillway. Case No. 1513, *op. cit.*

[263] Allan Boysen to Commissioner Claude L. Draper, December 6, 1923, in response to Draper's letter of December 5. Public Service Commission files.

[264] Mary J. Stoughton's notes increased to a total of $39,620.24 at the end of 1923. Wyoming Power Co. financial statements, Public Service Commission files.

[265] The 1924, 1925 and 1926 Wyoming directories listed Allan Boysen as manager of the power plant, but the man in charge of day to day operations may have been Allan's brother-in-law, William Sayles, who was married to Darlene Boysen. We know that William Sayles was "in charge" of the plant in January, 1925 (Asmus still made important decisions), when he was served in Case No. 1513. Case No. 1513, *op. cit.*

It was while Asmus was employed at the plant that his project left a very personal scar on a member of his family. Kathryne's son, Raymond Boysen, who was a student at the University of Chicago, visited the plant one summer, and while there he entered an area where the power was supposed to be shut off. Unfortunately, the power was on, and Raymond was severely burned on his legs. Asmus carried Raymond away to be treated, but the young man carried the scars from this incident the rest of his life.[266]

In 1923 there was a formal indicator that the era of Asmus Boysen had ended. Many Wyoming corporations that were no longer operating still held charters and in February, 1923, the legislature provided for the forfeiture of the charters of those that had not filed the required annual reports. In the fall of the year, the Secretary of State purged from the list a large number of corporations, including some involved in the several Boysen projects in Wyoming, leaving only the Fremont Power Company and the Wyoming Power Co. still officially in existence, and both were in bad shape financially.[267]

The new highway through the Wind River canyon finally opened early in 1924, so that there was now a tunnel on either side of the Boysen dam, with the railroad on the west and the highway on the

---

[266] Asmus Boysen worked in the power plant from June 1923 until October, 1924. According to Allan Boysen, he and two other relatives (whom we take to be Asmus Boysen and William Kyne) worked without pay in April, 1924. Allan Boysen to Wyoming Public Service Commission, June 18, 27, 1924. Public Service Commission files. Information regarding Raymond's injury was obtained in a telephone interview with Raymond's son, William Boysen of San Pedro, Calif.

[267] Chapter 69, effective February 26, 1923. *Session Laws of the State of Wyoming Passed by the Seventeenth State Legislature* (Cheyenne, 1923), 88-90. In November, 1923 the charters of the Asmus Boysen Mining Company, the Big Horn Power Co. and Dannebrog Investments Company were revoked, followed by the Riverside Irrigation Company and the Shoshoni Power & Electric Company (former Shoshoni Power & Irrigation Company) in December. The charter of the Fremont Power Company was revoked on July 19, 1927, and that of the Wyoming Power Co. was revoked on June 18, 1931.

east. To commemorate the opening of the road, the Utah Construction Company hosted an elk dinner for 73 people at the Boysen station of the railroad, but there was no indication that any Boysens were invited. When the ice broke up the following month, the river had the last word on the highway construction project, and carried away a bridge the contractor built to remove steam shovels from the canyon.[268]

It is interesting that flooding by the river is not mentioned in the accounts in 1924, which was also an active flood year, although not on the scale of 1923. The river peaked early in April, in late May, in early June, and for a fourth time in mid-June, but apparently did no reportable damage.[269]

We have noted that the Boysen power plant resumed limited production after the 1923 floods, but mud and debris behind the dam continued to clog the trash racks, and the plant once again shut down in March of 1924. The shutdown, which lasted until August, interrupted power supply to Shoshoni, and the Popo Agie plant again supplied the town with power. While this stopgap measure supplied the market, the financial result for the Boysen plant was very bad, as the cost of purchased power, plus the required debt service on the transmission line was far more than the revenues from Shoshoni.

Power deliveries in 1924 declined 43% and revenues of only $16,700 were down from the previous year by nearly $5,000. The $3,500 cost of purchased power ballooned the net loss to $6,100. Labor costs had to be trimmed, and James Rodgers, the lead electrician, was laid off. Boysen family support for the operation increased as brother-in-law

---

[268] The state highway commission reported the total cost of the canyon highway at $581,999.46 in 1924, but a later history of the road gave the total at $700,000, of which $345,955.08 was paid by the Federal government. *Fourth Biennial Report of the State Highway Commission of the State of Wyoming, For the Period Beginning October 1ˢᵗ 1922, Ending September 30, 1924* (Cheyenne, 1924), 6ff.

[269] The river flow at Thermopolis peaked at 17,900 feet per second on April 7 and 8, again at 15,700 feet per second on May 31, again at 14,000 feet per second on June 8, and finally at 18,500 feet per second on June 18. *Seventeenth Biennial Report of the State Engineer, op. cit.,* 15.

William Sayles joined Asmus at the plant, and the three family members sometimes worked without pay. To meet the debt service requirements, Mary Stoughton sent another $6,200, which included the money for the last payment to the Akron group. To deal with this financial crisis, Allan Boysen asked the Public Service Commission to authorize an increase in rates for the town of Shoshoni, to permit the company to realize a modest profit of $250 per month on that account. He hoped this would keep the company in business until the plant could be restarted.[270]

During high water periods, the river deposited silt behind the dam, and we are told that this layer of silt eventually reached some eight feet above the *crest* of the dam, and extended some six miles upstream. When the water flow was low, the river cut a narrow channel down through the mud, flushing mud through the plant intakes. After shutting down more than once in 1923, and starting up for some of 1924 (although far below full capacity), the plant was once again overwhelmed in 1925, when mud again filled the intakes, and halted power production again.

The people in Riverton were unhappy with the interruptions of service from the Boysen plant, and they now had an alternative source to turn to. Just before the Boysen shut down in 1925, the Pilot Butte power plant, located 23 miles northwest of Riverton, came onstream, and Riverton bought power from the new plant. Shoshoni also purchased power from the Pilot Butte plant until the Boysen plant resumed production.[271]

---

[270] Wyoming Power Co. financial statements. Public Service Commission files. One of the elements of the financial deficit was the line loss in the system. In the month of May, 1924, Wyoming Power purchased over 13,000 kwh from the Popo Agie plant, but was able to bill for only 9,150 kwh, a loss of about 30%. Allan Boysen to Wyoming Public Service Commission, June 18, 27, 1924. Public Service Commission files.

[271] Construction of the Pilot Butte power plant began in September, 1923, and the plant started delivering power on January 8, 1925. In the first year two-thirds of the output was supplied to government draglines working on the Riverton project. *New Reclamation Era* Vol. 16, No. 4 (April,

The transition of Shoshoni to the Pilot Butte plant was not as smooth as it was for Riverton, because although the town distribution system in Shoshoni received power over the transmission line that extended to Riverton, the town pump was only connected to the Boysen plant. As a stopgap measure, the Shoshoni water system was connected to the Northwestern railroad water tank, and when a fire struck the business district at the beginning of February, the makeshift water system did not have enough pressure to reach the second story of buildings. Many businesses, including the bank, were wiped out.[272]

The first effort to reduce the silt behind the Boysen dam did not come at the instance of the operators of the power plant, but from Albert Farlow of Lander, a former employee of the Boysen plant, who operated an ice business in Lander and also supplied ice to the Burlington railroad at Boysen. The silt accumulation behind the dam destroyed his ice business and he decided to do something about it.

Farlow and two other former employees of the plant built a cofferdam in the mud behind the dam, to hold back the water so they could reach the underflow gate below the intakes. They then chiseled through the timbers plugging the gate, and on April 21, 1925, set off a blast to clear the passage. They heard the walls of the dam crack, which could have been disastrous to them, and to many others, but the structure held. The blast created an opening measuring 10 x 11.6 feet, and the accumulated mass of mud behind the dam began washing down the river. The river cut a deep channel through the mud, lowering the water level behind the dam more than 40 feet.[273]

1925), 58 and (October, 1939), 279. In 1929, a second generating unit was installed in the Pilot Butte plant, to meet the commercial demand formerly served by the Boysen plant. *Thermopolis Independent Record,* August 2, 1973.

[272] The Pilot Butte plant was not immune to interruptions of service, for that plant shut down from March 8 until April 6. *The Riverton Review,* February 9, April 9, May 14, 1925.

[273] The other two Lander men who opened the passageway were Howard S. Crispen, a stone mason, and George Vaughn. *Thermopolis Independent,* April 24, 1925 and *The Wyoming State Journal* (Lander), April 28, 1925.

It is very clear that this audacious act was not authorized by either Allan Boysen or William Sayles, both of whom were working at the plant, but was directed by Asmus Boysen, himself. Despite the fact that he was not a shareholder, director or officer of Wyoming Power, Asmus decided all the critical issues, and in his testimony on July 31, 1925, Asmus Boysen said that he was at the dam when Farlow and his men opened the one gate, and even gave precise dimensions of the opening.[274]

The June high water of 1925 came and went with no water flowing through the railroad tunnel, because of the new opening under the dam (and also because the spring runoff was not high). Unfortunately, flushing the accumulated mud down the river created serious problems downstream. At Worland, the river became so muddy that the Wyoming Sugar Company plant could not use the water, and at the beginning of September, 1925, the sugar company obtained permission from the State and the railroad to reinstall a gate in the dam. After some difficulty, a new gate was placed in the dam, halting the flushing of silt. Nevertheless, as the large quantity of silt flushed from behind the dam made its way downstream, it raised the level of the riverbed and contributed to flooding in subsequent years, until it was finally washed downstream.[275]

The underflow gates under the dam were built as diversion for the river during construction and were then closed. Breniman testified that they were filled with concrete, but three other sources, including the railroad engineer, said they were closed with heavy timbers. While one newspaper account speaks of "floodgates" that were dynamited, both an engineer for the railroad and Asmus Boysen himself testified in 1925 that only one of the three under-flow gates was opened. D. J. Nelson, superintendent of the railroad gave the information that the tunnel did not flood in 1925. Case No. 1513, *op. cit.*

[274] When asked what the size of the opening was, Asmus said that it was "ten feet by eleven feet seven and one-quarter inches." Case No. 1513, *op. cit.*

[275] *The Wyoming State Journal* (Lander), October 7, 1925. The peak flow rate for the river at Thermopolis in 1925 was 10,700 feet per second on July t. *Eighteenth Biennial Report of the State Engineer to the Governor of*

Incredibly, the Wyoming Sugar company actually got permission from *both* the State of Wyoming and the railroad to close the underflow gate in the dam, which Allan Boysen must have seen as a gift from heaven. After four months of flushing, much of the silt behind the dam was carried away, and, now that the gate was once again in place, the plant could start up again. Wyoming Power commenced supplying the town pump at Shoshoni in November, 1925, and later the company resumed power supply to Shoshoni from the Boysen plant.

As one would expect, Wyoming Power Co. lost a lot of money in 1925. Output from the plant was nearly 77% below the low level of 1924 and revenues were only $9,300, but expenses exploded. Power purchases were $3,100, lawyers and engineers cost almost $1,400, and the crushing debt load generated nearly $8,800 in interest charges. William Sayles was the highest paid laborer, receiving $1,500, and wages and salaries were only $3,200, but the net loss was $12,800. Mary Stoughton advanced another $9,200 to keep the rickety financial ship afloat, raising the total of her notes to $61,400.[276]

We have noted that Allan Boysen refinanced the debt on the Riverton transmission line in 1922, on a note with Bankers Mortgage Company that required $700 monthly payments. In fact, the company made only one $700 payment in 1922, and none of the six payments in 1923 was as much as $700. After receiving four payments in 1924 and three in 1925, the lender was out of patience, and something had to be done. This time, the rescue came from another family member, William Kyne, who was then president of Keith Lumber Company in Casper. Kyne purchased the Bankers Mortgage Company note in October, 1925, removing the threat of another foreclosure.[277]

Now that he was again generating power at the dam, Allan Boysen moved to try to recover the right to serve Riverton. Wyoming Power had a negotiating point on the Riverton business, because it still

---

Wyoming, 1925-1926, 19. Also, *Thermopolis Independent,* September 4, 1925.

[276] Wyoming Power Co. financial statements. Public Service Commission files.

[277] Case No. 4218, *op. cit.*

owned the substation in Riverton that was being used to supply that town. However, the subsequent negotiations were complicated by the fact that the Popo Agie Light & Power Company, which owned the Riverton distribution system, had transferred its business to the Midwest Public Service Company. When Boysen asked the officials of the Midwest company to commence buying power from the Boysen plant, they were agreeable to having a second power source, but were limited by the terms of their contract with the Bureau of Reclamation plant at Pilot Butte. In December, the Midwest officials went to the Boysen plant, where they met "the old gentleman," Asmus Boysen (he was actually only 57). At that meeting, the Midwest company offered to try to get government permission to divide their business between the Boysen plant and the Pilot Butte plant.[278]

Asmus Boysen handled the negotiations with the Midwest company and there was much haggling over the terms of a contract, but everything was dependent on getting the government to consent. In the end, the negotiations accomplished nothing, because the Bureau of Reclamation refused to approve the offer made by the Midwest company.[279]

Harry C. Chappell of the Midwest company delivered this bad news to Allan Boysen in Shoshoni, who advised him to tell the story to his father, who was at the dam. Asmus exploded when he heard Chappell's report. Declaring that relations with the Midwest company were at an end, he called in a young man to witness his demand that the Midwest company vacate the Riverton substation by July 1. The date was later extended to July 15, and Allan Boysen gave the Midwest

---

[278] Description of the negotiations with Asmus Boysen is given in the testimony of H. C. Chappell, vice president of Midwest Public Service Company, before Commissioner Maurice Groshon at Riverton on September 25, 1926. Public Service Commission files.

[279] Docket No. 532, Public Service Commission files. The "young man" was never identified, and lacking other reasonable possibilities, he may well have been Raymond Boysen.

company another fifteen days later, so that Midwest could obtain the necessary materials to build their own substation.[280]

Despite the fact that the Wyoming Public Service Commission had turned him down before, Allan Boysen again decided to apply again directly to the commission, to recover the right to supply the City of Riverton. Of course, the Midwest company opposed the application, and a hearing was held in Riverton on September 25, 1926. The arguments detailed above were hashed out in the hearing, and when it was over, the commission affirmed the Midwest company's certificate for Riverton.[281]

In 1926, the Boysen plant generated power for the Shoshoni accounts in every month, but the financial results continued to be unfavorable, and the company lost $11,500 on revenues of $8,500. The total of salaries and wages reported to the Public Service Commission was back up to $4,600, but it is unlikely that any such sum was actually paid out. Most of that total consisted of $1,500 each for Allan Boysen, Asmus Boysen and William Sayles, the last two being listed as engineers. Poor Mrs. Stoughton contributed another $19,800, bringing her total to $80,200.[282]

Operations at the dam were quiet in 1927, continuing the pattern following the flushing of silt in 1925. The lights were still on in Shoshoni, the meters were read and the bills sent out by the Wyoming Power Co., where Asmus Boysen and William Sayles were the engineers and linemen. Revenues were about $7,400, interest expense was $10,400, and the loss for the year was $11,800. The notes payable increased, but probably only by the amount of the interest that was accrued but not paid. The two secured creditors were members of the family (William Kyne and Mary Stoughton), as were all but one of the men working for the company. The company was moribund, but not entirely dead.[283]

---

[280] Testimony of H. C. Chappell, *Ibid.*

[281] Docket No. 532, Public Service Commission files.

[282] Wyoming Power Co. financial statements. Public Service Commission files.

[283] Employees of the company were the two Boysens, William Sayles and James W. Stuchell, the secretary (who was paid $60). Wyoming Power

The power plant at the Boysen dam continued to operate in the spring of 1928, still with no hope that it could ever make money. In any case, the dam and plant were soon to be sold at auction, and Allan Boysen was not going to be there to bid. He shut down the power plant on May 24, marking the end of fifteen tumultuous years. It is significant that the final shutdown was occasioned by the transfer of the remaining customers to another power source, and not by the intervention of any court. This time, the town of Shoshoni was not left without power, as the Mountain States Power Company took over the supply of electricity to the area formerly served from the Boysen plant.

In order to acquire the distribution system of both the Wyoming Power Co. and the Shoshoni Light & Power Company, Mountain States had to lift the remaining liens against those properties. Two members of the Boysen family, Mary J. Stoughton and William Kyne, had secured interests in the Shoshoni distribution system and the transmission line from Riverton. Mary Stoughton released her lien on the Shoshoni properties, and we do not know how much she was paid for the release, but it was certainly much less than her outstanding loan balance of $84,600.[284]

Allan Boysen filed the final financial statements for the Wyoming Power Co. with the Wyoming Public Service Commission on January 3, 1929. Revenues for the period ended May 24, 1928 were about $5,000, and the company paid $1,400 to purchase power. William Sayles was gone from the list of employees, but Asmus Boysen was still there, as was James Stuchell, the faithful secretary of the company. Two part-time employees collected a total of about $600, and the loss was $2,800, a mere whimper in the company's history. Remaining on the books were some used furniture ($700), a 1920 Dodge truck

Co. financial statements. Public Service Commission files.

[284] *The Riverton Review,* September 27, 1928. Mary J. Stoughton's notes secured by the Shoshoni distribution and transmission line totaled $69,838.49, and she held additional notes of $14,800.82. Public Service Commission files.

($200), some uncollected receivables ($360), some inventory items and $107.43 in the Casper National Bank.

The people involved in the Boysen project over the years scattered widely. Asmus Boysen's brother, Nis Peter Boysen left Wyoming and moved to Des Moines, where he enrolled in Highland Park College. Niels Brorson represented Boysen in the early days of the copper play, and then moved to Chicago to run his office there, but when the office closed in 1910 he was out of a job. In 1920 we find him working as a druggist in Blair, Nebr.

Charles E. Breniman, Boysen's "prince of entertainers" from happier days, served the Boysen cause well both in Iowa and Wyoming, and he deserves a more extensive footnote. He later left to take up an exciting life with the U. S. Bureau of Investigation, the predecessor of the FBI.[285]

---

[285] Charles Breniman was in Tucson, Arizona and San Antonio in 1916, where he was watching agents of the Mexican Secret Service, who were trying to keep Mexican rebels from acquiring arms in the United States. It was later alleged that the BI agents interfered with the arms traffic until their superiors intervened, and that Breniman was thereupon transferred to a new post because of his action. Michael M. Smith, "The Mexican Secret Service in the United States, 1910-1920," in *The Americas,* Vol. LIX (July 1, 2002), 65-85, and *The New York Times,* March 8, 10, 1924. In 1924, Breniman testified before a congressional committee regarding the 1916 Mexican intrigue. *The New York Times,* March 8, 10, 1924. He died in California, April 15, 1960.

THE WARS IN THE COURTS

13

THE PARTNERS
WIN A SHARE

As we have already noted, the beginning of power production at the Boysen plant, the years of struggling to make it a profitable company, and the decline and collapse of the business went forward without any direct interference from the several courts that presided over Boysen's legal woes. Now that we have traced the story of Boysens' unsuccessful efforts to develop a viable business from their venture in Wyoming, we now resume the account of the legal struggle that took place, always at some distance from the dam in northern Wyoming.

While construction on the dam went forward in the summer of 1908, Boysen received one piece of good news from the federal court in Cheyenne, as U. S. District Judge Riner finally got around to issuing his decision in the 1906 case brought by Boysen's syndicate members. The judge decided that the conflicting arguments demonstrated that there was no enforceable contract among the members of the syndicate, and he dismissed the case. The disgruntled former partners appealed, but for the time being Boysen could claim a win, one of the few among what became a long list of losses.

Two years later, a bombshell from St. Louis hit Boysen when the 8th Circuit Court of Appeals decided that Judge Riner was wrong when he dismissed the case of the syndicate members. The appellate court decided that the syndication agreement *was* a valid contract, and it did entitle the members to share in the land Boysen received in exchange for the coal lease. Judge Willis Van Devanter dissented, which may have comforted his old law partner on the federal bench in Cheyenne, but it was no help to Boysen.[286]

This was bad news, but was not as bad as it could have been. Since Boysen only held one of the sixteen shares in the syndicate, there was a real risk he might be cut back from 100% ownership to only 6.25%. But the decision adopted a more Solomonic approach to the matter, holding that each of those members of the old syndicate who *accepted* the syndicate agreement were entitled to a one-sixteenth share in the land, and that the remaining shares belonged to Boysen.

The court decided that there were only six "accepting" members other than Boysen, and only five of them had sued for a share in his land. (The share of Josef Weis, who also accepted the agreement but did not join in the suit, was left in limbo for a time.) Moreover, the court decreed that the five "accepting" members who were plaintiffs in the suit must pay their share of Boysen's costs in acquiring the land. The effect of this decision was to convey 31.25% of the land to the five accepting shares, and leave Boysen with all of the remaining interest. Boysen was also entitled to be reimbursed for 31.25 % of his costs—and cash would certainly have been welcome for the financially beleaguered Boysens.

Leaving aside unanswered questions that were only resolved years later, Boysen only owned 11/16 (68.75%) of the tract conveyed to him in 1907, so when he conveyed his interest to the Asmus Boysen Mining Company, he only conveyed an 11/16 interest, and the subsequent conveyance of the 88-acre dam site to the Big Horn Power Co. was similarly limited to the same fraction. The Clarke group owned the remaining 5/16 interest (31.25%) in the entire tract.

Although the plaintiffs in the case before the 8th Circuit included five of the accepting partners of the syndicate, John Clarke spearheaded the assault on Boysen's legal position for many years, and over the years he acquired the shares of all except a half share of Robert C. Wertz. Accordingly, for convenience we shall refer to those entitled to an

---

[286] Judge Riner ruled for Boysen on July 11, 1908, and the 8th Circuit Court of Appeals reinstated the case against him on May 7, 1910. Case No. 288, *op. cit.*

interest in the Boysen land as the Clarke group, or simply the Clarkes. Clarke was 49 in 1910, and he had great confidence in his legal abilities, plus tenacity that was the equal of Boysen's. Unfortunately, Clarke did not realize that this 1910 decision in his favor was the high point of his contest with Boysen. The court awarded him a share in Boysen's land, and all he had to do to receive a deed was to pay his share of Boysen's cost of acquiring the land. Unfortunately, Clarke and his partners did not receive deeds for their land, because they did not agree with all of the elements of the court's decision, they did not pay their share of Boysen's costs, and they continued to fight.[287]

While Boysen did not ultimately win the legal battle, in the end, neither did the Clarke interests, for other opponents, notably the railroad and the State of Wyoming, proved more formidable than the original contestants. And, as we have said, an unmentioned party in the conflict was Delay, a fickle spirit that sometimes favored one side, and sometimes favored the other.

This decision answered a lot of questions, but new facts had appeared in the years after the syndicate members first brought suit in 1906. For one thing, Boysen's costs to acquire the tract were more than trivial. As we have already noted, Boysen identified $102,678.10 in costs he had incurred, and even when this total was reduced by $39,125 of proceeds he realized from sale of mining company stock, there was still a net of $63,553.10. The accepting partners thus owed Boysen nearly $20,000. In what was to become a familiar response, the Clarke group refused to accept the accounting. They particularly

---

[287] The six accepting members (other than Boysen) were Jacob E. House, Charles J. Woodhurst, Robert C. Wertz, William J. Broatch, John T. Clarke and Joseph Weis. Weis accepted the agreement, but was not a plaintiff in the 1906 suit, and was joined as a defendant; the court did not adjudicate his interest. Maurice Gordon Clarke, younger brother of John T. Clarke, acquired one-third of the Weis share on November 15, 1913, and John T. Clarke acquired the remaining two-thirds in 1916, but when they claimed the Weis interest in Boysen's land on December 9, 1920, it was barred by the Wyoming ten-year statute of limitations. *Clark vs. Boysen, et. al,* 285 *Federal Reporter* 122.

objected to the $12,000 legal fees Boysen paid in the case against Wadsworth, which gave him the right to explore on the reservation before the surveys were completed. After considering these arguments, the appellate court noted that Boysen had suffered "much expense and toil" which he had not included in the numbers he submitted, and accepted Boysen's accounting for his costs.[288]

Considering the difficulties the Boysens experienced in getting the generating plant underway, it is puzzling that John Clarke was so eager to share in those troubles. Nevertheless, once Boysen's project ceased being a minerals speculation and became a power plant, John Clarke apparently wanted to become involved in running that business. His father had been one of the incorporators of the first electric power company in Omaha, and John Clarke worked in the company in 1884.[289]

John Clarke said that he became "active" in the Boysen operation in 1910, although we do not know what he meant by that, for by his own testimony in 1931, he admitted that he had never been in the dam, and that his most recent observation of the dam was from the passenger car on the railroad. Yet, he testified in exaggerated details to events he could not have been involved in. Regarding an incident, which must surely be the action of April, 1925, he said "after the flood in the Big Horn River in 1923," he had the "timbers" removed from

---

[288] Broatch, *et. al, vs.* Boysen, *et. al,* 236 *Federal Reporter* 516. In the testimony before the State Engineer, Lacey said that $14,000 worth of stock was issued to Baldwin for legal services, but the difference between that number and the accounting to the court was not explained. Perhaps the lower figure reflects a discounted value for the stock. Broatch, Wertz, Woodhurst and Clarke tendered more than $13,000 to Boysen's lawyer in 1917, asking to receive deeds, but this offer was not accepted. Case No. 288, *op. cit.*

[289] The Northwestern Electric Light Company built the first power plant in Omaha in 1883, and John T. Clarke said he was involved with this operation the following year. His testimony was given on October 6, 1925, before the Special Master in Case No. 288, *op. cit.* Also, Sorenson, *op. cit,* 634.

the three openings under the dam, creating three passages through the dam of about 11 x 12 feet each. Clarke was mistaken in the number of passages opened through the dam (only one was opened), and he was also wrong about authorizing Farlow to open the underflow gate. Unfortunately, John Clarke often described matters as he would like them to be, rather than as they were at that moment.[290]

In 1911 (in a flashback to the events of 1899), Boysen tried to negotiate what appeared to be and indirect settlement with John T. Wertz. Wertz had never been a member of the old syndicate, and there is no indication that Boysen was willing to settle with that group, but obviously he felt Wertz was owed something for helping him acquire the coal lease. We have assumed that the special treatment of Wertz's father-in-law, Jacob House, in the agreement was really compensation to Wertz, and Boysen's offer to House's widow in 1911 is consistent with that assumption. The timing of Boysen's offer to Mary House may also have had something to do with Wertz's financial situation, which was grim, for the National Mining company had run out of money, and could not even pay Wertz's expenses for managing the company.

Boysen offered to settle the Jacob House claim to the Boysen tract, by giving Jacob's widow a quitclaim deed to 1/16 of the land still owned by the mining company (excluding the power company's 88-acre tract), which might have appealed to John Wertz, because it included the mineralized land, and excluded the dam and power plant, which was increasingly becoming a liability. However, since the St. Louis court had already decided that Mary House was entitled to 1/16 of the entire Boysen tract, *including* the power company land, she did not accept Boysen's offer.[291]

The appellate court in St. Louis directed the U. S. District Court in Cheyenne to determine how the so-called "accepting" syndicate members could receive their share of Boysen's tract, and at the end

---

[290]   Clarke's deposition was dated September 12, 1931, in John T. Clarke *vs.* Asmus Boysen, *et. al.,* Case No. 980, U. S. District Court, Cheyenne, and his testimony was on August 21, 1931, Case No. 1513, *op. cit.*

[291]   The offer to Mary House was made August 21, 1911. Case No. 288, *op. cit.*

of 1913, the Cheyenne court effectively left Boysen with an 11/16 interest in the tract (including that of Josef Weis), and ordered four of the other five "accepting" members to pay their share of Boysen's costs. Under the old syndicate agreement, the House interest did not have to contribute money to the syndicate, and so was not required by the court to share in Boysen's acquisition costs. Therefore, after the court's decision in 1913, the special master issued a deed to Mary House for her late husband's share of the Boysen tract. She promptly sold her share of the tract to John Clarke, and if she realized any significant amount from this sale, she would have been one of the few to profit from that conflict-ridden transaction.[292]

While the litigation between the Clarke group and Boysen did not end at this point, the future wrangling mostly involved details of the complex situation. The courts clearly were telling the Boysens that they had minority partners in all the land outside the power plant tracts. Title in the power plant tract was doubly confused. The effect of the federal court ruling was that Boysen had conveyed only an 11/16 interest to the Big Horn Power Co., but the power company ownership was subject to the trust deed in favor of the bondholders (although the trust deed was not a lien on the Clarke and Wertz interests). Finally, the lumber company lien was not yet decided, and there was the matter of the unpaid taxes, which could ripen into a tax deed, but only for the power company interest in the land.

At this time, John Clarke was confident that he could defeat Allan Boysen's title to the dam and power plant, and that his several lawsuits would eventually give him control of that facility. In anticipation of that eventuality, Clarke attempted to obtain Thermopolis as a customer for the Boysen power plant by trying to negotiate a business combination with the Hot Springs Light & Power Company, which then supplied the town of Thermopolis from a nearby plant on the river. While he did not reach an agreement with the Hot Springs company, he learned enough about their operation to become involved in that company's later troubles. Clarke never said that he represented Boysen in those negotiations, and it is most likely that he was acting on the assumption

---

[292] The judgment in Case No. 288 was handed down November 10, 1913.

that he would soon have the authority to approve any subsequent agreement. After this one attempt, Clarke seems to have lost interest in adding to the Boysen plant's limited market for power.[293]

The title to the Boysen tract and the associated dam and power plant was now encumbered by a number of conflicting claims, so that an unbiased observer would have concluded that its value was declining, not increasing. However, the Clarke family had a more optimistic view of the potential value of the Boysen project, and in January, 1916 they made another effort to chip away at Boysen's title to the land around the dam. Back in the fall of 1913, Josef Weis, the enigmatic Boysen partner who had accepted the old syndicate agreement, but didn't ask for a share in the land, transferred one-third of his share of the agreement to Maurice Gordon Clarke. Maurice Clarke was the youngest brother of John T. Clarke, and was the second Clarke family member to enter the lists against the Boysens. The younger Clarke was then 35, and had been an accomplished athlete before taking up the law and opening a practice in Okmulgee, Oklahoma sometime before 1905.

Maurice Clarke's intervention in the Boysen cases involved peripheral issues that never came to dominate the judicial scene, but continued to complicate the process of bringing the legal war to an end, becoming a sort of side show to the main drama. Maurice Clarke's 1916 petition (on behalf of Weis and himself) attacked Boysen's title on two bases. First, he asked that the Weis share in the Boysen tract be revived. Then he also asked that the 9/16 interest represented by all of the non-accepting members be sold and the proceeds distributed for the benefit of the seven accepting interests. If the first argument succeeded, Weis and Clarke would have a 6.25% interest, and if the second argument also succeeded, they would effectively have a 14.3% interest. Weis also asked for an accounting by the Boysen interests for their use of the lands. Edgar Fourt represented the Boysen interests,

---

[293] On March 10, 1919, Harlan J. Thompson, who was the majority owner of Hot Springs Light & Power Company, testified that John T. Clarke had been trying for "three or four years" to combine the Hot Springs company with the Boysen operation. Docket No. 104, Public Service Commission files.

and he filed a demurrer, saying the petition did not state a cause of action.[294]

Maurice Clarke's case eventually reached the 8th Circuit Court of Appeals in St. Louis, and late in 1922, that court acknowledged that Weis once had the right to a share of Boysen's land, but noted that he refused to join in the suit by the other partners in 1906, and in the ten years afterward he did not assert any claim to the land. Since Wyoming law only gave him ten years to assert his claim, he could not prevail.[295]

Despite the decision in the appellate court, the case did not die. The Lander judge removed Maurice Clarke's suit on the Weis interest from the active docket in 1925, because nearly eight years had passed without any action, but Clarke asked that it be reinstated, and it was. The following month, a new Lander lawyer came forward to represent the plaintiffs, but nothing further happened until 1928, when the judge dismissed the Weis/Clarke suit for the second time. Once again, Clarke asked that the case be reinstated, and once again, it was. This strange drama continued for twelve more years.[296]

In the summer of 1918, Judge Riner became weary of the delaying tactics on both sides of John T. Clarke's case against Boysen, and issued a number of orders. John Clarke and Robert C. Wertz had not paid

---

[294] Joseph Weis and Maurice Gordon Clarke *vs.* Asmus Boysen, *et. al.,* Case No. 2105 filed January 31, 1916, Fremont County District Court. If the Weis share were revived, Boysen's share would be reduced from 68.75% to 62.5%, and if the non-accepting shares were distributed over the accepting shares, Boysen would only hold 14.3%, with the remainder in the hands of the Clarke group.

[295] Clarke *vs.* Boysen, *et. al,* decided November 18, 1922, 8th Circuit Court of Appeals, 285 *Federal Reports* 122.

[296] Case No. 2105, *op. cit.* In Lander in the spring of 1934, Judge Fourt again dismissed the case, and this time, Clarkes' lawyer, Arthur Maxwell, agreed, but returned the next day, telling the judge the dismissal was "inadvertent," and the judge again reinstated the case. In the spring of 1936, the parties were back in court with more pleadings, but Judge Murane again dismissed the case on May 15, 1940. John T. Clarke pleaded for one more reinstatement, but this time the court turned him down.

the money they owed Boysen for their share of his expenses, and the judge ordered them to deposit the money with the court, on pain of having their case dismissed. Clarke thereupon deposited the money for the Woodhurst interest he had purchased and for the half interest he had purchased from Robert C. Wertz, and the judge then dismissed the case as to the remaining three shares of Clarke and the half share of Wertz. As we have come to expect, Clarke immediately appealed all of the Cheyenne judge's orders to the Eighth Circuit court in St. Louis. However, the Special Master did issue deeds to Clarke for the 9.375% interest he had paid for, but Clarke and Wertz had to await another day to get deeds for the remaining 21.875% interest they were entitled to.[297]

There were so many lawsuits pending that the Clarkes could choose which one to file pleadings in. At the end of 1920, Maurice G. Clarke decided to try to advance his effort to revive the Weis share in the Boysen land by attaching that question to the 1906 suit against Boysen, which was still pending in the Cheyenne court. He asked Judge Riner to let him intervene in that suit, and Riner turned him down at the end of 1920. Consistent with Clarke family tradition, Maurice Gordon Clarke mounted his own appeal to the 8th Circuit Court of Appeals in St. Louis.

At the end of 1927, John T. Wertz, that ubiquitous negotiator, and architect of the entire complicated mess, died in Thermopolis. Wertz's National Mining company drew attention in the newspapers from time to time, when Wertz showed the editor "small" samples of promising ore, when he brought prospective investors to look over the operation, or when he brought the prediction that "active work" would "soon begin." In 1909, he even went so far as to give the Washington *Herald* a list of ten shareholders, in an apparent effort to attract other investors. This list only included one of the political figures he often bragged about, and that one was no longer in the Congress. But the pot of gold, he hoped to find under the next rock never appeared, and

---

[297] The money John T. Clarke deposited with the court was paid to John Lacey for the account of the Asmus Boysen Mining Company, and the deeds were dated June 18, 1918. Case No. 288, *op. cit.*

by 1910 there was no money to pay his expenses, and we hear no more about the company, which had its charter revoked in the middle of 1927.[298]

John Wertz and his second wife were living in Thermopolis in 1927, and early in December he took a carpenter up to Willow Creek, to do some work up there. He died on December 18 and his widow said that his estate consisted of only about $300, which he held as agent for owners of mining claims having only "speculative value." So it was, that the coal lease John Wertz designed for Asmus Boysen, with its attractive-looking mineralization on Willow Creek, could not be used to look for copper, and when it was exchanged for a mile-square section of mineral land, that parcel over on the canyon also proved lacking in mining potential, and only lured Boysen into financial ruin. Moreover, even though Wertz was later able to get a second chance at exploiting the Willow Creek play on the coal lease (although Boysen also got a piece of it), for him it also was only a seductive call for more money, until there was no more. For the man who was once said to control most of the claims on Willow Creek—and for the other owners of those claims—the end was a whimper, not a bang.[299]

---

[298] *Wind River Mountaineer* (Lander), March 27, 1908 (quoting the Shoshoni *Gazette*), December 17, 1908 *The Washington Herald*, November 5, 1909. John Wertz assigned his $1,309.32 claim against the company to his brother, who sued the company to recover. Robert C. Wertz *vs.* The National Mining and Development Co., Case No. 1376, filed March 13, 1911 in the Fremont County District Court and dismissed without prejudice on June 24, 1912.

[299] *The Shoshoni Enterprise,* December 9, 1927. Also, Estate of John T. Wertz, Case No. 436, filed February 2, 1928, Hot Springs County District Court.

14

ELLA CLARKE
JOINS THE FRAY

Boysen's efforts to realize value from the dam and power plant were seriously complicated by the threat posed by the company's unpaid creditors, an important one of which was the Shoshoni Lumber Company, whose bill was badly overdue. By the end of May, 1909, the arrearage on that bill was nearly $8,000, and although Boysen sent two checks totaling $3,500 later in the year, the lumber company continued to press for payment of the balance. On May 10, 1910, the company's owners called a meeting with Boysen in the lumber company's offices in Shoshoni, hoping to receive some payment, or security for payment of the balance.[300]

At the meeting, where both Charles H. King and Peter Nicolaysen were present, Boysen said that he would try to raise the money to pay off the balance of some $5,200, but that if he could not, he would be happy to see the lumber company file a mechanic's lien on the dam and power plant. He explained this rather surprising response by saying that if the lien were filed it might help him to get the company's bondholders and stockholders to put up additional money.[301]

---

[300] The balance due the Shoshoni Lumber Company on May 31, 1909 was $7,994.49, and Boysen paid $2,000 on June 26 and $1,500 on September 17. Some small purchases were made subsequently, so that when the lien was filed the unpaid balance was $5,206.79.

[301] Case No. 1372, *op. cit.*

Asmus Boysen did get the attention of his bondholders, even before the lumber company filed its lien, although their attention to his affairs was not favorable to his business plans. As we have noted, the gold bonds were backed by a lien on the power company's assets, and if the bonds were not paid, the bondholders were entitled to foreclose on that lien. In fact, the power company paid only the first three coupons on the gold bonds (one payment in 1908 and two in 1909), and the bondholders soon clamored for their money.

In May and June, 1910, Iowa bankers representing bondholders came to Shoshoni to see Boysen. Boysen and Breniman showed the bankers the large irrigation projects under consideration in the Riverton valley—which could not have impressed them—and told them the area could be served by building a $20,000 power line to Riverton. Boysen quickly learned that the bankers were chiefly concerned about their missing interest payments, and although they listened to his sales pitch, when they learned how small the existing market for power was, they would not commit more money to a bad use. During this visit to Wyoming, Milo Gabriel, cashier of a Lyons, Iowa bank, also met Charles H. King of the Shoshoni Lumber Company and told King that he represented the bondholders of the power company, effectively putting King on notice that the company had other secured creditors.[302]

Faced with the Boysen's failure to raise money from the Iowa bankers, the lumber company filed its lien on September 9, 1910. The lien, to secure payment of $5,200 for construction supplies, plus interest, covered the dam and power plant. The next step was for the lumber company to foreclose on the lien, but before that could happen, there were more pleadings in 1913 in the Shoshoni Lumber Company's foreclosure case, but still no decision. To get the right to sell the dam and power plant, the lumber company had to join the trustee for the holders of the Big Horn Power Co. bonds as a defendant, and in response, Edgar Fourt, arguing for the trust company, contended that

---

[302] *Riverton Republican,* June 17, 1910. Milo J. Gabriel was the cashier of the First National Bank of Lyons. Gabriel said he was in Shoshoni in May, 1910, so there may have been two separate delegations of Iowa bankers. Case No. 288, *op. cit,* and Case No. 1372, *op. cit.*

the trust company lien was superior to that of the lumber company. The judge took the matter under advisement, leaving the matter for decision after another two years.[303]

Finally, in September, 1915, Judge Winter decided that the lumber company lien was superior to that of the bondholders. The delinquent account of the lumber company contained only six purchases made in the three days before the trust company filed its own lien on the Big Horn Power Co. assets. These purchases (mostly for feed) totaled just $39.61, but the judge gave the lumber company priority on that basis. This judgment for the lumber company set the stage for it to have the dam and power plant sold to satisfy the lien.[304]

We do not know when the Boysens conceived of the lumber company lawsuit as a way to wipe the slate clean of all contenders for the power company site, including the former syndicate partners, the creditors, and the bondholders, but that strategy now emerged. At the beginning of December, 1915, Allan Boysen took assignment of the judgment from the Shoshoni Lumber Company, and it appears that this assignment was a very friendly transaction between debtor and creditor. Allan Boysen immediately asked that the dam and power plant be auctioned to pay the judgment, and on December 22, 1915 the court ordered that the property be auctioned off.[305]

Before the dam could be sold the property had to be appraised. One of the appraisers of the dam and power plant was none other than Jesse E. Keith, the manager of the Shoshoni Lumber Company and the former roommate of Allan Boysen's two brothers-in-law. There is no indication that any of the appraisers had any expertise in valuing

---

[303] William J. Broatch, *et. al, vs.* Boysen, *et. al,* 8th Circuit Court of Appeals, 175 *Federal Reports* 702, decided January 7, 1910 and Case No. 1372, *op. cit.*

[304] Case No. 1372, *op. cit.*

[305] Judge Charles E. Winter made his finding of fact and law on September 11, 1915, and gave judgment for the lumber company on the same day. The assignment to Allan Boysen was dated December 8, 1915, execution was ordered the same day, the appraisal and sale were on January 4, and the sale was confirmed January 31, 1916.

power plants and concrete dams, but they set a value of $90,000 on the dam and power plant. This action cleared the way for the sheriff's sale, which was held on January 4, 1916. The sheriff knocked down the property to Allan Boysen for $7,300, who borrowed the money from his aunt, Mrs. Mary J. Stoughton.[306]

While the price Allan Boysen paid for the dam and power plant at the sheriff's sale was a steep discount from the appraised value of $90,000, it was just the amount he needed to pay the Shoshoni Lumber account, including accrued interest. The court confirmed the sale at the end of January, 1916. Allan Boysen now owned something, but it is important to ask what he owned.

The Boysen dam, with a power plant inside was mostly located on the streambed of the river, and we have already noted that the streambed was not a part of Boysen's land. The only indication of legal ownership of the dam was the permit issued to Asmus Boysen by the State Engineer. Arguably, the foreclosure on the dam and power plant also included the permit, although no effort was made to change the ownership of the permit for five more years. Moreover, the foreclosure did not affect the title to the approaches to the dam from the Boysen land on either side (but Allan also had a plan to take care of that). After this remarkable transaction, and for a couple of years later, the Boysens were able to hope they had put the scary financial past and the pesky legal opponents behind them. Unfortunately, the first doubts about this rosy scenario appeared the very next year.[307]

The first threat to Allan Boysen's financial coup in the sheriff's sale arose in the summer of 1916, when the sale of the dam and power plant came to the attention of one of the Big Horn Power Company's bondholders. Bernard P. Wickham of Council Bluffs, Iowa, owned 20 of the $500 bonds and 100 shares of stock in the company. The face

---

[306] In the 1910 census, Jesse Keith was living in a house in Shoshoni with Fred Aishton and William Kyne.

[307] The sheriff's deed was dated February 1, 1916. Case No. 1372, *op. cit.*

value of the bonds was $10,000, but he may have paid less than that, and he would have received the stock as a part of the deal.[308]

Wickham heard about the $90,000 appraisal, and he was incensed when he learned that Allan Boysen had purchased the dam and power plant for a mere $7,300. In the summer of 1916 he sued Allan Boysen and the Big Horn Power Co. in the Cheyenne Federal district court for collusion and fraud. While this might have been worrisome to Allan, the case did not produce any real threat for a couple of years, and then only because of John Clarke, who then had a new litigation partner.[309]

Having purchased the dam and power plant at auction, Allan Boysen took another step in the fall of 1916 to gain a clear title to most of his father's preference tract. Four years had now elapsed since Allan purchased the tax certificates on most of the Boysen tract, and the Fremont County Treasurer issued deeds to Allan for all of the Boysen tract except one lot on the east side of the dam. This tax deed gave Allan Boysen an 11/16 interest in the rest of the Boysen tract, including the 88-acre tract owned by the power company (although there were more questions regarding title to the 88-acre tract).[310]

The Clarke group took no action in response to the tax deeds. At least on paper, Allan Boysen owned all of the former Boysen tract, except for the parcel immediately adjacent to the dam on the east side. Moreover, he hoped that his purchase of the dam and power plant in

---

[308] Wickham's family also had more than a passing knowledge of northern Wyoming, as a cousin had been embroiled (on the prosecution side) in one of the cattle rustling cases back in 1892. John T. Wickham was a stock detective working at Otto Franc's Pitchfork Ranch in the Big Horn Basin when two prisoners, Jack Bedford and David A. "Dab" Burch were killed on their way to be tried for theft in Buffalo, Wyo. Wickham fled to Montana after the incident, and then lived out his life in Jefferson County, Mont., not further troubled by Wyoming law officers.

[309] Bernard P. Wickham *vs.* Big Horn Power Co. and Allan Boysen, Case No. 882, filed July 5, 1916 and dismissed November 12, 1918, U. S. District Court, Cheyenne.

[310] The four deeds from the Fremont County treasurer to Allan Boysen covered all except Lot 7, Section 4, Township 5 North, 6 East of the Wind River Meridian, and were dated September 15 and 25, 1916.

the Shoshoni Lumber Company foreclosure gave him clear title to that facility, against the many claims on those assets. At this point, Allan Boysen must have hoped that he could have a fresh start in running the power plant.

Even if his title were secure—by no means a sure thing—he faced other formidable challenges. Most immediately, the company operating the plant was bankrupt, and he needed to find a way to make money selling power. And the river was always an unpredictable threat, triggering interruptions at the power plant, and causing trouble for the railroad.

The next conflict involving the Clarkes arose from Allan Boysen's efforts to show the State that he could operate the dam without flooding the railroad. He hired a surveyor to design waterways, tunnels, open cuts and flumes to relieve the floodwaters above the dam during periods of high water. The land he needed to use to construct these proposed works was that part of the Boysen tract west of the dam, now partly owned by the Clarke group. To clear the way for the proposed construction, the Wyoming Power Co. commenced condemnation proceedings on this land at the beginning of 1918. However, by then, the validity of the lumber company judgment had been challenged (of which more later), and the judge refused to rule on Allan Boysen's condemnation case while the title to the dam was in dispute.[311]

In the fall of 1921, Allan Boysen tried again to clear the way for some flood control construction, withdrawing the 1918 case and filing a new case to condemn less than four acres of rugged terrain lying east of the railroad right of way and west of the dam. (The new petition named more than 25 defendants—some more than once—which later complicated the pleadings in the case.) The land to be condemned was

---

[311] The condemnation proceedings were filed in the Fremont County District Court, on January 12, 1918. The pleadings for this case have not survived, but the history of the case is given in the pleadings of Allan Boysen in Case No. 1154, *op. cit.* In the matter of the application of the Wyoming Power Co. to condemn property, Case No. 2283, filed January 31, 1918, and decided September 1, 1921, Fremont County District Court.

to be used to construct tunnels and other works west of the dam to alleviate flooding. The railroad was not named as a defendant, and we are not told how a tunnel to move excess water could be constructed west of the dam without interfering with the railroad's right of way and tunnel.[312]

The new condemnation attempt immediately ran into trouble from the Clarkes, and their opposition must have puzzled Allan Boysen. Back in 1919, when the secretary of the public service commission asked him about the threat of the Clarkes' litigation, he said, "Well, I don't see what any one would gain by trying to stop it. There's a chance to go ahead and make that dam pay an income. They [*i.e,* the Clarkes] have a chance to get some money, but if they fight it, they have no chance." Unfortunately, the Clarkes were not thinking about compromise. Instead, they thought they were playing a zero-sum game, where somebody had to win, and somebody had to lose, and it never occurred to them that both participants in the game might lose.[313]

John Clarke first tried to thwart the condemnation by claiming the rugged land was worth "several thousand" of dollars per acre. When the appraisal of the tract set a value of only $50 on the four acres, Clarke attacked the amount of the award. He also attacked the condemnation on procedural grounds. Hoping to stop the action before it could come to trial, Clarke instructed Porter B. Coolidge (his Lander lawyer) to point out to the court that two of the defendants were dead. "Knock out condemnation proceedings there, save appeal cost," he said in his telegram. Later, the Clarkes added the objection that the "numerous" bondholders of Big Horn Power Co. were not notified of the action. The power company deposited the $50 condemnation award with the

---

[312] From Allan Boysen's pleadings in Case No. 1154, *op. cit,* we know that case No. 2283 was dismissed without prejudice on September 1, 1921. The new case was filed on November 25, 1921. In the matter of the application of the Wyoming Power Co. to condemn property, Case No. 3061, filed November 25, 1921 and decided January 21, 1931, Fremont County District Court.

[313] Allan Boysen's testimony was taken in Thermopolis on March 10, 1919. Docket No. 104, Public Service Commission files.

court, but the objections of the Clarkes tied up the matter, so that this case also languished on the court docket until May, 1930, when the judge dismissed the case and returned the $50 deposit.[314]

In the spring of 1923, Allan Boysen tried once again to do something about the flooding problem. This time he proposed to condemn about 66 acres, including the dam, the area covered by the reservoir above the dam and on either side of it, and a portion of the stream bed and west wall of the canyon downstream from the dam. John Clarke filed an eight page answer to Boysen's petition, in which he recited the history of his title to an interest in the Boysen tract, and the history of the Shoshoni Lumber Company foreclosure, which he said was done without notice to him. Then he declared that the land to be condemned was already devoted to the purposes Boysen wanted to accomplish, so that the only reason for the condemnation was to deprive the Clarkes and others of their title to the property. This answer was filed with the court on the same day as Allan Boysen's petition, indicating that Clarke had some advance notice of what Boysen was doing. After these initial pleadings, nothing more was done regarding Boysen's third condemnation case until May, 1930, when it was also dismissed.[315]

To further complicate the tangled mess involving the Boysens, John Clarke filed another of those "side show" lawsuits in the summer of 1918, to modify the suggestion first advanced by brother Maurice Clarke in the 1916 suit with Josef Weis. As we have noted, the courts had left Boysen with his own share of the land, plus the shares of Weis and the nine partners who did not accept the agreement, and the Weis and Clarke suit asked that the shares of these nine partners not be given to Boysen, but be sold, with the proceeds distributed to the remaining partners. John Clarke's suit in Federal district court in Cheyenne suggested that instead of being sold, the shares of the

---

[314] William J. Broatch died September 10, 1922 and Samuel G. Collins, another defendant, died January 12, 1922. The Clarke wire to Coolidge is in the case file for Case No. 3061, *op. cit.*

[315] In the matter of the application of Wyoming Power Co., a corporation, to condemn property, Case No. 3301, filed March 1, 1923, the Fremont County District Court.

non-accepting partners should be distributed among the "accepting" partners. This formula would give John Clarke 75% of the Boysen property (as compared with 64.3% if his brother's suit succeeded), and reduce Boysen to one-sixth, or one-seventh, depending on the outcome of the Weis/Clarke suit. John Clarke might even get a larger share, for he asked the court to give him a lien on Wertz's share (for legal expenses advanced on account of Wertz).

For good measure, in this suit Clarke also asked that all of his claims include the railroad right of way. The railroad right of way was a very small portion of the Boysen lands, and Clarke seemed not to care that by challenging the railroad's title he guaranteed that he would have a well-financed opponent in court. After the railroad filed its answer in the case, the court granted the first of many continuances in what became yet another long-running case.[316]

In the fall of 1921, John Clarke launched still another legal challenge to the Boysen interests. On the records of the State Engineer, Asmus Boysen was still the sole owner of the permit to build the dam, and since John Clarke had a legal interest in the Boysen tract, he wanted his share in the dam itself, which was not on the Boysen land, but on the riverbed owned by the government. Clarke first filed a notice with the State Engineer that he had an interest in the permit and followed up with a formal lawsuit in the Cheyenne federal court, asking the court to give him the same percentage ownership in the dam permit as he held in the surrounding land of the Boysen tract. While John Clarke's lawsuits were never simple matters, this one was unique, in having only one plaintiff (John Clarke) and one defendant (Wyoming Power Co.). In its answer in the fall of 1922, the Wyoming Power Co. said that when Boysen acquired his land he did not intend to build a dam and

---

[316] To advance all of these claims, Clarke had to name all the other claimants. John T. Clarke *vs.* Asmus Boysen, The Asmus Boysen Mining Company, Allan Boysen, Big Horn Power Co, Chicago Title & Trust Co, C. B. & Q. Railroad Co, Big Horn Railroad Co, Shoshoni Power and Electric Co, Maurice G. Clarke, Joseph Weis, Carl H. Tiedemann, Robert C. Wertz and the Midwest Power and Light Co, Case No. 980, filed June 17, 1918 in the U. S. District Court in Cheyenne.

use his land as a power site, and therefore denied that Clarke had the right to a share of the permit. After these pleadings were filed with the court, nearly seven years passed without action.[317]

On March 9, 1928 Judge Neblett in the Cheyenne federal district court awarded Clarke a 9/32 interest (28.125%) in the permit, together with the associated water rights, and awarded a 1/32 interest (3.125%) to Robert C. Wertz. In July, the Special Master issued the assignments directed by the court, and he also assigned the remaining 11/16 (68.75%) interest to Wyoming Power Co. Nevertheless, John Clarke was not *entirely* satisfied, and served notice that he was appealing this decision.[318]

Two other "side show" Clarke lawsuits were filed in the Cheyenne federal court, in 1922. In the first, Ella R. Clarke sued to recover from the Big Horn Power Co. the unpaid interest from 352 coupons on the gold bonds she held. Later in 1922, trustees for the bondholders brought an action for the payment of the bonds, and asked that a receiver be appointed for the Big Horn Power Co., Allan Boysen and the Asmus Boysen Mining Company. Obviously, the timing of this suit was in response to pressure from the Clarke group, who held a majority of the bonds, so this is clearly a Clarke lawsuit brought by a different party. While the receiver was appointed, we have pointed out that the power plant continued to operate under two other power companies, and the receiver never had a role in operations.[319]

---

317 Case No. 1291, *op. cit.*

318 Case No. 1291, *op. cit.* Although John T. Clarke went through some of the motions of carrying an appeal of Case No. 1291 to the Circuit Court of Appeals, it appears that he did not actually do so. His argument with Judge Neblett's decree had to do with the interest of the so-called "lapsed" shares, and that issue was already present in other cases on appeal to the Circuit Court.

319 Ella R. Clarke *vs.* Big Horn Power Co, Case No. 1281, U. S. District Court, Cheyenne. The court appointed Thomas Hunter as receiver for the Big Horn Power Co. Case No. 1320, *op. cit.* Trustees for the bondholders were Henry Pogson, a New York lawyer, and Augustus R.

An important chapter of the Boysen story opened with the marriage of John Clarke in 1917. Helena Elizabeth Rauch Tiedemann, who was always known as "Ella," was the eldest daughter of Charles Rauch of Cleveland, the president and major owner of the Rauch and Lang Carriage Company, makers of carriages, and later of electric automobiles. Ella was also the widow of August Tiedemann, the son of a Cleveland banker. We do not know how much she inherited from her husband and her father, but it is apparent that she was comfortably able to invest and also to finance litigation. John Clarke was 56 when he married, and Ella was 49. Ella Tiedemann Clarke brought to the marriage a fresh enthusiasm for litigation, and ample means to support that passion.[320]

The Clarkes' new tactic for surrounding Boysen's financial situation by using the defaulted power company bonds was first used in 1916, before they married. Boysen borrowed nearly $9,000 from a Clinton, Iowa, bank at the beginning of 1911, and gave 24 ($12,000 face value) of the power company bonds as collateral. He made only a payment of one year's interest, and in the fall of 1916, the bank auctioned off the collateral, which was purchased by Ella Tiedemann, who gave $360 for them, or just $15 for each $500 bond. Sometime during the next year John Clarke took assignment of the note from the bank and lodged a counterclaim against Boysen for the value of the note.[321]

This is the first occasion when John Clarke and Ella Tiedemann acted together against Boysen, and also involved a new motive for

---

Smith, owner of a New York hotel. Henry Pogson also represented Henry T. Clarke in his suit against the Wyoming Power Co. in 1924.

[320] Hannes Tiedemann, who was president and co-founder of the United Banking & Savings Co. of Cleveland, died in 1908. In 1913, Rauch & Lang produced an electric sedan that sold for $3,200, but Kettering's invention of the self-starter marked the end of the electric automobile boom. Rauch died in 1913.

[321] Because John T. Clarke was a part owner of the Boysen tract, Maurice G. Clarke and Weis had to join him as a defendant, albeit a "friendly" one, and it was in this suit that John Clarke made his counterclaim against Boysen. Case No. 2105, *op. cit.* Also, Case No. 1372, *op. cit.*

their lawsuits. We can only speculate regarding the reason John Clarke wanted to get involved in the power generation business, but Ella Clarke was clearly more interested in the speculative profits she might earn from buying bonds at deep discount.

Ella Clarke's first direct intervention in the Boysen litigation was in the fraud case Bernard Wickham brought in the Cheyenne federal court in 1916, because she held some of the bonds of the Big Horn Power Co. She was not permitted to intervene in this case, which was just as well, because Wickham apparently decided not to continue his attack on Boysen when Ella Clarke was ready to press on—and pay for—her own much more elaborate lawsuits. In any event, the Wickham case never came to trial, and was dismissed in the fall of 1918, for lack of prosecution.[322]

Ella Clarke's strategy—a much more direct challenge to the Boysens than the Wickham suit—was to foreclose on the security for the bonds she held and get possession of the company's assets. However, before she could do that she had to eliminate Allan Boysen's purchase of the dam and power plant at the 1916 auction. In the fall of 1918, she contested the Shoshoni Lumber Company foreclosure in the Fremont County court, arguing that the bondholders had no notice of the foreclosure.[323]

Allan Boysen was still in the Army when Ella Clarke filed her suit, and on his return from the Army in the spring of 1919, he abandoned any hope of basing his ownership on his father's chain of title, and now based his entire claim on his purchase of the dam and power plant at the Shoshoni Lumber Company foreclosure. Since the dam was constructed across the river, on land excluded from Boysen's section of land, Allan Boysen asked the court to find that the dam was not a part of the property in dispute. As a fallback defense, he asked that if

---

[322] Bernard P. Wickham *vs.* Big Horn Power Co. and Allan Boysen, U. S. District Court, Cheyenne, Case No. 882, *op. cit.*

[323] Ella Clarke's motion to set aside the Shoshoni Lumber Co. judgment was filed August 29, 1918. Case No. 1372, *op. cit.*

the court should find against him, the Clarkes should be required to contribute to the cost of the dam and its equipment.[324]

In her pleadings, Ella Clarke disclosed some of her purchases of Big Horn Power Co. bonds. Her earlier pleadings were based on only four $500 bonds but she continued aggressively to buy up others, eventually accumulating $215,000 face value of the bonds, more than 60% of the $350,000 issue.[325]

One of the bondholders who sold her bonds to Ella Clarke was none other than Lida Leet, Anna Boysen's sister-in-law. While this fact might sound odd at first, considering that Lida did not figure in the troubles with Anna in 1908, there was another reason for her to dislike Asmus Boysen. It will be remembered that Asmus was the guardian of Lida's son William, and in the spring of 1909, Asmus filed suit against Lida and her daughter Helen, to force them to convey a one-third interest in Frank Leet's estate to the boy. For whatever reason, by 1920, Lida Leet was on the Clarke side against Boysen.[326]

Judge Charles O. Brown came to the bench of the Lander court in 1921, and at the end of June he finished wading through the pleadings on Ella Clarke's motion to upset the foreclosure of Shoshoni Lumber Company's lien. In a brief order, Judge Brown overruled her motion, giving Allan Boysen a momentary victory, and Ella Clarke promptly appealed to the Wyoming Supreme Court.[327]

The Wyoming Supreme Court finally heard Ella Clarke's appeal of the lumber company case in the spring of 1924. There it developed that her lawyers had done a poor job in crafting the case, because for

---

[324] Allan Boysen's military service ran from May 29, 1918 to February 13, 1919. His answer was filed April 4, 1919. Case No. 980, *op. cit.*

[325] The largest bondholder on Ella Clarke's list was Burghard H. A. Henningsen, who owned 106 of the bonds with a face of $53,000 at the time of his death. Case No. 1372, *op. cit.*

[326] The Boysen suit against Lida Leet and her daughter was filed in Carroll County District Court on March 5, 1909, and settled on November 29, 1915.

[327] Judge C. O. Brown overruled Ella Clarke's motion on June 28, 1921. Case No. 1372, *op. cit.*

some reason her case was based only on the four bonds she said she was entitled to receive from the estate of James Knox Sebree.[328]

James K. Sebree, who owned the Saratoga Hotel in Chicago, bought four of the $500 bonds at face value in 1909, and also received 20 shares of the Big Horn Power Co. stock. In the same year Sebree loaned $1,000 to Asmus Boysen, who gave four more bonds as collateral for the loan. The loan was never repaid, and the eight bonds, having a face value of $4,000, together with the shares, were still in Sebree's estate when he died in 1913. Sebree had a large estate, and the extremely drawn-out probate was snarled in an ugly battle between the legatees named in the will and Sebree's last mistress, who claimed to be his common law wife, so that it was the spring of 1919 before the executors could wind up the probate.[329]

Ella Clarke agreed to pay $800 for the eight bonds in May, 1919, but she did not receive then until eight months later. When she intervened in the lumber company case in 1918, she swore that she owned four of the bonds, and this discrepancy was fatal to her appeal to the Wyoming Supreme Court. The court determined that Ella Clarke had no interest in the four bonds until she actually received them, and dismissed her case. Naturally, she was not satisfied by this answer, and she immediately asked the United States Supreme Court to hear her side of the story.[330]

---

[328] Clarke *vs.* Shoshoni Lumber Co, *et. al*, decided April 15, 1924, Wyoming Supreme Court, 31 *Wyoming Reports* 205. We do not know how Ella Clarke's connection with the Sebree estate came about. The Chicago Title & Trust Company was one of the executors of the Sebree estate, and of course that company was also the trustee for the Big Horn Power Company bonds, but that need not suggest a connection with Ella Clarke. In the Matter of the Estate of James K. Sebree, deceased, Case No. 15536 in the Probate Court of Cook County, IL.

[329] The Sebree transactions are detailed in the affidavit of N. C. Brorson dated September 10, 1916, in Case No. 1372, *op. cit.*

[330] Sebree's estate amounted to over $340,000, and he made provision for his first wife and his two children, as well as his "housekeeper," who then renounced the will and claimed a share of the estate as his common law widow. The Circuit Court of Cook County denied her claim on March

The Supreme Court was headed by former President William Howard Taft, and with him on the bench was Justice Willis Van Devanter, who heard two Boysen cases when he was a judge in the Eighth Circuit Court of Appeals in St. Louis, and early in 1928, Ella Clarke's appeal finally got to the court—or at least to the door of that court. There are only a few instances in which a party has the *right* to appeal to the Supreme Court, and in all other cases, the Supreme Court has to consent to issue a writ of *certiorari*. Generally, an appeal to the U. S. Supreme Court would have been allowed only if it involved a Federal question, and the court did not spend much time on Ella Clarke's case, for it could not find a federal question in it, and dismissed the appeal for lack of jurisdiction.[331]

Allan Boysen had hoped that he avoided his creditors by buying the dam and power plant at auction in the Shoshoni Lumber Company foreclosure, but in March, 1928, Judge Neblett in the Cheyenne federal court destroyed that strategy. The judge voided the sale to Allan Boysen and gave judgment to the trustees for the bondholders in the enormous sum of $944,502.44, consisting of unpaid principal and interest.

This decision cleared the way for the bondholders to have the Big Horn Power Co.'s 11/16 interest in the 88-acre tract, plus the dam and power plant sold at auction. In authorizing the sale of the company's property, the judge did give the Boysen interests two liens on the proceeds from the sale. Allan Boysen was given a lien for the $3,893.72 he borrowed from Rosa Thompson in 1914, to redeem the property for unpaid taxes. The second lien was for the $7,383.65 paid by the Wyoming Power company for the dam and power plant in the lumber company sale. These small concessions to the Boysens were a very small consolation for a major disaster.[332]

25, 1919. Case No. 15536, *op. cit.* Ella Clarke's affidavit dated August 29, 1918, said that she was "a holder and owner" of the bonds. Case No. 1372, *op. cit.*

[331] Ella R. Clarke *vs.* Shoshoni Lumber Co, Case No. 96, decided on February 21, 1928 in the Supreme Court of the United States.

[332] Case No. 1320, *op. cit.*

15

THE CONDEMNATION CASES
AND A FEW OF THE OTHERS

Boysen was involved in several other lawsuits that were only peripheral to his troubles with the Clarkes, the State of Wyoming and the Burlington railroad. These cases were those that arose from the need to compensate people whose property was flooded by the dam, and also those cases involving the many unpaid bills.

Before he closed the underflow gates to start generating electricity, Boysen decided to condemn two parcels, one that was already partly flooded, and another he expected to be flooded later, particularly when the panels were erected atop the dam. The power company had the authority to condemn—and pay for—the flooded areas, but of course that cost money, which was in very short supply. In the spring of 1909 the company filed two condemnation actions in the Fremont County district court.

Boysen did not hire high-priced lawyers in Omaha or Cheyenne for these actions, and instead he engaged a 32-year-old Lander attorney named John Dillon. Dillon had earlier been a sheepherder at Hat Creek, but now he was following in the steps of his father, who was a judge in St. Louis. John Dillon had already been elected county attorney for Fremont County, and he was to get a fair amount of legal experience with the Boysen cases. It is hoped that he was paid for his work.

The first of the 1909 condemnations involved a 160-acre homestead owned by Frank E. Martin, about four and a half miles upstream from the dam. In the spring of 1900, Frank came to Fremont County, where he later filed on his homestead, fenced the 160-acre farm, erected buildings and corrals and pumped water from the river to irrigate until he could construct a ditch for that purpose. Then, in May, 1909, three months before he received his patent for the land, the power company condemned the entire farm. The company agreed that Martin could remove his log buildings and other improvements before the farm was flooded, but in fact, some of the farm was already under water.

Three appraisers set a value of $20 per acre for the land, for a total of $3,300, assuming that Martin would remove his improvements, but the power company objected that the appraised value was high, because some of Martin's land was low-lying and submerged before the lake reached it. The company asked for a jury trial, and when the judge accepted the appraisal anyway, Boysen did not pay the award. There the matter lay for awhile, the court having decreed that the power company could take Martin's land, but leaving Martin without the payment he was entitled to, so that Martin had no land and no money.[333]

In the spring of 1912, Frank Martin finally lost patience over the delay in getting paid, and sued to try to get his money. He was then living in Thermopolis, and he painted a grim picture of his situation. He said that the power company had agreed to let him remove his improvements, but before he could do so, the lake flooded all but five acres of his farm, destroying his improvements. He said he "often" demanded that the company pay him, to no avail. Martin's lawyers devised a draconian remedy for their client, asking that Boysen be forced to shut down the power plant and open the underflow gates until the condemnation award was paid.

Edgar Fourt argued for the power company that Martin should not recover, because the 1909 condemnation was based on the assumption that Boysen would build a 50-foot dam, and when the dam subsequently was limited to 35 feet, there was no need to condemn Martin's land. While this explanation at first sounds strange, Martin testified that he

---

[333] The judgment against Big Horn Power Co. was for $3,343.40 plus costs of $10.55. Big Horn Power Co. *vs.* Martin, Case No. 1145, Fremont County District Court, filed May 31, 1909 and decided December 6, 1909, and Case No. 1548, *op. cit.* Martin received his patent for his homestead on August 12, 1909.

was only being flooded for "four to six to seven weeks each season," implying that flooding occurred only during times of high water in the river. Still, it was not fair for Boysen to argue that Martin could farm fields that were flooded four to seven weeks during the growing season.[334]

Judge Charles Carpenter heard the testimony from both sides and at the end of June he issued the injunction Stone and Winslow requested, but he stayed the injunction so that Edgar Fourt could appeal the decision to the Wyoming Supreme Court. In the meantime, the power plant could continue to operate—actually, for quite awhile, because the answer from the Supreme Court would not come any time soon. First, all of the important papers in the case had to be copied and the transcript forwarded to the appellate court. Then each side needed time to prepare its arguments to the Supreme Court. After all of this paper work was in place, the court would set the date for a hearing, and after the hearing was completed, the judges would ponder all of the information they had received. Finally, sometime later, the court would issue its opinion. Since Boysen wasn't winning many cases, buying time was a way to avoid losing.

The Boysens did enjoy a partial win in the Martin case in the fall of 1916, when the Wyoming Supreme Court decided their appeal of Frank Martin's judgment for the condemnation award. The court agreed that Frank Martin was entitled to be paid for his land, but was not entitled to force Boysen to shut down the plant. Martin thus again went away with the empty affirmation that he had lost his land, but was still due some money.[335]

Frank Martin partially avenged himself on the Boysens when Allan Boysen named him as a defendant in another condemnation case, apparently because his award had not been paid. Martin was in no mood

---

[334] Big Horn Power Co. filed its answer on April 30, 1912. Case No. 1548, *op. cit.*

[335] The Wyoming Supreme Court reversed the Fremont County decision in the Martin case on October 16, 1916. Big Horn Power Co. *vs.* Frank E. Martin, Case No. 757, Wyoming Supreme Court, 24 *Wyoming Reports* 400.

to be cooperative, and in his response he asked why he was named, and he also questioned (among other things) how the Wyoming Power Co. could own a dam located on federal land on the river. Martin still did not get any money, but perhaps the satisfaction that his questions may have interfered with Allan's efforts may have been some compensation to him.

The second of the power company's 1909 condemnation cases was no more successful for Boysen than the first one, but it did provoke a response that resulted in payment. About three miles upstream from the dam, the lake was expected to flood a portion of the land allotted to a Northern Arapaho, Alto L. Hanway, the son of Rose Hanway (whose Indian name was Walks in the Night), the daughter of Plenty Bear, an important Arapaho headman (who had a long history of friendship with the government).[336]

Alto Hanway received his allotment on the river upstream from Boysen's dam in 1907, when he was only 17. About 120 acres of the allotment was along the river (part was on higher ground), and it was this parcel that the power company sought to condemn. Boysen's lawyer served papers on Hanway's father as his guardian, and on Henry E. Wadsworth, the Indian agent on the reservation (because actual title to Hanway's allotment was held in trust for him by the United States government).[337]

---

[336] When the tribes ceded the hot springs at Thermopolis to the U. S. government, Plenty Bear was a member of the Arapaho delegation at the negotiations held in April, 1896. Virginia Cole Trenholm, *The Arapahoes, Our People* (Norman, Okla., 1970), 256, 261, and Dorothy G. Milek, *The Gift of Bah Guewana: A History of Wyoming's Hot Springs State Park* (Thermopolis, Wyo., 1975), 32-33. Paul/Alto Hanway was born October 1890. Also, Tacetta B. Walker, *Stories of Early Days in Wyoming: Big Horn Basin* (Casper, Wyo., 1936), 196. Alto Hanway's father was Paul Hanway, a Pennsylvanian who had worked at Fort Robinson before coming to Fort Washakie.

[337] Big Horn Power Co. *vs.* Alto L. Hanway, Case No. 1146, filed May 31, 1909, in Fremont County District Court. Alto L. Hanway received his allotment on June 6, 1907. Under the Dawes Act, title to allotments was

179

The three men who appraised the Martin land also appraised the riparian portion of Hanway's allotment at the beginning of June, and they valued Hanway's land at $1.25 per acre, as compared with the $20 per acre value they placed on the Martin land. Wadsworth promptly appealed the amount of the award in the Lander court, where he asked for a trial by jury. The Lander court did not act on this request, and the matter dragged on for four years, when lawyers for the U.S. government removed the case to Federal court in Cheyenne.[338]

In the autumn of 1913, the U. S. government finally got around to dealing with the matter of the flooding of Alto Hanway's allotment. The government ignored the power company's lawsuit and brought its own suit against the Big Horn Power Co. in the U. S. District Court in Cheyenne, asking for damages of $15 per acre for the 42 acres that were flooded, for a total of $600. The court gave judgment for $600 in its decision in the case in 1915, and also declared that if the judgment was not paid within 60 days, the power company was to so alter the "character and structure" of the dam so as to remove the water from Hanway's allotment. Simply stated, the company had to pay up, or bring the lake down.[339]

The Big Horn Power Co. didn't have $600, and this creditor was not prepared to wait for its money. Faced with this terrible threat, Allan Boysen explained his plight to William Tracy, who was then the mayor of Shoshoni, and Tracy readily understood the gravity of the situation, for if Boysen lowered the lake to satisfy the Hanway judgment, the town of Shoshoni would lose its power supply. Since time was of the essence, Tracy paid the judgment from his personal funds (the Town of Shoshoni eventually reimbursed him for this outlay). Allan Boysen

---

to be held in trust for 25 years, to guard against speculative exploitation of the allottees.

338 Case No. 1416, *op. cit*, and United States *vs.* Big Horn Power Co., Case No. 765, filed October 21, 1913 and decided July 1, 1915, U. S. District Court, Cheyenne.

339 Case No. 765, *op. cit.* Normally, the Federal district court would not hear a case involving less than $3,000, but in this case the government itself was the plaintiff and not subject to that limitation.

assigned an insurance policy on his life to the town, to secure payment of this debt, which grew over the years to $1,260, including interest and other costs. Unfortunately for the town, Boysen did not pay the debt, nor did he die, so that the municipality was financially embarrassed, leaving this embarrassment to be addressed in yet another case, but only after thirteen years.[340]

Thirteen years later, after he shut down the power plant, Allan Boysen delivered his inventory of more than 4,000 pounds of copper wire to the town of Shoshoni in the summer of 1928, apparently expecting the town to sell it and give him the money. The town did sell the wire to Mountain States Power Company for $360, but kept the proceeds, and in 1929 Boysen hired a lawyer to retrieve this sum, with interest. In its defense, the town of Shoshoni responded that Boysen still owed the town $600 plus interest (a total of $1,260) for its payment back in 1915 to keep the U. S. government from shutting down the power plant following the flooding of Hanway's allotment. The town acknowledged that Boysen had taken out a life insurance policy in favor of the town, to secure the $1,260 debt, but, of course, he was still very much alive, and there was no immediate prospect of payment from that source. Following these pleadings, the matter rested without action for another four years, when Allan Boysen's suit was dismissed.[341]

The 1911 floods that damaged the new railroad tracks raised the level of the lake considerably, as we have noted, flooding additional farms located upstream from the dam. Two of the landowners in that area sued the power company for the resulting damage, one in the fall of 1911 and the other the following spring. The first case was filed in the fall of 1911 by Myron E. Walker, whose farm of about 160 acres was some seven miles south of the dam. He asked for damages of $4,500. The second case, filed the following spring, was that of Samuel W.

---

[340] The account of the involvement of the town of Shoshoni in the Boysen finances is given in Allan Boysen *vs.* Town of Shoshoni, Wyoming, Case No. 4331, filed March 29, 1929 and decided January 14, 1933, Fremont County District Court.

[341] Case No. 4331, *op. cit.*

Hardman, whose homestead was about six miles south of the dam, and a mile or so north of Walker's land. Hardman asked for $5,000.[342]

Boysen hired Benjamin Sheldon to represent the power company in the Walker case. Most attorneys were now using typewriters for their pleadings, but Sheldon, who was then 65, had been a storekeeper and a bookkeeper before settling into the practice of law, and he wrote his pleadings in an elegant longhand. Although the Hardman case involved the same issues, Boysen hired Edgar H. Fourt to represent the company in that case. Fourt had already been involved in two other Boysen cases, albeit on the other side. After the initial filings, both cases were laid over to be heard the following June, when the Hardman and Walker cases came up for trial on the same day, using the same jury.

In the Hardman case, where the power company was defended by Edgar Fourt, the jury awarded Hardman $3,055, plus costs. In the Walker case, Sheldon tried to show that the flooding complained of resulted from the usual high water in the river, and was not caused by the dam. He asked the judge to give the following remarkable instruction to the jury:

The Court instructs the jury that it is a principle in nature and the law of hydrostatics that water when impounded or dammed up, ceases to flow, and that the current ceases to exist and that in such case there could be no damage from the current.

The judge refused to give this instruction, and Sheldon then asked him to have the jury determine whether the flooding was caused by the "regular high water periods" in the river. The jury replied that this was not the cause of the flooding, and returned a verdict of $3,242 for Walker.[343]

Boysen hired Fourt to file motions for a new trial in both cases, to no avail, and there the matter rested for awhile. Of course, the company had no money to pay many things, including these two judgments, and

---

[342] Myron e. Walker *vs.* Big Horn Power Co., Case No. 1481, filed October 19, 1911 and decided June 10, 1912,; and Samuel W. Hardman *vs.* Big Horn Power Co., Case No. 1544, filed on March 30, 1912 and decided June 10, 1912, both in Fremont County District Court.

[343] Cases No. 1481 and 1544, *op. cit.*

consequently, Hardman and Walker were not paid, nor did they pay their lawyer, Ralph Kimball. In March, 1914, Kimball filed attorney's liens against both judgments, hoping to get paid if any money were found.

The sheriff tried to collect the Hardman and Walker judgments in 1917, and in 1922 he tried again, without success. Both men were now willing to give up the fight, until 1922, when Ella Clarke appeared on the scene and took assignment of both judgments. We do not know how much she paid for the two judgments, but it was at least enough to pay the legal fees of both men, for Ralph Kimball later said that he had been paid. Ella Clark now pressed to sell the farms securing these judgments, as well as *all* of the Big Horn Power Co.'s property. In preparation for the sale, the two farms and the properties of the Big Horn Power Co., were appraised in May, and the value for the three properties was set at $579,500. Ella Clarke immediately challenged the appraisal, saying (among other things) that the Big Horn Power Co. assets were subject to the mortgage in favor of the bondholders. The judge then ordered a new appraisal, which lacked a good deal in arithmetic accuracy, but is important for its effect on the cases.[344]

In the new appraisal, the two farms were valued at $1,200 each, and the gross value of the Big Horn Power Co. assets, was set at $715,150, without any detail as to how that figure was arrived at. The amount owing to the bondholders consisted of the $350,000 initial face, plus the unpaid interest coupons of $140,000, plus interest on the unpaid interest and principal after the maturity of the bonds of $101,150 and $126,000 respectively, for a total of $717,150. Of course, this value is greater than the $715,150 appraisal given for the power company assets, which should have yielded a negative value for this item. However, the summary of appraisal said that subtracting $717,150 from the gross appraised value left a net value of $800 for Big Horn Power Co.'s assets. This number, when added to the value of the farms, gave a total net appraisal of $3,200. With the required appraisal in hand, the sheriff

---

[344] Hardman was living in West Virginia when he assigned his judgment to Ella R. Clarke on February 23, 1922; Walker's assignment to her was dated June 5, 1922. Case No. 1481, *op. cit.*

then conducted the sale, in which he auctioned off the two farms and the 11/16 interest of Big Horn Power Co. in the 88-acre tract. The sheriff said the power company tract was subject to a mortgage of $717,350 (not the $717,150 used in the appraisal) in favor of the bondholders.[345]

This is one of the few occasions when we know that Allan Boysen and Ella Clarke were both present in the same place at the same time. Ella Clarke appeared and bid a total of $4,075 for the three properties. Allan Boysen, bidding on behalf of the Wyoming Power Co., offered $5,650, for the three properties, winning the auction. The good news was that when the court confirmed the sale, the company would be entitled to a deed for the dam and power plant, but the bad news was that the sale was subject to a mortgage of $717,350. Ella Clarke was in a position to foreclose that mortgage, which explains why she let Allan Boysen win the auction. In effect, Allan Boysen got nothing of value for his $5,650, and it was now clear on the record that he really did owe the bondholders.[346]

Allan Boysen got the money to outbid Ella Clark from his aunt, Mary J. Stoughton. Mary Stoughton put up the money for Allan to buy the dam back in 1916, and now she supplied the money to buy it again, subject to a huge mortgage. And she also loaned Allen the money to make the annual payments to buy out the Akron group. Even though Allan Boysen's bid was more than the $3,200 appraised value of the three properties, it did not come close to covering the Hardman and Walker judgments, with their attendant interest and costs. So Ella Clarke still was owed money from these judgments, and at the beginning of 1923, the court awarded her an additional judgment against the Big Horn Power Co. for $8,096, plus costs.[347]

---

[345] The first appraisal was dated May 22, 1922, and the second was dated June 28, 1922. Case No. 1544, *op. cit.*

[346] The sheriff's sale was held on August 26, 1922. Case No. 1544, *op. cit.*

[347] The Hardman judgment was $3,055 and the Walker judgment was $3,242, both of which were entitled to interest from the date of the judgment. Case No. 1481 and Case No. 1544, *op. cit.*

On May 4, 1923, the Lander judge confirmed the auction of the previous year, and directed the sheriff to issue a deed to the Wyoming Power Co. for the Martin, Walker and Big Horn Power Co. tracts. This action brought an immediate reaction from Ella and John Clarke, who were in Lander by May 22. Ella Clarke went to Porter Coolidge's office and assigned the Hardman judgment to Henry T. Clarke, Jr, (John Clarke's brother, and another of the Clarke lawyers).[348]

Henry Clarke then used this unsatisfied judgment to claim the property Allan Boysen had won in the auction by tendering $6,075 (which was Boysen's bid of $5,650, plus 10% interest), to the Fremont County sheriff to redeem the property. The sheriff refused, saying that the judge had already confirmed the sale, and had ordered him to issue the deed to the Wyoming Power Co. While the sheriff did not let Henry Clarke redeem the property, he didn't issue the deed to Wyoming Power Co., either. Henry T. Clark, Jr. then brought his own lawsuit in the Cheyenne federal court against the Wyoming Power Co. at the beginning of 1924, demanding that the Fremont County sheriff be prevented from issuing a deed to the Wyoming Power Co.[349]

This case soon became a comedy of errors, when the U. S. Marshal refused to serve the subpoena because Henry Clarke had not paid the necessary fees. After John Clarke paid the fee, the marshal finally served Allan Boysen at Shoshoni, and Asmus Boysen at the dam. The marshal also served Sheriff Lawrence Bruce Gaylord in Lander, but referred to him as "Bob Gaylord," rather than L. B. Gaylord, as the writ required, so more papers were filed to make clear that "Bob" was indeed "L. B." While all this was going on, none of the defendants bothered to

---

[348] Ella Clarke's assignment was dated and notarized by Porter Coolidge on May 22, 1923. The typist omitted the "Jr." after Henry T. Clarke's name, and the correction was made in the unmistakable handwriting of John T. Clarke. Case No. 1544, *op. cit.* The details of Henry T. Clarke's actions are given in Henry T. Clarke *vs.* Wyoming Power Co., Case No. 1430, U. S. District Court, Cheyenne.

[349] The three lawyers in addition to Henry T. Clarke, Jr. were Clyde M. Watts, Albert D. Walton and Henry B. Pogson, the last of whom was also one of the trustees for the bondholders. Case No. 1430, *op. cit.*

respond, and this was another instance were delay saved the Boysens money and trouble.[350]

Even though the seasonal floods of 1913 were not bad, there was still flooding from the lake, and in the fall of 1913, another farmer upstream from the dam sued the Big Horn Power Co. for flood damage. Carl Wagner's homestead was located across the river from Myron Walker's place, and he asked for $6,690 for the loss of two houses, a barn, and other improvements, plus the permanent loss of the value of the land for farming or grazing. Once again, the power company did not appear to oppose the lawsuit, and the following June Judge Winter awarded Wagner $3,500, plus costs. Of course, Wagner didn't receive any money as the result of this judgment.

There were other suits to collect unpaid bills from Boysen. The London Guarantee & Accident Company sued in 1910 for unpaid premiums on the workmen's compensation insurance policy on the project, and this creditor was one of the more persistent. The Big Horn Power Co. did not appear to contest the action, and the judge issued a default judgment against it, but the London company was not able to collect. In the spring of 1916 the London company tried again to collect, without success, and by the time of the London company's last attempt, in 1922, the judgment had grown with interest to over $3,800. This time, the sheriff found Asmus Boysen somewhere in Fremont County and served the notice on him, but no one paid the judgment.[351]

In 1914, the S. Morgan Smith Co., another of Boysen's unpaid creditors, tried to avoid the expense of suing in the district court in Lander by getting a justice of the peace in Fremont County to give them a judgment for $97.90 plus $11.00 costs against the Big Horn Power Co., thus adding a justice court to our list of cases. Years passed with no payment, and the Morgan Smith company then took the

---

[350] After the case was dismissed in 1935, the clerk returned the balance of the fees to John T. Clarke. Case No. 1430, *op. cit.* Big Horn Power Co. was a defunct corporation, its charter having been revoked the previous year.

[351] Case No. 1317, *op. cit.,*.

matter into the Fremont County District Court in the spring of 1922, but there was still no money to be found, and the case was finally dismissed in May, 1930.[352]

The Akron group had not been paid for all the money they loaned to the power company during the period when they were operating the power plant, and in 1914, Fred Lane, a member of that Akron group, sued the Fremont Power Co. to collect on a total of 69 delinquent notes (including his own), totaling $13,834. When the case came to trial in the fall of 1915, the company did not appear, and the judge issued a default judgment for $13,823 plus $677 interest, but the sheriff found no property to satisfy the judgment.[353]

Finally, there was a case we could call a "friendly" lawsuit, because it was just a family affair. When William Kyne paid off the note for the Riverton transmission line and the Riverton substation, he also took assignment of the bank's mortgage on the property. He sold his lien to the Mountain States company for $15,000, and applied the proceeds to the balance of the note. The remaining deficiency on his note was nearly $30,000, and Kyne sued the Wyoming Power Co. to recover this deficiency. Kyne surely knew that Wyoming Power did not have any significant assets, and this suit undoubtedly was intended to cover the unlikely event that something good would later turn up. Allan Boysen was served in this case in Shoshoni, and Wyoming Power did not respond. In the spring of 1929, Judge Edgar Fourt gave Kyne a default judgment for his deficiency, and four days later, Sheriff Gaylord advised the court that he could find no property to satisfy the judgment.[354]

---

[352] S. Morgan Smith Company *vs.* Big Power Company, Case No. 3185, filed May 13, 1922 and decided May 12, 1930 Fremont County District Court. In Wyoming, the justice courts could hear cases not involving title to real estate or money actions exceeding $200. Sections 5185 and 5186, *Wyoming Compiled Statutes Annotated, 1910*, (Laramie, Wyo., 1910).

[353] Fred A. Lane *vs.* Fremont Power Company, Case No. 1904 in the Fremont County District Court, filed October 19, 1914 and decided November 20, 1914. The sheriff's return of execution was dated March 9, 1915.

[354] William Kyne took assignment of the note on October 28, 1925 and received the proceeds of the mortgage foreclosure and sale on July 7,

None of these cases affected the outcome of the major issues pursued by the chief contenders in this story, and except for the case of Alto Hanway's allotment, they also yielded nothing for the plaintiffs.

1928. He filed his action in the Fremont District Court on July 9, 1928, Allan Boysen was served personally in Shoshoni on July 10, 1928, Judge Fourt's judgment was dated May 13, 1929 and Sheriff L. B. Gaylord's return of the attempted execution was dated May 18. Case No. 4218, *op. cit.*

16

THE STATE AND THE SUPERSTRUCTURE

At the end of 1913, the case that was the most serious threat to the Boysen operation was back in the Lander court. This was the 1909 case filed by Attorney General of Wyoming against Boysen and the Big Horn Power Co., claiming that the dam did not conform to the specifications in the permit. In November, 1913, Attorney General Preston filed his answer to the 1909 response from the Boysen side. Asmus Boysen was a defendant in the original case, but in 1913 he did not even hire a lawyer to represent him personally. The Big Horn Power Co. hired Ben Sheldon to represent it, and in deference to new technology, he used a typewriter to submit his pleadings.

Sheldon's answer made a frontal attack on the State's case. He said the State had no interest in the matter that would permit the case to be brought, and that in effect the railroad was using the State as its legal department. He also claimed the dam was in fact built in accordance with the requirements of the permit and that there was no evidence that the superstructure had damaged the public.

The judge gave short shrift to Sheldon's work product, and ruled that all the State's allegations were true, and that the superstructure was an unlawful obstruction of the river. He also ordered that until the superstructure was removed, the bridge over the dam was not to be used, and for good measure, Boysen was to open the underflow gates, as well. This, of course, meant that the plant would have to halt power generation, and faced with this awful result, Sheldon moved for a new trial on December 11. Mercifully, that motion could not be

189

heard until the court met the following February, giving Boysen a little more time.[355]

In February, 1914, the judge denied Ben Sheldon's request for a new trial, but did stay the injunction to permit Sheldon to appeal the case to the Wyoming Supreme Court. This time there was a price tag on Sheldon's request, for in order to appeal the judgment, the Big Horn Power Co. had to post a $500 bond, and the company did not have $500.

On paper, the Big Horn Power Co. should have been able to raise that much money, as it was supposed to be receiving a $10,500 annual rental from the Akron group's companies operating the plant, but as those companies were also out of money, the rental was clearly not being paid. Sheldon needed time to raise the money for the bond, and he went back to the judge, who gave him another month.

To raise the $500, Boysen had to borrow from his friend (and Shoshoni saloonkeeper) Barney Aronson, and his son-in-law, William Kyne. To shore up the legal talent for the appeal, Boysen hired another lawyer to help Ben Sheldon. The man he selected was Porter B. Coolidge (who sometimes wrote poetry when he was not practicing law), and together the two lawyers filed the power company's petition for review of the case by the Wyoming Supreme Court.[356]

At the hearing in Cheyenne before the Wyoming Supreme Court, Boysen's two lawyers used all the arguments they could think of to keep the superstructure in place, even contending that the dam really was built according to the specifications in the permit. However, the deputy state engineer who inspected the dam on July 10, 1909 found violations of the permit, one of which was clearly a technicality. We have noted that the State Engineer did not reduce the length of the spillway when the height of the dam was reduced from 50 feet to 35,

---

[355] Judgment was handed down December, 2, 1913. Case No. 1154, *op. cit.*

[356] Aronson was secretary of the Big Horn Power Co. when the sheriff served him with the summons in Carl Wagner *vs.* Big Horn Power Co. Case No. 1791, Fremont County District Court. The petition to the Wyoming Supreme Court was dated July 27, 1914. Case No. 1154, *op. cit.*

but since the spillway at the lower point in the canyon was a lot shorter than the 143 feet called for in the permit, this was cited as a violation. The other violation noted by the court was the unauthorized extension of the piers on top of the dam (the so-called superstructure), which further obstructed the spillway.

The court based its decision on both violations, and Boysen's arguments were unavailing. On June 1, 1915, the Wyoming Supreme Court declared that the superstructure would have to go, and as a further small financial insult to the insolvent company, the court assessed $25.90 in court costs for the appeal. When he later mentioned this decision in his testimony, Asmus Boysen said, "That ended the hopes of the Big Horn Power Co. and Asmus Boysen . . . ."[357]

However, the decision only ended Boysen's hopes, for it did not bring down the superstructure, did not halt power production and did not cause the Boysens to concede defeat. Instead, like so many other decisions involving the Boysen interests, this decision by the highest court in the State of Wyoming merely gathered dust ignored by the Boysens for another six years.

Time finally ran out for the Boysens in the fall of 1921, when the Wyoming Attorney General asked the Fremont County court to hold the Boysen interests in contempt for failure to remove the superstructure. The judge took the matter under advisement, but did note that he would order some sort of relief for the railroad.[358]

The Wyoming Power Co. was now in possession of the dam and power plant, and it answered the complaint—with a list of excuses. The general excuses were that the postwar depression made it impossible

---

[357] Big Horn Power Co. *vs.* State of Wyoming, Case No. 806, filed November 2, 1914 and decided June 1, 1915, 23 *Wyoming Reports* 271. Boysen's quote is from his testimony in Case No. 1320, *op. cit.*

[358] Testimony regarding traffic levels on the railroad was given by A. W. Parker, chief dispatcher of the railroad. Case No. 1513, *op. cit.* The State of Wyoming filed a motion in the 1909 case (Case No. 1154) on August 24, 1921. Attorney General W. L. Walls hired the Cheyenne firm of Roderick N. Matson and T. Blake Kennedy to assist him in prosecuting the case.

for the power company to raise capital, the Lander court calendar was congested (and was suspended during the influenza epidemic at the end of World War I), and three different judges heard the Boysen cases in as many years. For good measure, the company added the observation that in "normal" seasons, the river didn't flood, anyway. (From the data we have provided, it will be seen that there were few "normal" seasons at the Boysen dam.) Then three more years passed.[359]

At the end of 1924, the Burlington railroad lodged a comprehensive complaint against the Clarkes, the Big Horn Power Co. and other judgment creditors of the Boysen dam and power plant, in the Federal district court in Cheyenne. For the first time in the Boysen dam litigation, no Boysens were named, and the Big Horn Power Co. was represented by Thomas Hunter, the court-appointed receiver. This suit had the dual objective of eliminating the flooding problem and clearing the railroad's title to its right of way. Pending resolution of the suit, the railroad asked for a temporary injunction to keep the operators of the dam from any action maintaining the dam in violation of the original permit. This injunction would prevent the operators from installing obstructions (*i.e.,* wooden panels) in front of the piers on the dam to increase the flow through the power plant.[360]

Judge T. Blake Kennedy, who was now in Judge Riner's place as the Federal district judge in Cheyenne, could not hear most of the Boysen cases because of a conflict of interest and he immediately recused himself from the new railroad case and assigned it to Judge J. Foster Symes of the Colorado district. However, passing Boysen cases to

---

[359] Allan Boysen's answer dated October 29, 1921, was filed in the case of The State of Wyoming *vs.* Asmus Boysen and Big Horn Power Co., Case No. 1154.

[360] Case No. 1513, *op. cit.* Midwest Power and Light Co. was a defendant because of a conveyance from John T. Clarke on February 28, 1916, and Clarke Land and Loan Co, Frederick A. Williams, G. C. Whittall, Ella R. Clarke, Harry F. Clarke and Henry T. Clarke, Jr. were defendants because John T. Clarke issued mortgages on his interest to them, and Kinnear Manufacturing Co. and Carl Wagner were defendants because they had unsatisfied judgments against Big Horn Power Co.

judges sitting in other federal districts created yet another opportunity for the Clarkes to complain.[361]

Judge Symes issued a warning order, stating that he was of the opinion that the railroad's request should be granted, and gave the defendants until January 31, 1925 to respond. He specifically authorized personal service on John and Ella Clarke, and permitted service by publication on the other defendants. This ruling immediately formed the basis for still another procedural clash with the Clarkes, who were defending the case as potential owners of the dam and power plant.[362]

The Burlington railroad lawyers learned that the Clarkes were in Cheyenne (testifying in another case in federal court), and issued subpoenas to both of them in Wyoming. The Clarkes immediately protested that they were exempt from service while testifying in federal court, and Judge Symes then quashed the subpoenas, forcing the U. S. Marshal to serve the Clarkes at the Touraine Hotel in New York. Thereupon, Ella Clarke contended that Judge Symes' warning order was void because she was a resident of New York, but this time the judge did not agree with her.[363]

Although the Clarkes had been legally served, they continued filing objections until the end of July, 1925, when the case came to trial, and this time it was a full dress affair. For some reason, at this point the Clarkes hired Albert D. Walton of Cheyenne to represent them at trial (at one point Walton asked for leeway from Judge Neblett, saying,

---

[361] When he was in private practice in Cheyenne, Kennedy assisted the Attorney General in the appeal of Boysen's permit case to the Supreme Court. Because of that conflict of interest, Kennedy recused himself from most Boysen cases that came before the Cheyenne federal court.

[362] The judge also authorized personal service of Frederick A. Williams, who held a mortgage on John T. Clarke's interest, but on January 29, 1925 he disclaimed any interest in the lands involved in the suit. Case No. 1513 and Case No. 980, *op. cit.*

[363] Case No. 1513, *op. cit.* The Clarkes lived in hotels in New York City, one of which was the Hotel Touraine, at 9 East 39th Street, which was demolished in 1927, and another was the Barclay. *New York Times,* September 4, 1927.

"Your Honor knows I never heard of this case until last night"). The railroad brought ten employees to testify regarding the right of way title, and to the damage caused by flooding at the Boysen dam (there was 74 pages of that testimony). Then the court heard from Asmus Boysen and John Clarke.[364]

John Clarke described his association with the Boysen project, starting with the lease of 1899, and his later "help" to get the Boysen preference enacted by the Congress. Walton asked if he had any deeds to the Boysen land, and Clarke replied, ". . . as I explained to you, I didn't think that the court had any jurisdiction." As to the railroad's problems with the dam, Clarke referred to an offer he had made to "obviate any trouble there," but the railroad attorneys objected to that line of inquiry, and we do not know what that offer might have entailed.

On cross examination, Clarke admitted that his closest approach to the dam was when he went through the canyon on the railroad two or three years earlier, although he said he was on the 88-acre tract two years earlier. Then the railroad lawyers tried to learn if Clarke had any property they might attach later on. Clarke claimed that he owned 7/8 of the Boysen tract, thus laying claim to all except two shares (presumably those of Boysen and Wertz). Then he acknowledged owning a lot in Plainfield, NJ and "hundreds of lots" in Belleview, Nebr.

The railroad lawyer then asked Clarke whether he had done anything to correct the problems at the dam, and Clarke snapped back, "There is no reason why I should donate anything to the Chicago, Burlington and Quincy Railroad." When he asserted that the railroad had never brought a suit to abate the nuisance, the railroad lawyer said, "There is one here now," and Clarke retorted, "This one will not get far." That conclusion was very wrong, but the quotation gives us an insight into the Clarkes' attitude toward their opponents in many of the lawsuits swirling about them. After this testimony, there was no further action in this case until 1928, but there were other cases the federal judges had to deal with.[365]

---

[364] Case No. 1513, *op. cit.*
[365] Case No. 1513, *op. cit.*

Judge Kennedy assigned the two cases brought by John Clarke and the one brought by Henry T. Clarke, Jr. against the Boysen companies to Judge Symes. John Clarke was unhappy with this action, because he wanted to go to trial, and Judge Symes had a busy docket, so Judge Kennedy transferred those cases to Judge Colin Neblett, of the New Mexico district.[366]

Judge Neblett looked at the tangled arguments in the cases, and decided to summon some help. At the end of July, 1925, he appointed William E. Mullen, a Cheyenne attorney and former Attorney General, as Special Master to sort through four cases, and report to the court on questions of fact and law. The cases were the original case brought against Boysen by the syndicate partners, two cases brought by John Clarke, and the case brought by the trustees for the power company bondholders. The judge gave Mullen a deadline of October 1, which was later extended.[367]

By the time he issued his report at the end of September, 1926, the Special Master had presided over more than 41 days of testimony, which took up 960 pages in the record. In his report on John Clarke's 1918 suit for an interest in the so-called "lapsed" shares in the Boysen tract, the Special Master concluded that the Circuit Court of Appeals had already determined that the interests represented by these shares

---

[366] On March 3, 1925, Judge Kennedy assigned Clarke's case asking for a share in the permit (No. 1291) to Judge Symes, and according to that order, Symes was to hear the case in Cheyenne, unless the parties stipulated otherwise. On April 25, 1925, Kennedy also assigned Clarke's 1918 case asking for a share in the "nonaccepting" participations (No. 980) and Henry T. Clarke's case foreclosing on Ella Clarke's judgments (Case No. 1430) to Judge Symes. On May 9, John T. Clarke complained about Judge Symes' schedule, and asked that he be deposed for Case No. 1291, because he lived in New York and would unlikely be able to attend hearings in person. Apparently in response to this request, on May 11, Kennedy reassigned Case Nos. 980 and 1291, as well as Case No. 1430, to Judge Neblett.

[367] Mullen was Attorney General of Wyoming in the years 1905-11. The four cases assigned to the Special Master were Case Nos. 288, 980, 1291 and 1320.

could not be revived. He therefore recommended that the court dismiss Clarke's claim on that issue. The Special Master did not offer any conclusions of fact or law regarding ownership of the railroad right of way, leaving that issue to be determined by the court. John Clarke filed exceptions to the Special Master's report, as did the railroad, and so that controversy continued to drag on.[368]

Judge Neblett issued his decision in the cases he had assigned to the Special Master in the spring of 1928. The judge ruled that the railroad had only an 11/16 interest in its right of way through the Boysen tract. As to the matter of the superstructure on the dam, the judge decided it was a nuisance, and ordered that it be removed within six months. John Clarke promptly asked for a rehearing of the case, which was denied by the judge at the beginning of May, and then Clarke appealed. The railroad also appealed the issue of the title to its right of way.[369]

We have noted that Judge Neblett gave the bondholders of the Big Horn Power Co. the right to have the company's property sold to satisfy their large judgment. In June, 1928, Special Master Mullen held the sale of the Big Horn Power Co.'s 11/16 interest in the 88-acre tract, setting a minimum of $35,000 for bids. Ella Clarke was the only bidder, and she paid $35,000. Together, Ella R. Clarke and John Clarke now owned 96.75% of the 88-acre tract, less the Burlington railroad's original right of way through the property. The dreams of Asmus Boysen and Allan Boysen thus officially ended, but Allan Boysen was

---

[368] The railroad asked that the special master be requested to report on the facts and law of the right of way question. Case No. 980, *op. cit.*

[369] Judge Neblett had presided over the case for three years, but now he was sitting in the Denver court, so that the parties had to agree for him to take the Clarke case to Denver. In order to give Clarke an interest in the right of way, the court adopted the strange view that the law opening the reservation to settlement somehow suspended the earlier law permitting railroad rights of way across the reservation. The decree was issued March 9, 1928. Case No. 980, *op. cit.* The issue of the railroad's right of way was involved in Case No. 980, as well as case No. 1513, so the 1928 decision affected both of them.

in the process of shutting down the plant anyway, having transferred all its business to the Mountain States Power Co.[370]

Asmus Boysen's appearance before the Special Master was the last time he appeared personally in these legal wars, and it is appropriate to remember at this point is an incident which gives a glimpse of the burden the endless litigation must have been, in addition to all of the other stresses he faced in his pursuit of a Wyoming fortune. He was once asked—not for the first time—to produce for the court some of the records of his two corporations. Boysen replied that he carried these corporate records to Cheyenne in 1913 in connection with earlier testimony, and afterward returned them to his room in Chicago's Stratford Hotel, since he had closed his Chicago office at the beginning of 1910, and had no other place for the safekeeping of business papers. He placed the papers involving the power company and the mining company, as well as other papers belonging to his wife and to him, in a trunk, which he left with his good friend William Lick, the hotel's desk clerk. The clerk was a friend of many years, and he assured Boysen the papers would be waiting for him. Unfortunately, years passed before Boysen was once again called to produce the corporate papers. When he returned to Chicago to recover these papers in December, 1924, he found the hotel had been torn down and replaced by an office building, and his papers were irretrievably lost.[371]

---

[370] The public sale was held June 9, 1928 and the award was made by Special Master William E. Mullen on June 12. Case No. 1320, *op. cit.* Robert C. Wertz still owned 3.25% of the 88-acre tract.

[371] Case 1513, *op. cit.* The Stratford Hotel, on Chicago's Michigan Avenue, was torn down in 1924 and replaced by the Straus Building.

17

THE CLARKE (BOYSEN) DAM

The Boysen dam was now really the Clarke dam, but it was not clear what value they could attach to their winnings. Although the plant still could theoretically operate, all of its former customers were being served by the Mountain States company. The newspaper account of the auction sale quoted the new owners as saying they would open the floodgates as soon as the river subsided, and then overhaul the plant and install new equipment. This information was apparently provided by Byron H. Smith of Shoshoni, who was part owner of a grocery store there, and now on the Clarke payroll, as well. Unfortunately, the account was sheer puffery, not unlike the puffery the Boysens often engaged in, and it ignored the ongoing lawsuit involving the dam they now owned. Indeed, with the change of ownership, the Clarkes merely replaced the Boysens as the focus for the railroad's attacks on the facility.[372]

John Clarke believed that the Boysen interests owed him a good deal of money for his trouble, and he continued his efforts to get a court to agree with him. But long before Clarke stopped trying, the raging river, the railroad, the State of Wyoming and numerous lawyers had long ago carried away all the remaining money the Boysens had. John Clarke's siblings also continued to contest the title to land that was owned by Allan Boysen under his tax deed. They seemed not to realize

---

[372] The newspaper account said the dam was purchased by J. T. Clarke and his brothers, and did not mention Ella Clarke. *Riverton Review,* June 12, 19, 1928.

that even if they could find a judge who agreed with them, the land was mostly suitable only as pasture for the mountain sheep that now graze there. Indeed, even after the Boysens and the Clarkes disappeared from the scene, there continued to be tax sales of the land, as subsequent owners refused to pay the nominal taxes to retain title to it. Despite a lack of any obviously logical purpose, the Clarkes continued to hire lawyers—a lot of lawyers—and pursue their legal crusade. But they were now much closer to the point where judges turned a deaf ear to their arguments.

Back in 1915, the State of Wyoming ordered the Boysens to remove the superstructure from the dam, and Judge Neblett in the Federal court issued the same ruling in 1928. The Boysens forestalled the unfavorable decisions by endless delays, but could not alter the result, and it was the Clarkes' bad luck to perfect their claim to ownership in the—almost—final stages of that ponderous process. But first, there were more delays.

John Clarke's appeals from Judge Neblett's 1928 rulings were finally decided in 1930 in one grand consolidated case before the 10th Circuit Court of Appeals in Denver, a new court organized in 1929 for the area that included Wyoming. The decision consolidated ten appeals in four different cases involving the Boysen (now Clarke) interests. The cases were heard before a three-judge court, and Judge Orie L. Phillips wrote the opinion for the unanimous court.[373]

John Clarke's first appeal from previous decisions asked for recovery of reasonable rental value of his share of the property used by the Boysens. On this appeal the court awarded him a judgment of $35,279 against Allan Boysen, the Asmus Boysen Mining Company, the Fremont Power Company and the Wyoming Power Co., with interest at 6% from March 9, 1928. To say this judgment was of doubtful value is to overstate the situation, for the Boysen mining company and the Fremont Power Company were officially defunct, and the financial

---

[373] The appeals involved the cases considered by the Special Master, Case Nos. 288, 980 and 1320, and Case No. 1513.

condition of Allan Boysen and the Wyoming Power Co. was not much better off.[374]

Clarke's second appeal again asked for his proportionate interest in the nine elapsed shares of the old syndicate. The court rejected Clarke's request and upheld the 1910 decision of the 8th Circuit Court of Appeals, which concluded that the nine shares had never come into existence. The court also noted that Clarke was too late in asking for this participation, having waited until Boysen had spent large sums improving the property before making his claim.[375]

The third and fourth appeals dealt with the effort of the trustees for the bondholders to foreclose their lien on the dam and power plant. The Denver court upheld Judge Riner's decision voiding the lumber company sale for the mechanics' lien, and upheld the lien of the bondholders. It also upheld Allan Boysen's senior lien for the money borrowed from his aunt, but struck down the Wyoming Power Co.'s lien for the money spent to acquire the dam in the lumber company sale.

The fifth appeal was a desperate effort by the Clarkes to avoid removing the superstructure. They had unearthed an interesting document that was filed by the railroad at the time it obtained its right of way across the allotment of Alto Hanway. The document was not entered in the record, but the Clarkes contended that it referred to an agreement between the railroad and the Big Horn Power Co. regarding the height of the dam, and the erection of the superstructure atop the dam. The railroad objected to this interpretation, and the appellate court agreed with their objection, turning back the Clarke initiative.

The last appeals from four cases involved the railroad right of way and the matter of the Boysen dam being a nuisance. As to the right of way, the court reversed the Cheyenne court's finding regarding the railroad right of way filed in 1905, holding that the railroad's filing created a valid 100-foot right of way, and was therefore superior to any claims from the Boysen tract. However, the railroad's right of way

---

[374] Appeal No. 40 from Case No. 288, *op. cit.* Clarke *vs.* Boysen, 39 *Federal Reporter, Second Series* 800.

[375] Appeal No. 42 from Case No. 980, *op. cit.*

through the Boysen tract was wider than 100 feet; it was 300 feet wide where the Boysen station was located and 150 feet wide elsewhere. The Clarkes did prevail in arguing for a 5/16 interest in the additional right of way, and the railroad had to pay for the value of that land.

As to the nuisance question, the Clarkes were now the owners of the dam, and they argued hard that the superstructure should be left intact. They contended that the dam was built in accordance with the permit issued to Boysen, and alternatively that the State Engineer didn't have jurisdiction over a dam on Indian lands. Moreover, they argued that the State Engineer couldn't limit the height of the dam unless it was unsafe, and finally, they argued the railroad had no standing in the case because the dam was built before the railroad arrived.

None of these arguments convinced the court, and the only remaining question was who should remove the nuisance. The trustees for the bondholders argued they should not be responsible, and the court agreed with them, saying they only loaned money to the enterprise, and did not create the nuisance. This placed the onus for removal on Clarke, who was the only remaining solvent party. Clarke argued that he should not have to abate the nuisance because he had received no notice from the railroad, but the court found that he had plenty of knowledge of the nuisance. Moreover, since he had fought hard and obtained title to a share of the property, and argued for a share of rents and profits, he must now share the responsibility for abating the nuisance. The Circuit Court sent the case back to the Cheyenne court to be implemented, and on June 17, 1930, Judge T. Blake Kennedy issued an injunction giving Clarke six months to remove the superstructure from the dam. Unfortunately, this still did not mean that superstructure would soon come tumbling down.[376]

At this time, the old dam and power plant were not just worthless properties, but also expensive liabilities, and once Ella Clarke became the owner of the Boysen dam, she was no more obedient to court orders than the Boysens had been. Meanwhile the river was oblivious to the change of ownership and in the summer of 1930, flood waters ran six feet over the spillway, and logs and trash were still lodged on

---

[376] Appeals 41-48 from Cases No. 288, 980, 1320 and 1513, *op. cit.*

the superstructure in February of the following year. The Burlington railroad once again asked the Federal district court in Cheyenne to have the superstructure removed, and this time, fifteen years of delay came to an end (although the lawsuits did not end after the superstructure was gone).

The Cheyenne court ordered the U. S. Marshal to remove the superstructure, if it had not been removed by the first of April, 1931. The cost of removal was estimated at $7,500-10,000, and the railroad had to deposit a bond of $15,000. John Clarke intervened once again, in a frantic effort to save the last vestiges of the prize he and his wife had tried so long to possess. He said the dam and power plant was worth $425,000, and asked that the superstructure be permitted to remain, with a bypass opening. He gave no justification for his valuation, and since the plant had no customers, his number was simply preposterous. Anyway, the time for argument had finally passed, and the judge denied Clarke's motion.[377]

On March 31, 1931, the U. S. Marshal invited bids for the work to commence on May 1, and the lowest of the three bids submitted was for $6,850, only 37% of the next higher bid. The marshal determined that the low bid omitted some required work, and negotiated a revised bid of $14,136, which was then confirmed by the court on April 13. The work was completed on July 24, 1931, and the cost was charged against the railroad's $15,000 deposit. John Clarke tried to reduce his liability by criticizing the marshal's handling of the demolition. First, he said that he had not received notice, because his lawyer was not available for the hearing. Then, he complained that the marshal unnecessarily inflated the cost of the project by increasing the contractor's bid to include additional work, without seeking new bids.[378]

---

[377] John T. Clarke asked for a stay of removal on January 3, 1931, and the court denied this petition on March 20. Clarke gave the estimate of value in a letter dated February 25, 1931, to Burlington general solicitor J. C. James. Case No. 288, *op. cit.*

[378] Details of the bid letting are from Clarke *vs.* Chicago, Burlington & Quincy Railroad Co., Case No. 656, in the 10th Circuit Court of Appeals, 62 *Federal Reporter, Second Series* 440. Also, Case No. 288, *op. cit.*

Before ruling on Clarke's latest arguments, Judge McDermott performed a judicial act no other judge of a Boysen case ever did: he went up to Fremont County to see the Boysen dam, arriving there near the end of July, 1931, after the demolition of the superstructure was completed. Back in the court room on September 15, Judge McDermott approved the report of the U. S. Marshal, declared that the marshal's costs were reasonable, and ordered John Clarke to pay the railroad $16,968.01, plus interest from July 30, 1931, within 30 days, or have the dam and power plant sold at auction.[379]

It will come as no surprise that the Clarkes did not pay the judgment, whereupon the U. S. Marshal levied on the 88-acre tract, together with the dam and power plant. The sale of the Clarke property was set for February 18, 1932, but once again John Clarke received an extension of the time to appeal, and further delay occurred in the fall of 1932 because of illness. He wired the Cheyenne court from New York City, saying that he was under doctor's care and was unable to hire local (Wyoming) counsel. However, this infirmity by no means meant that the Clarkes had left the legal battlefield.[380]

In his appeal, John Clarke again objected to the action of the U. S. marshal in negotiating with the contractor who removed the superstructure, resulting in increased cost for the work. Also, he criticized Judge McDermott for signing orders on behalf of the Cheyenne court while sitting on district court cases in Topeka. (Federal judges often did this sort of thing but John Clarke thought it was wrong.) Finally, Clarke contended that the railroad should have also tried to recover the cost of removing the superstructure from Robert C. Wertz (who still had half a share in the property), as well as from the Clarkes.

To the railroad, it looked as though it would have to wait a long time to recover the money it had advanced to have the superstructure removed, and said so in its petition to the court in November, 1932.

---

[379] Judge McDermott visited the dam after issuing his order of July 24, which allocated costs to Clarke, and before July 30, when he approved the Marshal's report. Memorandum on Petition for Allowance of Appeal, apparently written about February 3, 1932, Case No. 980, *op. cit.*

[380] Clarke's wire was dated November 29, 1932. Case No. 288, *op. cit.*

Clarke was challenging every point, however small, in order to avoid having his interest in the real estate sold at auction. But the railroad also pointed out that selling the property at auction would not yield any money, since the land and the dam were appraised at about $32,000, and were encumbered by mortgages of about $100,000. Moreover, Clarke lived in New York, and avoided coming to Wyoming, where he could be held in contempt for failing to obey court orders.

Then, in a stroke of extraordinary good luck, the railroad discovered a way to recover the money the Clarkes owed.

18

THE CLARKES FIND SOME OTHER CHEAP BONDS

The Boysens were not the only Wyoming target of the Clarkes' legal team, and in the spring of 1926, the Clarke family took on another cause, which was also an effort to earn a windfall profit from some discounted bonds—this time the bonds of the Hot Springs Electric Light & Power Company. This case now became entangled with the Boysen cases in a way the Clarkes could not have anticipated.

John Clarke first met Harlan Thompson, the majority shareholder of the Hot Springs Electric Light & Power Co., back in 1915 or 1916, when Clarke was trying to persuade the town of Thermopolis to buy power from the Boysen plant, and he continued to watch the decline of the Hot Springs company's fortunes. At the end of 1919, the Hot Springs company authorized a $200,000 issue of 7% gold bonds, to facilitate the sale of the company to Maurice Singer, a broker from New York. Since the company was not a good credit risk, its bonds sold at a deep discount (estimated at 60%), implying a total realization from the bond issue of perhaps $80,000. The company did not pay the interest on the gold bonds, and there were undoubtedly bondholders who were willing to sell out well below 40% of face value. The Clarke family, sensing the opportunity for a good profit, purchased some $50,000 (face value) of the bonds. The Hot Springs company became essentially insolvent, and in December, 1925 Rufus J. Ireland bought up the property at the tax sale, and transferred the Hot Springs company's operations to the Monument Hill Co.[381]

To protect the Clarke family investment in the Hot Springs company bonds, Henry T. Clarke, Jr. filed a lawsuit in the Cheyenne federal court in March, 1926, opposing the transfer of the business of the Hot Springs company to the Monument Hill company, and asking for an accounting of the funds of both companies. The story of the Hot Springs company judgment was a vintage Clarke performance, beginning in the summer of 1927, when the case was delayed because John Clarke was unable to attend the trial. He was suffering from neuritis and lumbago, and from treatment of a large abscess in the "gluteal region," which must have given him the sort of pain he often visited on others.[382]

In 1928, there were motions for continuance, the case was dismissed, the case was reinstated, and finally came to trial. The upshot of all of this maneuvering was a decision in which Ireland and the Thermopolis power company were ordered to pay into the court a total of $92,000 for the benefit of the bondholders. Included in the award was $10,000 that was allocated for the Clarkes' attorney's fees. However, payment was not made because John Clarke was unhappy with the size of the award, and with the fact the court gave him nothing for his own legal work on the case. The Clarkes took their appeal to the U. S. Tenth Circuit in Denver.[383]

---

[381] Henry T. Clarke, Jr. owned $5,000, John T. Clarke had $15,000, and other family interests owned $30,000. Henry T. Clarke *vs.* Hot Springs Electric Light & Power Co., Case No. 1659, U S. District Court, Cheyenne.

[382] Herman Reher of New York, the proprietor of a café, also owned $36,000 face value of the bonds, and he associated himself with Clarke's suit. Case No. 1659, *op. cit.*

[383] Case No. 1659, *op. cit.* Henry T. Clarke *vs.* Hot Springs Electric Light & Power Co, Case No. 1811, U. S. District Court, Cheyenne, and Clarke, *et. al, vs.* Hot Springs Electric Light & Power Co, *et. al,* Case No. 493 in the 10th Circuit Court of Appeals, 55 *Federal Reporter Second Series* 612.

The Denver court heard evidence on the valuation question, and refused to interfere with the lower court's decision on that point. Regarding the matter of legal fees, the Denver court instructed the Cheyenne court to decide whether Clarke should recover for his time and expenses.

The Clarkes immediately mounted another appeal to the U. S. Supreme Court, asking that court to overrule the portions of those decisions of the Denver appellate court that had gone against them. As Ella Clarke found out in 1829, the Supreme Court did not find a Federal question in the Hot Springs case, either, and refused to grant *certiorari* in October, 1932.[384]

In March, 1932, the Hot Springs case was back in Cheyenne from the Denver appellate court, to determine whether Clarke should recover legal fees, and in July, John Clarke asked the court to award him $4,400 for his time. He told the court he had spent several thousand dollars on the Hot Springs cases and devoted 100 days of his own time to preparation. The Cheyenne court was obviously not entirely persuaded, but in December, 1932 did award Clarke a total of $1,293.98 for his expenses and preparation time. John Clarke did not agree with this result, but for a time did nothing about it.

The December, 1932 decision of the Cheyenne federal district court brought the Clarkes closer to receiving money from the Hot Springs case, but the story did not end that way. After waiting five months, John Clarke asked the Federal district court to reopen its 1930 decision and give them interest on their judgments for the time the case had been argued since 1930. The judge denied this request.

At this point, the defendants in the Hot Springs case concluded that as far as they were concerned, all of the open items in the case were settled (although there were still appeals pending), and they then paid $92,160 into the court in Cheyenne to satisfy the judgments. Now, money was actually in Cheyenne, and at this point the Clarkes could have received their share, but it was not to be. Instead of taking the

---

[384] The writ was denied October 10, 1932. Maurice G. Clarke, Henry T. Clarke, John T. Clarke, *et. al*, *vs.* Hot Springs Electric Light & Power Co, *et. al.* 287 *United States Reports* 619.

money, the Clarkes appealed the issue of interest on the judgment to the Denver appellate court.[385]

Judge McDermott, who sat on the Circuit Court in Denver, did not hear the appeal, because he had been acting in the district court below, but Judge Phillips again wrote the opinion, which was brief. Since he and Judge McDermott were responsible for most of the actions the Clarkes complained of, it is not surprising that he reached the opinion he previously held, and affirmed all of the lower court decisions. Once again, the Clarkes promptly asked the U. S. Supreme Court to hear them, and in the fall of 1933, the Supreme Court once again declined to do so. This was the situation in the Hot Springs case when the Burlington railroad lawyers were looking for money to pay for the demolition of the Boysen dam superstructure.[386]

The Burlington lawyers asked the court to let the railroad recover its money for demolition of the superstructure from the Clarkes' award in the Hot Springs case, and Judge Symes, who was then acting in the railroad case, set December 10 for a hearing on that petition. Notice of the hearing, dated December 1, reached John Clarke in New York on December 6 and he immediately asked the court to delay the hearing until at least December 30, because he had no counsel in the West, his Denver firm having withdrawn from his cases, in a dispute with him over *their* fees. Clarke also filed an affidavit asking Judge Symes to disqualify himself, because of bias against John Clarke. The basis for this claim was an incident in connection with the Hot Springs case, where Judge Symes refused to name a receiver for the Hot Springs company because John Clarke did not pay his expenses in one of the

---

[385] Clarke, *et. al, vs.* Hot Springs Electric Light & Power Co, *et. al,* Case No. 1140 filed May 8, 1933, in the 10th Circuit Court of Appeals, 76 *Federal Reporter Second Series* 918.

[386] Case No. 656, Clarke *vs.* Chicago, Burlington & Quincy Railroad Co, *et. al,* Case No. 657 (same title), decided December 19, 1932, 62 *Federal Reporter Second Series* 440 and Case No. 57, John T. Clarke *vs.* C B & Q Railroad Co, Case No. 58 (same title) and Case No. 59, Ella R. Clarke, *et. al, vs.* C B & Q Railroad Co, 290 *United States Reports* 629, decided October 9, 1933.

Boysen cases. It seemed that John Clarke had trouble making friends in the legal profession.[387]

Judge Symes did not delay the hearing, nor did he disqualify himself, and on December 10 he issued a temporary injunction freezing the Clarkes' share of the Hot Springs case judgment, so that this money would be available to satisfy the railroad's judgment, if and when the appellate court determined how much money could be paid out.

While the Clarkes' latest appeal in the Hot Springs case was going forward, they continued to haggle with the Cheyenne court as to how the money from the judgment should be paid out. The judge in Cheyenne ordered the clerk to pay outside counsel $10,673.80 for their expenses and services, and John Clarke objected, on two counts. The lawyers involved were his Denver law firm, and Clarke had already advanced some of their fees, and he wanted to get his money back, but also, as we have noted, he objected to the amount of their fees. The court allowed Clarke to recover his advances, but he was still not satisfied, and filed an appeal to the Denver appellate court on that issue. So the money from the Hot Springs judgment remained on deposit with the federal court in Cheyenne.[388]

The two Hot Springs case appeals from the Cheyenne district court were heard in Denver in the spring of 1935. The first was John Clarke's claim for $4,400 for his own legal fees and services, and on that issue he told the court that he was the best judge of the value of his services, saying his services were "much more expert than many lawyers

---

[387] The exact amount the Clarkes were entitled to receive from the Hot Springs case does not appear from the record, but the railroad's petition indicates that the judgment involved a payment of $407.43 on each $1,000 bond. Since the Clarkes owned at least 50 bonds, they would have been entitled to more than $20,000, which would have been more than sufficient to satisfy the railroad judgment before it was increased by interest. The railroad petition to apply the Hot Springs case funds to its judgment was dated November 18, 1932. Case No. 980, *op. cit.*

[388] Clarke *et. al, vs.* Hot Springs Electric Light & Power Co, *et. al,* Case No. 1142, filed July 2, 1934 in the 10th Circuit Court of Appeals, 76 *Federal Reporter Second Series* 918.

could have given this kind of work." Judge McDermott, who heard this appeal, wryly remarked that District Judge T. Blake Kennedy in Cheyenne ". . . has had extensive opportunity to judge of the character and value of the services Mr. Clarke renders in litigation." He went on to say that if he were forced to accept Clarke's idea of value, it was fortunate Clarke didn't ask for $400 a day. After these playful remarks, the judge said. ". . . [I]t is well settled that a trial court is not bound to allow fees his own knowledge and experience tell him are exorbitant . . . ." Clarke was allowed $1,250 for his 110 days of work. Clarke's other expenses, including the cost of "many" trips to Wyoming were disallowed, because Clarke did not segregate his costs for this case from "much other litigation" he was pursuing in Wyoming.

On the issue of interest for the period since the 1930 judgment, Judge McDermott said that Clarke himself was responsible for the delays after the 1930 judgment and denied the appeal, saying, "There must be an end to litigation sometime . . . ." It is regrettable that this piece of sage judicial dictum came so late in the story. Not satisfied with this answer, the Clarkes once more asked the U. S. Supreme Court to hear their complaints, and in the fall of 1935, that court once more declined to hear him.[389]

In the summer of 1938, John and Ella Clarke made a final effort to keep the Cheyenne federal court from pressing them to recover the cost of removing the superstructure by trying to get the New York courts to intervene. They actually obtained an order from the Appellate Division of the New York Supreme Court staying the railroad case proceedings, which for a short time produced repercussions in Cheyenne. To avoid being in contempt of the New York courts, the railroad asked the Cheyenne court to vacate its order in the case, but Judge Alfred Murrah of Tulsa was in Cheyenne to hear the case, and he refused to vacate the order, ruling that the New York courts did not have jurisdiction. In the summer of 1938, Clarke's attorney in New York complained to Judge Murrah that Clarke was prevailing in the New York courts, but could

---

[389] Maurice G. Clarke, Henry T. Clarke and John T. Clarke *vs.* Hot Springs Light & Power Co, *et. al,* 296 *United States Reports* 624, decided October 21, 1935.

not stop the Wyoming cases from going against him, and Judge Murrah deposited that letter with the numerous other papers in the file.[390]

As the need for the Clarkes to pay the Burlington railroad for removing the superstructure refused to go away, John Clarke tried to reduce his obligation by sharing the cost with the Boysen interests. He obtained a judgment of $35,279 against the Big Horn Power Co., Wyoming Power Co., Fremont Power Co. and Allan Boysen. Of course, those defendants were all either defunct or bankrupt, and the judgment, like so many others in this story, went uncollected.[391]

In July, 1938, the time finally came for the railroad to be paid. Interest of more than $8,200 had swelled the judgment to more than $25,000, but the Clarkes' proceeds from the Hot Springs case paid most of that total, leaving only $445.56 which the Clarkes owed the railroad. Thus, ironically, the Boysen dam that John Clarke strove so long to possess finally became the mechanism to deny him the gain he could have realized from the Hot Springs case—his only profitable Wyoming speculation.[392]

The Clarkes' opposition to the railroad case did not end until after John Clarke's death. We do not know who paid the last $445.56, but on December 21, 1942, the railroad declared that its judgment had been satisfied. The final entry in the record of Clarke litigation against the Boysen interests came on March 27, 1957, when Judge Ewing T.

---

[390] Case No. 288, *op. cit,* and Case No. 1320, *op. cit.* The letter from Albert Adams of New York City to Judge Alfred P. Murrah was dated July 25, 1938. The New York cases were consolidated for appeal in that state, and Clarke's appeal was denied October 21, 1938. 7 *New York Supplement Second Series* 574. Judge Murrah's order was dated July 18, 1938. Case No. 980, *op. cit.* Judge Alfred Paul Murrah, whose name was given to the federal building destroyed in the Oklahoma City disaster, was appointed to the federal bench in 1936, at age 32, making him the youngest man to serve as a U. S. District Judge.

[391] Case No. 288, *op. cit.*

[392] Interest to July 18, 1938 amounted to $8,274.74, making the total judgment $25,242.75, of which $24,797.19 was recovered from the Hot Springs case. Case No. 288, *op. cit.*

Kerr of the Cheyenne federal court authorized the clerk to destroy any exhibits not claimed by the parties in four Boysen cases.[393]

At the beginning of 1934, Ella Clarke tried to realize something from the Boysen assets she had gone to so much trouble to acquire. Payment of the demolition judgment from the proceeds in the Hot Springs case left Ella Clarke with title to her 11/16 interest in the 88-acre tract, but when she put it up for auction there were no bids. After this abortive effort, she did not pay the taxes on the tract, and it was sold for unpaid taxes in the fall of the year. It was a sad end to an ambitious undertaking so tenaciously pursued.[394]

---

[393] The four cases covered by Judge Kerr's order were Nos. 288, 980, 1320 and 1513, *op. cit.*

[394] Ella Clarke's attempted sale of the 88-acre tract was on February 24, 1934. Case No. 1320, *op. cit.*

19

THE AFTERMATH

A short item in the July 22, 1938 Thermopolis *Independent Record* was headlined, "Here from Chicago." The item told of the arrival of "A. Boysen" from Chicago, to visit his daughter Anna Maria at the William Kyne residence, and we hope the Kynes drove up the river to let the 70-year-old Boysen see his dam, the superstructure now gone, but still stubbornly holding back the river. This time Boysen's interview with the newspaper was very brief. He did not comment on his legal or financial problems, but he could still dream, for he predicted that Wyoming would see more development in the next ten years than any other state in the union. It was fitting that his visit to Wyoming stirred enthusiasm within him, as his first visit also did, some 39 years before.[395]

Asmus Boysen only lived a little more than a year after his last visit to Wyoming. According to a telegram received by Anna Marie Kyne (who was then living on Owl Creek, in Hot Springs County), he died in his sleep of an apparent heart attack, the day after Thanksgiving in November, 1939. He was then still living in Chicago with his second wife, and his daughter Helena also lived there. His presence in Wyoming had faded so much that the newspaper headline announcing his death misspelled his name. He was 71.[396]

---

[395] *The Thermopolis Independent Record,* July 22, 1938.

[396] Boysen died November 24, 1939. The headline was "Amos Boysen Died in Chicago Friday." *The Thermopolis Independent Record,* November 30, 1939.

John T. Clarke died at the Hotel Barclay in New York City on November 10, 1941, having survived Asmus Boysen by only two years. He was a month short of his eightieth birthday, and he died without a will, leaving an estate of less than $10,000. Ella R. Clarke lived on until the spring of 1955, when she died in Atlantic City, N. J., and she still had some of her former wealth when she died—the only one of the three who was that lucky.[397]

After both the Clarkes and the Boysens left the legal battleground, the physical remnants of their many disputes remained. The Boysen dam was still in place across the river at the head of the Wind River canyon, between the railroad in its tunnel on the west side, and the new highway in its tunnel on the east side. It was a sad brooding hulk, and the only testimony to its presence was from the river, as it rushed over the dam on its turbulent journey down the canyon.

On either side of the dam was the Boysen tract, which continued its checkered history. At the end of 1930, Allan Boysen executed a deed to his sister, Helena Aishton, covering the entire original Boysen tract. This was a warranty deed, based on the tax title he purchased in 1916, but he might have had a chore establishing a clear title to all of that property. In any case, his sister only paid taxes on about 82 acres, on either side of the river south of the 88-acre tract, and she was the last Boysen to "own" a portion of the famous section of land that once belonged to her father. She held this land until 1961.[398]

---

[397] *New York Herald Tribune,* November 12, 1941. John T. Clarke was born December 28, 1861. Ella Clarke was granted letters of administration for his estate on November 24, 1941. Surrogate's Court in New York County, NY, File No. A-2399. The probate of Ella Clarke's will is recorded in the Atlantic County Surrogate's Court, Docket No. 28951. The final distribution of her estate consisted of securities worth $60,287.50 as of December 11, 1958, the income from the estate having been distributed earlier.

[398] The property retained by Helena Aishton under the 1930 deed was Lot 2 and Lot 3 in Section 4, a total of 82.63 acres, which were included in the treasurer's deed to Allan Boysen on September 25, 1916. Allan Boysen's deed to Helena Aishton was executed December 1, 1930, and conveyed

The rest of the Boysen tract, excluding the 88-acre tract transferred to the Big Horn Power Co., was sold for taxes in the summer of 1931 and the tax deed issued to Fremont County in 1935 wiped out both the Boysen and Clarke interests to that land. The 88-acre tract for which Ella Clarke paid $35,000 was sold for unpaid taxes in 1934, and the tax deed issued to Fremont County in 1938. So ended the Clarkes' ownership in the Boysen tracts.

In the spring of 1940, the Fremont County commissioners quieted the title of a number of properties they had acquired through tax sales, in preparation for auctioning them, and all except three lots included in the original Boysen tract were included in this action. The auction was held on February 15, 1941, and Raymond R. Purdum purchased the Boysen tracts, paying $150.00 for the parcels adjoining the dam, and $50.00 for the larger tract—a big discount from the $10 per acre Boysen paid when he bought the land. For the last time, all except two lots included in the 680-acre Boysen tract was united in a one person, although there were still clouds on the title that the Purdums needed to remove.[399]

Raymond Purdum was no stranger to the Boysen project. When Peter Dykeman sold control of the Riverton power plant early in 1918, Raymond Purdum came to Riverton to take charge of the electrical work in the plant, which began purchasing power from the Boysen dam in 1919. By 1921, Purdum was the manager of the Riverton plant, and he negotiated the arrangements to connect the town of Hudson to the grid, only months before the Boysen plant shut down. Thus, Purdum witnessed the death throes of the Boysen operation.[400]

---

an 11/16 interest in the land. Helena Aishton subsequently conveyed these two lots by deed on May 15, 1961.

[399] Lots 2, 3 and 4 in Section 4, Township 5 North, Range 6 East of the Wind River Meridian were not included in this sale. The Board of the County Commissioners of Fremont County, Wyoming *vs.* Helena B. Aishton, *et. al,* Case No. 5832, filed on May 25, 1940 in the Fremont County District Court and decided December 23, 1940.

[400] The Popo Agie Light & Power Company was organized in 1914, and Purdum was manager of the Popo Agie company plant until 1925, when

One problem with Purdum's title was the fact someone was "squatting" on part of the 88-acre tract as early as 1935, and in 1945 brought an action to acquire title by adverse possession. The occupants of this land brought suit against Ella and John Clarke, the Big Horn Power Co. and the Wyoming Power Co., none of whom responded, and the judge gave a default judgment to the plaintiffs. Ray Purdum cured this problem by exchange of quitclaim deeds in 1952.[401]

After Purdum died, his widow brought an action to quiet title against the many other former claimants to the land. To bring this action, her lawyer had to try to serve a summons on each of the twenty-six defendants named in the suit. Allan Boysen's signature acknowledging service on August 15, 1953, gives us the last Boysen signature on a legal matter involving the Boysen tract. The decree quieting title in Mrs. Purdum was handed down in the fall of 1953.[402]

After Boysen's power plant shut down, the first Boysen dam was only an irrelevant relic until the federal government became interested in building a new dam and power plant upstream from this location. Asmus Boysen lived long enough to learn that the Corps of Engineers

---

the company was purchased by Midwest Public Service Company of Casper. *The Riverton Review,* February 15, 1918, July 30, November 29, 1925, May 24, 31, 1928.

[401] The adverse possession case included Lot 2, Section 33, Township 5 North, Range 6 East of the Wind River Meridian, which was included in the 88-acre tract transferred to the Big Horn Power Co. Bertha L. Anderson, as Executrix of the Estate of Olof Anderson, deceased, and Brita Anderson, *vs.* Ella R. Clarke, John T. Clarke, Wyoming Power Co. and Big Horn Power Co, Case No. 6446, filed May 16, 1945 and decided September 11, 1945, Fremont County District Court. The quitclaim deeds were exchanged between Lucile Connaghan and Ray Purdum on March 7 and 8, 1952.

[402] Ray Purdum died February 20, 1953. The quiet title action was Gladys L. Purdum *vs.* Harry T. Clarke, *et. al.* Case No. 8296, filed August 3, 1953, and decided November 9, 1953, Fremont County District Court. The decision relied in part on adverse possession by the Purdums for more than ten years, thus avoiding the need to address the many legal arguments afflicting the properties over the years.

was interested in building a new dam near the one he built so long ago, for in 1939, the Corps of Engineers recommended that the new dam be constructed on Boysen's original site. A newspaper story said that surveyors from the Army Corps of Engineers were evaluating the possibility of building a 200-foot "power dam," at or near the old Boysen site. Curious as to the impact of placing such a large structure on the river, Fred Northern, the Shoshoni town marshal, consulted the local surveyor, who told him that such a dam would leave Fred Northern's home 70 feet under water. "What in Hell will become of me?" Northern expostulated.[403]

In the spring of 1939, the newspapers once again took notice of the Boysen dam (no mention was made of the former Clarke ownership). The Shoshoni *Independent's* story began,

"We expect that Mr. Boysen would be interested in a story that is prevalent here the last few days, so we are going to tell the story as we have gleaned it from various sources for Allan's benefit and then we are sending him a marked copy."

Newspaper stories speculated on the likely height of a new dam, and the possible effect on the railroad, the highway and the town of Shoshoni. In contrast with the long controversy over Boysen's little 35-foot dam, the 1939 public discussion of a 200, 250 or 280-foot monster structure was extremely positive on all sides. With the prospect of federal funding, all agreed that moving the highway presented no great problem, and there were also feasible solutions for the railroad. In July, it was reported that the railroad favored a five or six-mile tunnel as an alternative to its existing right of way south of the canyon. If the dam were 280 feet high, the town of Shoshoni would have to be relocated, but the Thermopolis *Record* pointed out that towns of 5,000 population—with large cemeteries—were moved for the TVA project, and compared with that example, moving the town of Shoshoni would be "very simple."[404]

---

[403] *Shoshoni Independent,* quoted in *The Thermopolis Independent Record,* May 4, 1939.

[404] *The Thermopolis Independent Record,* May 25, July 6, July 15, August 17, November 9, 1939.

The cost of the dam was shrugged off as "a couple of million dollars," and would be a bargain for the government. The looming world war interrupted consideration of the second Boysen dam, but when it was finally built, the earlier predictions were accurate, for it did not occasion years of litigation.[405]

There is still a Boysen dam in Wyoming, and the story of the new Boysen dam can be told quickly. After more studies in 1941-42, the Flood Control Act of 1944 authorized the concept of a new Boysen dam, located upstream from the old Boysen site. One of the elements of the Federal project was to remove the remnants of the old Boysen dam, and to do this it was necessary to get permission from the owner of the surrounding property. Fortunately, by then there were no contentious opponents to resist the government. In September, 1947, Raymond Purdum authorized the Bureau of Reclamation to clear the channel of the river, receiving $500 for this privilege. The first Boysen dam is gone, but an alert motorist driving through the Wind River Canyon when the river is low may be able to identify the remains of the footings of Boysen's dam.[406]

The new Boysen dam is located 1.5 miles upstream from Boysen's original structure, and although the new reservoir was not a threat to the railroad in the canyon, it would still flood the Burlington railroad tracks south of the new dam. We do not know the details of the negotiations that followed, but we do know there were no lawsuits, at all, because the federal government was a far more formidable opponent for the railroad than Asmus Boysen or John Clarke, and besides, the government was willing to pay for the privilege of having its own way. The railroad relocated its tracks to accommodate the new dam and lake, on an realignment carrying the tracks across the river, to enter a tunnel on the east side just below the new dam. The relocation, completed in August, 1950, involved 13.5 miles of tracks, seven bridges, two sidings

---

[405] *The Thermopolis Independent Record,* August 17, 1939.

[406] The actual site of the dam was in the stream bed of the river, which was never conveyed to Boysen, but Purdum owned the access to the dam on both sides.

and a tunnel—not five or six miles long, as was suggested back in 1939, but 7,100 feet, still the longest on the Burlington system.[407]

Relocation of the railroad and the highway cleared the way to begin construction of the new dam and power plant in the fall of 1947, and the new facility was complete at the end of 1952. The new earthfill dam was 220 feet high and 1,143 feet long at the crest, holding back a reservoir of nearly 1.5 million acre feet. One of the old railroad tunnels was incorporated in the new project, to be used as intake for the 15,000 kilowatt power plant. Once more, there was an operating Boysen power plant, which dwarfed Boysen's little plant.

Allan Boysen, who struggled so long to make his father's project financially viable, was in Chicago in 1930, working as a bookkeeper, but by 1934 he was in Scottsbluff, Nebr., working as a flagman for the Burlington railroad, and he was still there in 1953, when he acknowledged service in the Purdum quiet title action. When the marker commemorating the first Boysen Dam was dedicated at the dam site on November 28, 1965, Boysen's three daughters were all still living, although Allan had died. (William Sayles, Jr, grandson of Asmus Boysen, was present at the dedication.)

Darlene married William Sayles, son of Edward Sayles, one of the managers at the Casper oil refinery. Helena Boysen Aishton, who was divorced from Fred Aishton, was living in Chicago when Asmus died there in 1939, and she also later lived in Scottsbluff.

As we have noted, William Kyne was in the wool business after his marriage to Anna Marie Boysen, and in 1920 he was managing a lumber yard in Casper. However, by 1930 he was back on Owl Creek, again in the sheep business. After 1932, a Casper banker asked him to manage the large sheep ranch of Lucy Morrison Moore, and he later purchased this ranch. He and Anna Marie Kyne were living on that ranch in 1939 when Asmus Boysen died, but both later moved to California.[408]

---

[407] Overton, *op. cit*, 559.

[408] Dorothy Buchanan Milek, *Hot Springs: A Wyoming County History* (n.p, 1986), 62.

Asmus Boysen's second wife, Kathryne Fanning Boysen, died in Los Angeles in 1955, and Kathryne Boysen's son Raymond died in Torrance, Calif., in 1966.

Although Asmus Boysen is gone and the memory of his efforts in Wyoming dims, his name, increasingly disconnected from those real events, lives on in a number of places, the largest of which is the Boysen State Park, which surrounds the new Boysen reservoir. After the new Boysen dam was constructed, the State of Wyoming entered into an agreement with the Bureau of Reclamation to establish a state park on the Boysen reservoir. In the summer of 1965, Ray Purdum's wife conveyed part of the Big Horn Power Co.'s 88-acre tract to the State of Wyoming Parks Commission, to become a part of the park, and the park's Lower Wind River Campground is located on this parcel. The Bureau of Reclamation had already named their new dam for Asmus Boysen, so it was natural that the State Parks Commission should also attach his name to the state park. If the choice of the Boysen name involved any thought regarding the man himself or his tangled history, no record of such consideration apparently survives.[409]

Certainly the most prominent monument to the Boysen name is Boysen Peak, a 7,556-foot peak in the Owl Creek Mountains, northwest of the location of Boysen's own dam. Of Boysen's operations near his dam, little remains, although the dry creek behind his camp southwest of the dam site is named Boysen Creek, and the location of Boysen's camp site west of the dam is shown on the U. S. Geological Survey maps. The Boysen railroad station has completely disappeared, but the location of the railroad water tower, which served the steam engine boilers, still appears on the maps, and the concrete foundation of the tower is very much in evidence.

The old town of Boysen has disappeared entirely, although the history of its site is interesting. For a few months after the town was platted in 1907 until the dam begin creating its lake, the settlement along the river was above water. By the time the Wyoming newspaper editors visited the location in the summer of 1910, the town was

---

[409] Gladys Purdum to the State of Wyoming, Warranty Deed dated June 22, 1965, Fremont County Clerk's office.

completely flooded by the rising waters of the lake, and that was the situation until 1925, when the underflow gates were reopened to flush the excess silt from above the dam. When the Bureau of Reclamation finally removed the Boysen dam, the river flushed the rest of the silt from its former channel, leaving a flat tableland on either side of the river. After the State of Wyoming received title to the Boysen lands on the east side of the river and established the Boysen State Park, the Upper Wind River Campground was established along the river in the area where the old town of Boysen once was.

When Asmus Boysen came to the Wind River canyon, there were "plenty" of bighorn sheep living there, at home in the rugged mountains. In the years to come, these majestic animals declined in numbers, so that after the 1950s there was only a single sighting of them in the area. At the beginning of 1995, the Wyoming Game and Fish Commission relocated a small herd of sheep from the Whiskey Basin to the Wind River canyon, where they once again thrive in their native environment. When human visitors are not enjoying the Upper and Lower Wind River campgrounds south of the old Boysen dam site, occasionally the sheep come down from the mountain to frequent them as well. Of course, the level ground at the campgrounds is different from the former river bank, and is a reminder of the silt that accumulated above Boysen's dam. Withal, it is a happy use for some of Asmus Boysen's land.[410]

[410] Calvin King, quoting one L. Morrison, is the source of sighting of "plenty of sheep" on Copper Mountain in the 1890s. Calvin L. King, *History of Wildlife in the Big Horn Basin of Wyoming* (Cheyenne, n.d.), 20. The only recorded sighting of bighorn sheep in the canyon after the 1950s was in 1988, when two rams were reported there. On January 1, 1995, 32 ewes, 8 lambs and 3 rams were relocated from Whiskey Basin to the Wind River canyon. Kevin Hurley of the Wyoming Game and Fish Department supplied the information regarding the 1995 relocation of sheep and the earlier 20th century sightings in a telephone conversation with the author on February 10, 2006.

20

WHAT DO WE MAKE
OF THESE PEOPLE?

We have recounted an extraordinarily complex story involving the Clarkes and the Boysens as major opponents, each side striving to possess an asset of questionable value in a sparsely-settled region in a sparsely-settled state. These two opponents were also assailed by two other formidable opponents that were determined to destroy that same asset. The first of these formidable opponents, the Burlington railroad, was a common carrier endowed with the right of eminent domain, used to getting its own way, and financially capable of hiring as many lawyers as it needed (including those on its own payroll). The other formidable opponent was the State of Wyoming, which supported the railroad's claim, with all the power that sovereignty implies. Viewed in that light, one can readily see that the individual opponents in this story should both have deserted the battlefield and ceded the issue to the Burlington and the State.

But there was also another unseen party in the conflict. That party was delay, and its impact was formidable. One party or the other could seem to be winning, while the matter made its way in an appeal to another court. And delay was a deterrent not only to our individual opponents, but also to their formidable adversaries. So we may be a bit charitable to the Boysens and the Clarkes, for not recognizing for a long time that the cause was lost—for both of them.

It is interesting to see how outsized egos could lead intelligent men into this sort of mess. Asmus Boysen started out in Wyoming as a client of John T. Wertz, who suggested the land for the coal lease, and organized the syndicate to manage it, a syndicate dominated by close associates of Wertz and others from Omaha whom he selected. With railroad backing, the members of the syndicate could see the chance for a quick speculative return, but Wertz often had other motives as well, and part of the lease was also prospective for copper. However, Boysen did not follow Wertz's scenario, but instead elected to keep the lease in his own name, and perhaps as a consequence the syndicate never held a meeting to elect the board of directors and no one made the financial contribution required by the agreement. When railroad backing for the coal venture disappeared, Boysen was willing to look for other minerals—perhaps at Wertz's urging—and he asked the government to exchange the lease for the right to look for copper. At the time, there was no indication that the other syndicate members knew of or cared about this action. The lease exchange failed, but Wertz continued to be in the background, still talking to Boysen, while at the same time trying to organize other syndicates for other clients.

We can assume that Wertz was talking to Boysen at the time when Congress was considering opening the reservation to settlement, and of course, Boysen was well situated politically to raise questions about the old lease. Wertz would have been active behind the scene as well, not for love of Boysen, but in order to get the leverage to accommodate his other clients on the reservation. Before selecting his land, Boysen got caught up in the Copper Mountain play, but when he went to look for a site for his square mile of mineral land, he went back to his coal lease—although not to the spot Wertz considered most prospective. After the debacle with the diamond drill, he fell back on the place where he could see copper outcropping on the canyon walls, and he had the advice of recognized mining experts before he spent a lot of money looking for it.

By the time the search for copper failed, Boysen had spent a lot of money (although he still had a fair amount left), and most of the decisions he made from this point on were a vain effort to recover the money he had spent, When that was no longer possible, he was still driven by the conviction that it was not fair for his opponents to take what he had spent so much energy and money to acquire.

To be sure, his optimism for Wyoming was overblown. At first, he built the dam and power as a cheap source of power for the mining bonanza he anticipated, and when that bonanza failed to materialize, he expected to supply power to the small market represented by the nearby towns until increased power demand came from the rapid agricultural development after the reservation opened in 1906. Nor was he alone in these opinions, for others with experience in the field made similar bets. Many fortunes were lost on Copper Mountain and the government's planning for irrigation in the ceded area took a long time to develop, and even when it did, the state was caught up in the agricultural recession of the 1920s. The market enjoyed by the Boysen plant was too small to give the plant a return on its investment, and building transmission lines and distribution systems to serve other municipalities could not have been justified by the revenues they would earn—even if Boysen had the money to build them.

Boysen ignored the claims of his former partners in the coal syndicate, because he thought they were not entitled to a share when they had done nothing and he spent a fortune on his preference tract. And we should remember that Boysen had good legal advice that agreed with his conclusion about the syndicate agreement, a conclusion that was shared by Judge Riner in Cheyenne.

As to the railroad opposition to his project, Boysen said he had been told the railroad was not going to build through the canyon, and in fact we now know that assumption was not obviously wrong until his dam was already in place. To be sure, the Burlington railroad had a right of way dating back to 1905, but so did the Northwestern, and the Burlington had lots of rights of way filed that never were used. We now know that the Burlington itself did not make up its mind on the canyon route until after the Colorado & Southern acquisition (and didn't actually pay for the canyon right of way until February, 1909, when Boysen's dam was nearly completed).

What of the State of Wyoming? No one knew how disastrous the Boysen dam would be at times of high water in the canyon, so the question as to whether the dam should be 60 or 50 or 35 feet was mostly a matter of guesswork, but because Boysen built a superstructure on his dam and failed to get the state engineer to correct the length of the spillway on the permit, the State of Wyoming had a sound technical case to destroy what Boysen had built. But we have seen that the state engineer told Boysen he could build the dam higher if the railroad did not build through the canyon, and Boysen proceeded to construct the dam in an manner that could be economically extended upward, to the level where the spillway *would be* 124 feet long, using the piers as supports. Unfortunately, the State was the only party that had the luxury of hindsight to guide its case. It was not necessary to decide whether the dam ought to be 35 or 50 or 60 feet high, because it was clear that the dam was causing a lot of trouble for the railroad. Boysen thought this hindsight was unfair, but in this case fairness was not a legal concept.

So much for the Boysen side. What of the Clarkes? The Clarkes were strongly motivated to make small investments and parlay them into a windfall, and they were averse to paying full price for anything. They were also clients of John Wertz, and were in fact about to try to negotiate their own coal lease when Asmus Boysen stopped in Omaha to head them off, and tell them he would take care of them in his syndicate. John Clarke signed the agreement, but contributed nothing to Boysen's investments, and when he was forced to share Boysen's costs to receive a share of the land, he thought the price was too high. Clarke said he went to Washington to help Boysen with his efforts to get the section of land, but this may have been only another example of his many exaggerated statements. Boysen's feelings hardened as lawyer Clarke came up with one legal argument after another to deprive Boysen of the fruits of his investments.

After John Clarke married Ella Tiedemann, he gained both money and added enthusiasm for extracting gain from the tangled legal situation, and she was undoubtedly the inspiration to buy up the gold bonds that ultimately proved the downfall of the Boysen edifice. Like John Clarke, she didn't like to lose and her history in the courts was one of insisting on yet another appeal against every unfavorable decision, no matter how slim the chances of success might be. With Ella Clarke, the lawsuits soon took on lives of their own, apart from any consideration of financial gain.

The Burlington railroad summarized the Clarkes' actions in a 1930 brief:

"Boysen built the power dam in 1907 and 1908 at a cost to himself of $350,000. No decree has ever required Clarke or associates to contribute to the *great cost of the dam,* and they never have . . . . Circumstances indicate that Clarke has cleverly taken advantage of the mistake of Boysen in building the costly dam on the land in which Clarke established an equitable interest, and has carried on the litigation throughout the years pursuant to a studied plan ultimately to wrest the dam from the impoverished Boysen . . . . All this time Clarke has known that the unauthorized superstructure was a public nuisance [yet] . . . Mrs. Clarke purchased 11/16 of the dam and nuisance at foreclosure sale, for less than ten per cent of the original cost . . . . In view of the manner in which Clarke, by circumstances and Boysen's poor judgment, has been able to appropriate to himself property created by others, . . . there is nothing inequitable . . . in requiring them to correct [the nuisance]." [emphasis in the original][411]

It would have been impossible for either the Boysens or the Clarkes to write a synopsis as brief as this, because the long delays worked to change their perception of the chances of success month by month, until the years rolled by. We now can see that when Asmus Boysen and John Clarke and Ella Clarke died, their legal ventures were a total disaster, but it is unlikely that any of the three would have agreed with that assessment at the time. The major unanswered question is why the parties to this blizzard of lawsuits continued to hire lawyers to press on, when the State of Wyoming and the Burlington railroad had already destroyed any economic value to be gained from the property, and in any case, the sluggish economy in the Fremont County made any hope of profit a very remote possibility, even in the best of circumstances. We can never know the answer, but it is clear that somewhere along

---

[411] *Brief for Respondents, Chicago, Burlington & Quincy Railroad Company and Big Horn Railroad Company in Opposition to Petitions for Writs of Certiorari,* October Term, 1930, in the Supreme Court of the United States.

the way, the contest took on a life of its own, apart from the economic interests of the Boysens and the Clarkes.

In 1887, before Asmus Boysen came to Wyoming, the Sundance *Gazette* wrote, "When the angel Gabriel blows his horn, a vast array of lawyers will rise up and from sheer force of habit, move for a continuance of the cases before the court." That spirit was still alive in the days of Asmus Boysen and John T. Clarke.[412]

---

[412] *Sundance Gazette,* January 7, 1887 (quoting the San Francisco *Post*).

Holland America Line ship P[ieter] Caland, powered by both sails and steam, the ship that brought Asmus Boysen to the U.S. in 1886. Courtesy of the Library of Congress.

Asmus Boysen as a younger man, c. 1902. Courtesy of
William Boysen, San Pedro, Calif.

Anna Boysen. Courtesy of William Boysen, San Pedro, Calif.

Allan Boysen, who managed the Boysen power plant for a number of years, sometimes with "help" from his father. Courtesy of William Boysen, San Pedro, Calif.

Kathryne Boysen, Asmus Boysen's second wife, and her son Raymond Boysen. Courtesy of William Boysen, San Pedro, Calif.

John T. Clarke, Boysen's tenacious legal opponent, c. 1927. Courtesy of the Nebraska State Historical Society.

Ella R. Clarke, courtesy of Carl H. Tiedemann, New York, N.Y.

Charles Breniman, Boysen's first manager in Wyoming. Author's collection.

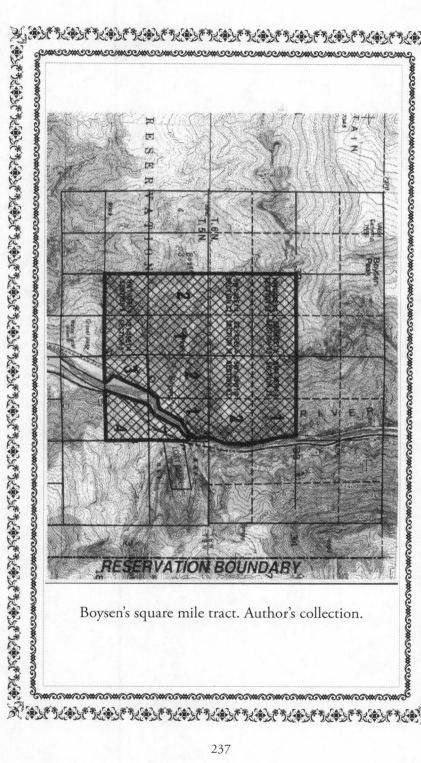

Boysen's square mile tract. Author's collection.

One of the mine shafts used in Boysen's
unsuccessful search for copper. Courtesy
of William Boysen, San Pedro, Calif.

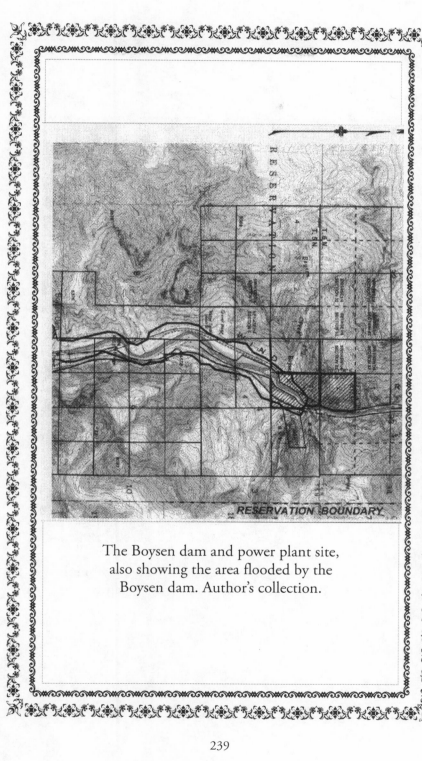

The Boysen dam and power plant site,
also showing the area flooded by the
Boysen dam. Author's collection.

Early dam construction, showing the buttresses in the river bed. Courtesy of William Boysen, San Pedro, Calif.

The lake upstream from Boysen dam, before the railroad was built, with the town of Boysen in the distance. The road from Shoshoni to the dam is the higher road on the hillside across the reservoir. Courtesy of William Boysen, San Pedro, Calif.

Looking south from the Boysen dam, with the
railroad station in the foreground. The position of
the upper road across the lake gives an idea of the
increased depth of the water, as the reservoir filled.
Courtesy of William Boysen, San Pedro, Calif.

Boysen dam, with superstructure in place. Courtesy of the Wyoming State Archives, Department of State Parks and Cultural Resources.

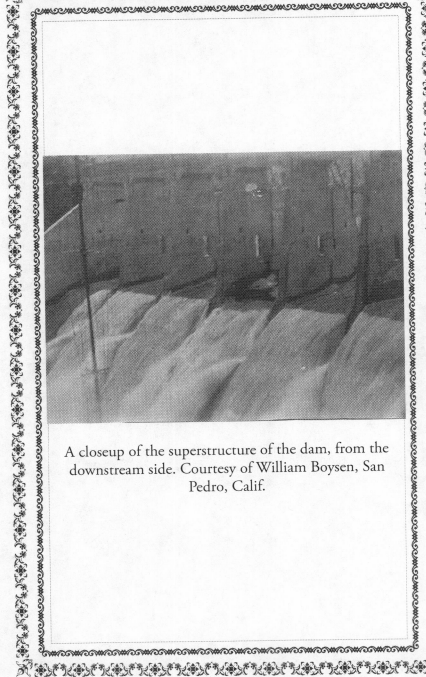

A closeup of the superstructure of the dam, from the downstream side. Courtesy of William Boysen, San Pedro, Calif.

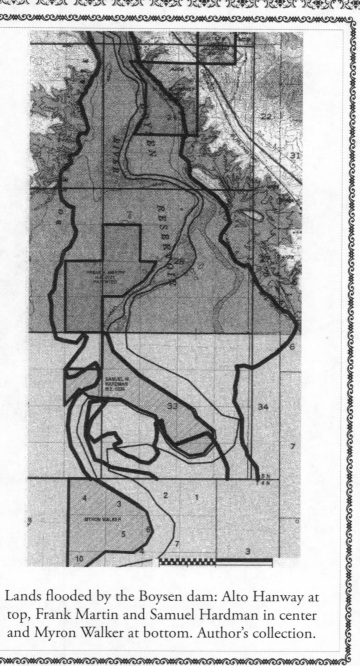

Lands flooded by the Boysen dam: Alto Hanway at top, Frank Martin and Samuel Hardman in center and Myron Walker at bottom. Author's collection.

A passenger train on the flooded tracks, facing the Boysen dam. Courtesy of William Boysen, San Pedro, Calif.

The Boysen advertisement in the April 4, 1912 issue of Den Danske Pioneer. Courtesy of the Danish Immigrant Archive at Dana College.

This is the Big Horn Power Co. interest coupon due July, 1913, on Gold Bond No. 147, one of many that were unpaid. Courtesy of William Boysen, San Pedro, Calif.

Bighorn sheep grazing in the Boysen State Park.
Courtesy of Kevin Hurley, Wildlife Management
Coordinator, Wyoming Game and Fish Department.

Asmus Boysen as an older man. Courtesy of Shirley
Obert, Casper, Wyo.

BIBLIOGRAPHY

COURT ACTIONS

Justice of the Peace Court, Fremont County Wyoming:

S. Morgan Smith Co. *vs.* Big Horn Power Co, decided April 10, 1914.

Wyoming District Court, Fremont County:

Big Horn Power Co. *vs.* Martin, Case No. 1145.

Big Horn Power Co. *vs.* Alto L. Hanway, Case No. 1146.

State of Wyoming *vs.* Big Horn Power Co, Case No. 1154.

London Guarantee & Accident Co. *vs.* Big Horn Power Co, Case No. 1317.

Shoshoni Lumber Co. *vs.* Big Horn Power Co, Chicago Title & Trust Co, and Charles H. Jackson, Trustee, Case No. 1372.

Myron E. Walker *vs.* Big Horn Power Co, Case No. 1481.

Samuel W. Hardman, *vs.* Big Horn Power Co, Case No. 1544.

Frank Martin *vs.* Big Horn Power Co, Case No. 1548.

American Hoist & Derrick Co. *vs.* Big Horn Power Co, Case No. 1700.

Carl Wagner *vs.* Big Horn Power Co, Case No. 1791.

Fred A. Lane *vs.* Big Horn Power Co, Case No. 1904.

Joseph Weis and Maurice G. Clarke *vs.* Asmus Boysen, *et. al,* Case No. 2105.

In the matter of the application of the Wyoming Power Co. to condemn property, Case No. 2283.

In the matter of the application of the Wyoming Power Co. to condemn property, Case No. 3061.

S. Morgan Smith Co. *vs.* Big Horn Power Co, Case No. 3185.

In the matter of the application of the Wyoming Power Co. to condemn property (2nd case), Case No. 3301.

William Kyne *vs.* Wyoming Power Co, Case No. 4218.

Allan Boysen *vs.* Town of Shoshoni, Wyoming, Case No. 4331.

Board of the County Commissioners of Fremont County *vs.* Helena B. Aishton, Asmus Boysen Mining Co, Big Horn Power Co, John T. Clarke, Ella R. Clarke, Maurice G. Clarke, Henry L. Clarke, Clarke Land & Loan Co, Chicago Title & Trust Co, Charles H. Jackson, Trustee, Wyoming Power Co, *et. al,* Case No. 5832.

Bertha L. Anderson, as Executrix of the Estate of Olof Anderson, deceased and Brita Anderson, *vs.* Ella R. Clarke, John T. Clarke, Wyoming Power Co. and Big Horn Power Co, Case No. 6446.

Gladys L. Purdum *vs.* Harry T Clarke, *et. al,* Case No. 8296.

Wyoming District Court, Hot Springs County:

Estate of John T. Wertz, Case No. 436.

Wyoming Supreme Court:

Edmore Le Clair *vs.* J. B. Hawley, *et. al.,* Case No. 578, 18 *Wyoming Reports* 23.

Big Horn Power Co. *vs.* State of Wyoming, Case No. 806, 23 *Wyoming Reports* 271.

Big Horn Power Co. *vs.* Frank E. Martin, Case No. 757, 24 *Wyoming Reports* 400.

Clarke *vs.* Shoshoni Lumber Co, *et. al,* Case No. 1132, 31 *Wyoming Reports* 205.

United States District Court, Cheyenne, Wyoming:

Asmus Boysen *vs.* Harry E. Wadsworth, Case No. 286.

William J. Broatch, Harry F. Clarke, Robert C. Wertz, Thomas Coughlan, Charles J. Woodhurst, John T. Clarke and Mary F. House, as heir to Jacob E. House, *vs.* Asmus Boysen, the Asmus

Boysen Mining Co, Adam Morrell and Joseph Weis, Case No. 288.

C. B. & Q. Railroad *vs.* Big Horn Power Co. and Asmus Boysen, Case No. 485

United States *vs.* Big Horn Power Co, Case No. 765.

Bernard P. Wickham *vs.* Big Horn Power Co. and Allan Boysen, Case No. 882.

John T. Clarke *vs.* Asmus Boysen, The Asmus Boysen Mining Co., Allan Boysen, Big Horn Power Co, Chicago Title & Trust, C. B. & Q. Railroad, Big Horn Railroad, Shoshoni Power & Electric Co, Maurice G. Clarke, Joseph Weis, Carl H. Tiedemann, Robert C. Wertz and Midwest Power & Light Co, Case No. 980.

Ella R. Clarke *vs.* Big Horn Power Co, Case No. 1281.

Henry B. Pogson, Trustee, and Augustus R. Smith, Trustee, *vs.* Big Horn Power Co, *et. al,* Case No. 1320.

Henry T. Clarke *vs.* Wyoming Power Co, Case No. 1430.

C. B. & Q. Railroad *vs.* John T. Clarke, Case No. 1513.

Henry T. Clarke *vs.* Hot Springs Electric Light & Power Co, Case No. 1659.

Henry T. Clarke *vs.* Hot Springs Electric Light & Power Co, Case No. 1811.

United States Eighth Circuit Court of Appeals:

Wadsworth *vs.* Boysen, 148 *Federal Reports* 771.

Broatch *vs.* Boysen, 175 *Federal Reports* 702.

Broatch *vs.* Boysen, 236 *Federal Reports* 516.

United States Tenth Circuit Court of Appeals:[413]

Clarke, *et. al, vs.* Boysen, *et. al,* 39 *Federal Reports Second Series* 800.

---

[413] Wyoming was in the U. S. 8th circuit from June 18, 1891 until the 10th Circuit was organized in 1929.

Clarke, *et. al., vs.* Hot Springs Electric Light & Power Co., *et. al.,* 55 *Federal Reporter*

Second Series 612.

Clarke *vs.* Chicago, Burlington & Quincy Railroad Co., 62 *Federal Reporter Series,*

Second Series 440.

Clarke, *et. al., vs.* Hot Springs Electric Light & Power Co., *et. al.,* 76 *Federal Reporter*

Second Series 918.

Probate Court of Cook County, IL:

Estate of James K. Sebree, deceased, File No. 15536.

New York Supreme Court, First Department:

John T. Clarke *vs.* C. B. & Q. Railroad Company

John T. Clarke and Henry T. Clarke, as Trustees of Clarke Land & Loan Company, a dissolved corporation, *vs.* C. B. & Q. Railroad Co.

Henry T. Clarke and John T. Clarke, as surviving directors of the Trustees for Clarke Land & Loan Company, dissolved (a Nebraska corporation), *vs.* C. B. & Q. Railroad Co.

George W. Wager and A. G. Clark, as Trustees, *vs.* C. B. & Q. Railroad Co.

New York Appellate Division:

John T. Clarke *vs.* C. B. & Q. Railroad Company

John T. Clarke and Henry T. Clarke, as Trustees of Clarke Land & Loan Company, a dissolved corporation, *vs.* C. B. & Q. Railroad Co.

Henry T. Clarke and John T. Clarke, as surviving directors of the Trustees for Clarke Land & Loan Company, dissolved (a Nebraska corporation), *vs.* C. B. & Q. Railroad Co.

George W. Wager and A. G. Clark as Trustees, *vs.* C. B. & Q. Railroad Co.

Supreme Court of the United States:

> Ella R. Clarke *vs.* Shoshoni Lumber Co. and Allan Boysen, 276 *United States Reports* 595.

> John T. Clarke *vs.* C. B. & Q. Railroad Co., and Ella R. Clarke *vs.* C. B. & Q. Railroad Co., 290 *United States Reports* 629.

NEWSPAPERS (WYOMING UNLESS NOTED OTHERWISE)

Audubon County Journal (Exira, Iowa).

Basin Republican.

Bill Barlow's Budget (Douglas).

Buffalo Bulletin.

The Cheyenne Daily Leader.

The Chicago (Ill.) *Daily Tribune.*

The Clipper (Lander) and *The Lander Clipper.*

The Cody Enterprise.

Copper Mountain Miner (Birdseye), *Copper Mountain Miner* (Boysen), *Copper Mountain Miner* (Hudson) and *The Miner* (Hudson).

Den Danske Pioneer (Omaha, Nebr.)

Fort Wayne (Ind.) *News.*

Greybull Standard.

Lake Benton (Minn.) *News.*

The Laramie Republican.

Manning (Iowa) *Monitor.*

Natrona County Tribune (Casper).

New York Herald Tribune (New York, N.Y.).

New York Times (New York, N.Y.).

Riverton Republican.

The Riverton Review.

The Shoshoni Enterprise.

Thermopolis Independent.

The Thermopolis Independent Record.

Thermopolis Record.

Wind River Mountaineer (Lander).

The Washington Herald (Washington, D. C.).

The Worland Grit.

Wyoming Derrick (Casper).

Wyoming State Journal (Lander).

The Wyoming Tribune (Cheyenne).

OTHER PRIMARY SOURCES

Congressional Record, XXXIX.

Eighteenth Biennial Report of the State Engineer to the Governor of Wyoming, 1925-1926.

Eleventh Biennial Report of the State Engineer of Wyoming to the Governor of Wyoming, 1911-1912 (Laramie, Wyo., 1913).

Fifteenth Biennial Report of the State Engineer to the Governor of Wyoming, 1919-1920 (Laramie, Wyo., 1921).

Fourteenth Biennial Report of the State Engineer to the Governor of Wyoming, 1917-1918 (Laramie, Wyo., 1918).

Fourth Biennial Report of the State Highway Commission of the State of Wyoming, For the Period Beginning October 1st 1922, Ending September 30, 1924 (Cheyenne, Wyo., 1924).

58th Congress, Third Session, House Report 3700 (Washington, D.C., 1905).

Francis E. Warren Collection, American Heritage Center, University of Wyoming.

National Archives RG 75, Special Cases No. 147.

Preliminary Examination of Reservoir Sites in Wyoming and Colorado, Document No. 141, House of Representatives, 55ᵗʰ Congress, Second Session.

Report on the Exploration of the Yellowstone River, by Bvt. Brig. Gen. W. F. Raynolds (Washington, D. C., 1868).

Seventeenth Biennial Report of the State Engineer to the Governor of Wyoming, 1923-1924.

Sixteenth Biennial Report of the State Engineer to the Governor of Wyoming, 1921-1922 (Casper, Wyo., 1923).

Third Biennial Report of the Public Service Commission of Wyoming 1919-1920.

Thirteenth Biennial Report of the State Engineer to the Governor of Wyoming (Laramie, Wyo., *1915-1916* (Laramie, Wyo., 1916).

Twelfth Biennial Report of the State Engineer to the Governor of Wyoming (Laramie, Wyo., 1914).

Wertz papers, Hot Springs County Museum, Thermopolis, Wyo.

Woods, L[awrence] Milton, *Sometimes the Books Froze: Wyoming's Economy and Its Banks* (Boulder, Colo., 1985).

Wyoming Public Service Commission files.

BOOKS

Bryant Butler Brooks, *Memoirs of Bryant B. Brooks: Cowboy, Trapper, Lumberman, Stockman, Oilman, Banker, and Governor of Wyoming* (Glendale, Calif., 1939).

Danstrup, *A History of Denmark* (Copenhagen, 1947).

Edgar, Bob and Turnell, Jack, *Lady of a Legend* (Cody, Wyo., 1979).

Gray Community History, 1881-1981 (n.p., 1980).

Harrison, Charles Yale, *Clarence Darrow* (New York, 1931).

Iowa State Register (n.p., 1900).

King, Calvin, *History of Wildlife in the Big Horn Basin of Wyoming* (Cheyenne, n.d.).

Larson, Taft Alfred, *History of Wyoming* (Lincoln, Nebr., 1978).

Milek, Dorothy Buchanan, *The Gift of Bah Guewana: A History of Wyoming's Hot Springs State Park* (Thermopolis, Wyo., 1975).

—*Hot Springs: A Wyoming County History* (n.p., 1986).

Mortensen, Enok, *The Danish Lutheran Church in America: The History and the Heritage of the American Evangelical Lutheran Church* (Philadelphia, 1967).

Overton, Richard C., *Burlington Route: A History of the Burlington Lines* (New York, 1965).

R. L. Polk's Wyoming State Gazetteer and Business Director for 1908-1909.

Sage, Leland, *William Boyd Allison: A study in Practical Politics* (Iowa City, Iowa, 1956).

Trenholm, Virginia Cole, *The Arapahoes, Our People* (Norman, Okla., 1970).

Urbanek, Mae, *Wyoming Place Names* (Boulder, Colo., 1967).

Walker, Tacetta B., *Stories of Early Days in Wyoming: Big Horn Basin* (Casper, Wyo., 1936.

Wyoming Business Directory, 1924 (Denver, Colo., 1924).

INDEX

Boysen, Hans Jes (Asmus'
father), in Aabenraa 3; in
Skanderup, 4.

Boysen, Helena (Asmus'
daughter),6; marriage to Fred
Aishton, 105; receives deed
to part of Boysen tract, 214.

Boysen, Ingeborg Matthiesen
(Asmus' grandmother), 3.

Boysen, Jacobi Frederik (Asmus'
brother), 4n., 6n.

Boysen, Kathryne Cecilia
Fanning (Asmus' second
wife), relationship with
Asmus, 86; marriage to
Asmus, 116-17; death, 220.

Boysen, Louis Koch, 35; and
Wyoming sulphur operation,
45.

Boysen, Maren Mathilde
Vildfang (Asmus' mother), 3.

Boysen, Nis Peter (Asmus'
brother), 4n., 148;
and Copper Mountain
exploration, 33-34, 36;
personal threats to, 41.

Boysen, Peter (Asmus'
grandfather), 3.

Boysen, Raymond Michael,
Kathryne's son, 116; injury at
power plant, 139; death, 220.

Boysen, Rosa Darlene (Asmus'
daughter), birth (1900), 7n.;
married William Sayles, 219.

Boysen, William, (son of
Raymond), 139n.

Boysen Peak, 220.

Boysen Creek, 220.

Boysen, town platted, 55;
inundated by the lake, 96-97;
part of state park, 220-21.

Bradford Exchange Bank, 21n.

Breniman, Charles E., manager
of Boysen companies in
Wyoming, 56, 64, 68, 76,
97; accident in the river, 57;
leaves the Boysen operations,
108-109; career with FBI,
148.

Brice, Edward L., and Wertz, 30,
31n.; and Willow Creek play,
54.

Broatch, William J., "accepting"
member, 153n.

Brodegaard, Fred, 98.

Brooks, Wyoming Governor
Bryant Butler, 68, 83.

Brorson, Niels C., and coal lease,
18; as manager of Boysen's
mining company, 46, 56, 63;
Boysen's manager in Chicago,
83; druggist in Nebr., 148.

Brown, Judge Charles O., 173.

Brown, J. C., 138n.

Buffalo Bill dam, 69n.

Burch, David A. "Dab," 165n.

Burdick, Charles W., 69.

Burke, Timothy F., U.S. attorney,
44.

Burlington railroad, see Chicago,
Burlington & Quincy
railroad.

Wagner, Carl, condemnation
suit, 186.
Wahaba town (renamed
Dannebrog), 99.
Walker, C. E., 130n.
Walker, Myron E., condemnation
case, 181-86.
Walls, Attorney General W. L.,
191n.
Walton, Albert D., 185n.,
193-94.
Warner, F. H., 114n.
Warren, Wyoming Senator
Francis E., 12n.; comment
on Boysen preference, 25-27.
Washakie, Shoshoni Chief, 12.
Watts, Clyde M., 185n.
Wedding of the Waters, 49.
Weis, Josef/Joseph, syndicate
member, 14-15, 17n, 18;
and syndicate members'
lawsuit, 52, 152, 157, 168;
"accepting" member, 153n.
Wertz, Edwin S., 55.
Wertz, John T[homas], allotting
agent, 11-12, 17; suspended
and terminated, 18; and
syndicate agreement, 20; and
Boysen preference, 29-30;
and National Mining &
Development Co., 30; and
Edward L. Brice, 31n.; and
Willow Creek play, 38, 41;
offer to Boysen, 41-42; and

lawsuit by Edmore Le Clair,
54; death, 159-60.
Wertz, Robert C., syndicate
member, 14; owner of half
share, 152; "accepting"
member, 153n.
Western Light, Heat & Power
Co., 104.
Wickham, Bernard P., 164-65,
172.
Wickham, John T., 165n.
Williams, Pueblo "Peb," 35.
Willow Creek play, 38, 41, 54.
Wilson, James, Secretary of
Agriculture, 8, 16.
Wilson, Dr. James M., 97-98.
Wind River, name confusion, 49.
Wind River Indian Reservation,
10.
Winter, Judge Charles E., 163.
Woodhurst, Charles J., syndicate
member, 14-15, 17, 20;
"accepting" member, 153n.
Woodruff, John D., 83.
Wyoming Power Co. chartered
to operate power plant, 120;
financial statements (1918),
121, (1919), 124-25, (1920),
126, (1921), 127, (1922),
127, (1923), 138, (1924),
141, (1925), 142, (1926),
146, (1927), 146-47, (1928),
147-48; obtained Riverton
franchise, 124; transmission